SAFEGUARDING
THE INSTITUTION

SAFEGUARDING THE INSTITUTION

How the Culture of the Church of England Facilitates Abuse

Stephen Kuhrt

First published 2025 by Dandelion Digital, an imprint of Paper Lion Ltd
13 Grayham Road, New Malden, Surrey, KT3 5HR, UK
www.paperlionltd.com

Copyright © Stephen Kuhrt 2025

Stephen Kuhrt has asserted his rights under the Copyright,
Designs and Patents Act 1988, to be identified as Author of this work.

All rights reserved. No part of this work may be reproduced, recorded or transmitted in any form, digital or mechanical, including photocopying or any information storage or retrieval system including for the training or use of AI, without the permission of the publisher in writing.

A catalogue record for this book is available from the British Library

ISBN
Paperback: 978-1-908706-54-6
eBook: 978-1-908706-55-3

Design: cover by Nathan Larkin, interior by seagulls.net

In memory of Neil Todd (1974-2012)
A victim of the culture of the Church of England

Contents

Preface ix
Acknowledgements xi
Foreword – A Survivor of Sexual Harassment xiii

CHAPTER 1 1
Delusions of Adequacy
Facing the Reality of Safeguarding in the Church of England

CHAPTER 2 16
It Takes a Village to Abuse a Child
The Inescapably Communal Nature of Abuse

CHAPTER 3 38
Pragmatism and Passive Aggression
How Problems are Approached in the Church of England

CHAPTER 4 63
Wilful Incompetence
The Wider Culture of the Church of England

CHAPTER 5 87
Captivity to Fear
Getting it Wrong About Safety in the Church

CHAPTER 6 112
Seen and Not Heard
Inconsistent Attitudes Towards Behaviour in the Church

CHAPTER 7 134
What Has Sex Got to Do With It?
The Impact of Dishonesty About Sex in the Church

CHAPTER 8 155
Prophets and Whistleblowers
The Courage Needed to Rock the Boat in Churches

CHAPTER 9 180
Tough on Safeguarding, Tough on the Causes of Safeguarding
A Vision for Restoring Truth to the Centre of the Church's Culture

Select Bibliography 231
Notes 232
Index 244

Preface

This book is the result of over half a century spent within the Church of England, the last twenty-two as one of its clergy. During this time, I have experienced much in this church that is wonderful. This book, however, is focused upon the darker side of the Church of England and specifically those aspects of its culture which have led directly to the very safeguarding scandals that have so blighted its reputation in recent times. It makes the case that, unless these cultural issues are recognised and confronted, the current 'improvements' to safeguarding within the Church of England will be superficial and result in little genuine change.

Much of the detail and analysis within this book will therefore sound extremely negative to many who love the church. It also has the potential to cause considerable pain to those invested in the Church of England, specifically. The intention, however, is not a destructive one. One of the signs of a good and loyal friend is when they have the courage to say what needs to be heard with clarity and honesty. The writer is more than a friend to the Church of England. Indeed, it has been a family he has belonged to throughout his life.

However, if anything, family bonds increase the responsibility to speak the truth when this is necessary, along with the willingness to endure a sometimes angry response. There is a great deal within these pages about the courage that is needed if truth is to be spoken to the culture of the Church of England, and the hardships that will then be suffered by those who speak this truth. This book is seeking to model the commitment to truth-telling that it promotes, plus the courage to accept the consequences that come from this.

But as well as reflecting the importance of truth, the intention here is to display an equally strong belief in redemption: specifically, the redemption that becomes possible once truth-telling is followed by repentance. Belief in the resurrection of Jesus Christ makes me dare to believe that instead of 'publish and be damned', the result will be 'publish and be blessed'.[1] When I say this, I am thinking less in personal terms than for the future of the church. My hope is that by presenting deeply uncomfortable truths about the current culture of the Church of England, this book will help it to undergo the painful process of death and resurrection that forms the path to followers of Jesus Christ receiving and sharing the blessings built on these gospel truths.

Virtually all of this book was written some time before the publication of the (much-delayed) Makin Review, with the details it revealed about the appalling crimes of John Smyth and their mishandling by various parts of the Church of England.[2] This, of course, led swiftly to the resignation of Justin Welby as Archbishop of Canterbury. Further resignations of senior figures within the church may still follow, correctly in my opinion. These events and the welcome discussion they have prompted about the culture of the Church of England make the publication of this book particularly timely.

To reinforce its aim, this book is dedicated to the memory of someone who was associated with an earlier safeguarding scandal involving the negligence of an Archbishop of Canterbury. Neil Todd was a young man who paid the ultimate price for multiple failures within the culture of the Church of England. I never met him in person, but he is on my heart. May he rest in peace and rise in glory.

Stephen Kuhrt
Easter 2025

Acknowledgements

There are many people to thank in connection with this book. Some because of the support they gave me through the period of suspension that forms a central part of its narrative, and others through encouraging the writing of the book itself. Many did both. Simon Blackwell and Penny Holroyde are old friends who were extremely wise and supportive during my suspension. More recent friends who helped in a similar manner are Tracy Borman, Lee Furney, Nikki Gough, Harriet Morgan, and Nicola Storey. The steadfast support of my colleagues and former colleagues at Christ Church ensured both my survival as its vicar and the production of this book, with vital roles played by Jon Cook, Helen Hancock, Elizabeth Hill, Anna and Nathan Larkin, David and Katy Loffman, Gill Mosquera, Sarah Parker, Kate and Robert Shrimpton, David Taylor and Luke Wickings.

Clergy from further afield who have contributed in various ways to this book and encouraged its writing include Steve Doel and Hugo Foxwood. Numerous other clergy in the Church of England have contributed just as fully to its contents, if somewhat less positively!

The path towards the publication of this book has been far from easy with some extraordinary factors involved. The expertise of Katy Loffman of Paper Lion Ltd has been vital in seeing it through to completion for which I am hugely grateful. Nathan Larkin used his skills in graphic design to create its cover. Thank you also to the Survivor who was willing to write the Foreword and understandably wishes to remain anonymous.

Finally, I wish to express my thanks to my family who, for various reasons, have had to endure much through the multitude of issues connected with this book over the last few years: my parents Gordon and Olive Kuhrt, my brothers Martin and Jon Kuhrt, my dear wife and children – Katie, Rebecca, James, and Abigail; and my son-in-law, James Connolly.

Seeing those close to you pay part of the cost for something that you believe in can be difficult. But in this case, it has been made easier by the conviction shared by all those named here in the rightness of challenging a church culture that has led to such catastrophic outcomes and seeking to be part of its remedy.

Foreword

*By a Survivor of Sexual Harassment
and its Mishandling*

I am more than happy to commend this book for a number of reasons that stem from personal experience and a deep conviction about the need for genuine accountability within the Church of England. Over the past three decades, I have known Stephen Kuhrt as a passionate advocate for the Christian faith – an advocacy combining intellectual depth with an unwavering commitment to authenticity. Stephen embodies true integrity, consistently standing up against injustice to illuminate truth and defend principles of fairness. As both a theologian and a vicar, he recognises that the church's credibility hinges on its ability to live out its proclaimed values.

When policies and procedures become mere paperwork, devoid of sincere implementation or transparent execution, the church's spiritual witness becomes hollow and meaningless. Stephen understands that Christian witness requires more than rhetoric – it demands committed, principled action that demonstrates genuine moral accountability. All of this is to say that I believe his work in this book represents exactly what the church needs most: a courageous examination of the deep-rooted causes of its systemic failures in safeguarding.

Tragically, we repeatedly encounter narratives of survivors of abuse having their experiences dismissed, minimised, or ignored. These people are frequently confronted with an impenetrable wall of institutional silence, driven more by a desire to protect the church's reputation than by a genuine commitment to accountability and justice. My personal journey illuminates precisely why this book is so necessary. While studying for ordained ministry in another part of the Anglican Communion, I encountered a deeply troubling situation that exposed the church's problematic tendency to prioritise institutional reputation over individual safety and justice. When a fellow student – a senior church leader – began making persistent and unwelcome romantic advances, I experienced firsthand the toxic institutional culture that Stephen examines in these pages.

Despite my clear and repeated communications rejecting romantic overtures, this senior cleric continued his pursuit. He sent romantic gifts, emails expressing inappropriate sentiments, and even attempted to set up a bank account in my name. These were actions that felt manipulative and deeply invasive. When I sought support from the theological college's leadership, I was met with shocking dismissiveness. The principal's response – "You are both adults, can't you sort this out yourselves?" – epitomised the very institutional mindset this book challenges.

What became most apparent was the institution's instinct for self-preservation. Rather than getting to the root of the substantive issues of harassment and inappropriate behaviour, the college leadership seemed primarily concerned with minimising disruption and protecting the institution's reputation. I was effectively portrayed as a troublemaker, a 'hysterical woman' who was overreacting to a situation that made me feel unsafe.

In this dark moment, Stephen was a beacon of support and theological wisdom. He listened deeply, validated my experiences, and provided critical theological perspective. When others suggested that I should 'keep quiet' or be 'more forgiving' – effectively asking me to sacrifice my own wellbeing for the institution's comfort – Stephen offered something far more valuable: affirmation, support, and a robust theological framework for understanding my response.

Stephen's support went beyond mere sympathy. As a gifted theologian with an encyclopaedic knowledge of the Bible, he helped me understand that challenging injustice is not only permissible but often necessary. He demonstrated how Christian witness becomes meaningless when the church fails to uphold its own proclaimed values of justice, transparency, and care for the vulnerable.

This book is the natural extension of that commitment. By examining the Church of England's safeguarding failures, Stephen is not attacking the church he loves but offering it a path to redemption. He understands that true Christian witness requires courage – the courage to look unflinchingly at systemic problems and work towards meaningful change.

The narrative and analysis contained in this book will likely make uncomfortable reading for many. They challenge the church to move beyond performative displays of concern to implement robust, transparent safeguarding policies and fundamentally alter its culture in order to allow these changes to take root. My own experience – where an atheist police officer showed more Christ-like compassion towards me than church leaders – starkly illustrates the urgent need for such change.

What makes Stephen's approach so powerful is his fundamental love for the church. This is not a work of cynical critique, but of hopeful challenge. He understands that communities can only grow and heal when they are willing to confront their deepest failures honestly. By documenting systemic issues in safeguarding and in the culture of the Church of England, he offers the church an opportunity for genuine transformation.

Notably, an external review conducted four years after my experience confirmed the college's mishandling of my complaint – a validation of the very concerns Stephen articulates in this book. Such independent assessments underscore the critical importance of his work.

For anyone concerned about institutional accountability, pastoral care, and the genuine embodiment of Christian values, this book is essential reading. It represents a crucial intervention at a moment when the church must choose between protecting its image and protecting its most vulnerable members.

I am profoundly grateful that Stephen has had the courage to write this book. His work represents hope – hope for people who have been mistreated and hope for everyone that the Church of England can change and become the compassionate and just community it claims to be.

CHAPTER 1

Delusions of Adequacy

Facing the Reality of Safeguarding in the Church of England

Watching the Peter Ball Documentary

In January 2020, like many clergy in the Church of England, I watched the two-part BBC documentary *Exposed: The Church's Darkest Secret*.[1] Most clergy in England (and many beyond) probably felt themselves compelled to watch a programme that examined the details surrounding the abuse of eighteen young men committed between 1977 and 1992 by Peter Ball, the ex-Bishop of Lewes and then Gloucester, and the response to this abuse by senior figures in the Church of England. Two and a half years previously, the independent report conducted by Dame Moira Gibb had concluded that the Church of England and its senior leaders had colluded with Peter Ball rather than seeking to help those he had harmed or assuring itself of the safety of others.[2]

The former Archbishop of Canterbury, Lord Carey, was notably singled out for particular criticism for his failure to pass on letters that he received about Ball to the police. Many details in the documentary were shocking, and one of its most distressing aspects was the story of Neil Todd. Todd was the young man who was denied justice when he first reported Peter Ball's abuse in 1992. Unable to go through this ordeal again when a more thorough response to Peter Ball's offences began in 2012, Neil Todd then took his own life.

As I watched the documentary, it provoked two responses within me. Both were extremely personal. The first and less important one came from the realisation that I had lived in considerable proximity to the place where some of Ball's crimes were committed. From January to September 1988, I worked as a lay assistant at a church called St John's sub Castro in Lewes. I was nineteen years of age, having just left school. The time in Lewes formed the bulk of my 'gap year' prior to going to university. While coming from a very different church tradition from most of the young men abused by Peter Ball, I was otherwise similar in age and in my desire to explore how God might be calling me to service in my future life. It was during those nine months that the possibility that God might be calling me to ordination first occurred to me. I remain grateful for everything that the experience of working at St John's gave me. But I also count myself fortunate that at no point during those nine months in Lewes did I ever meet with Peter Ball, let alone come under his influence. Seeing the locations where Ball abused many of his victims, the documentary brought home to me that things could have been very different.

However, there was a far more important response that the documentary also drew from me, and one just as personal. I felt ashamed of the Church of England. This was not because I was shocked by the documentary's revelations about the inadequate response that the church's senior leaders had made to the allegations against Peter Ball. It was because, on the contrary, I was totally unsurprised at what had occurred. At that stage, I had been an ordained minister in the Church of England for seventeen years. As I watched the programme, it was with mounting anger that I realised that it was reflecting much of my own experience during that time. This was very specifically with regard to safeguarding, but also in terms of the general culture within the Church of England. I recognised, with a disturbing degree of clarity, how this culture had led very directly, not just to the cover-up of safeguarding scandals such as that involving Peter Ball, but to such scandals occurring in the first place.

Among the specific factors that I particularly recognised was the culture of duplicity and dishonesty. In a press conference about the Ball case in 1992, Jeremy Walsh, then Bishop of Tewkesbury, declared that "One incident, however bad it might be, doesn't negate a lifetime's ministry".[3] It is difficult to believe that Walsh did not know at that stage that there was far from just one incident involving Peter Ball. The Archbishop of Canterbury, George Carey, was certainly aware that this was not the case. Yet for the sake of protecting both Ball and the reputation of the church, this representation was allowed to go uncorrected. The impression was deliberately fostered that the incident involving Neil Todd was a one-off aberration from an otherwise unblemished ministry. It would have been serious enough even if that had been the case, I should add. But things were in fact much worse.

Just as recognisable was the attitude shown by John Yates, then Bishop at Lambeth. When alerted to Ball's activities, Yates responded by saying, "What do you expect me to do?" This is just the sort of inadequate and evasive response that I had got used to, when I raised issues of importance within my diocese.[4] So too was the inertia that followed, as Yates failed to act in response to the complaints or communicate with those who made them. Worse in its familiarity, was the combination of fear, entitlement and hubris that led George Carey to think that he was qualified to judge whether the matter of Ball's reported offences was something that should or should not involve the police.

My annoyance with all of this was heightened by an even greater anger at the general crassness of the Church of England, within which these features were established. This included the exaggerated veneration accorded to the figure of Peter Ball and the irresponsibility of a culture that had made it 'normal' for him to live with scores of young men. Just as disturbing was the cosy interconnectedness between senior figures in the Church of England and other national figures representing entitled unaccountability. These included the then Prince Charles and other powerful men whose undue influence was critical in Ball's crimes not being dealt with properly.[5]

Most of all, I was furious at the complacent irrelevance of an organisation that had created such an insular subculture that it was totally unable to recognise the evil involved in privileging the safety of 'one of its own' over those for whom the church had a responsibility of care. By the end of the documentary, I was clear that the entire culture of the Church of England had played a role in the death of Neil Todd. I was equally clear that the culture that was so indifferent to the fate of this young man, was the very same one that I had experienced through my seventeen years of ordained ministry.

Personal Background

Recognition of all of these factors was not something that came easily to me. My father was an Anglican vicar who had served as an archdeacon in Southwark Diocese from 1989-96 and then Director of Ministry for the Church of England from 1996-2006. All of my life has been spent within this church, with overwhelmingly positive experiences. I married the daughter of another senior Anglican clergyman who had been Chief Secretary to the Board of Mission and Unity for the Church of England. In time, I was ordained into this church – as was my elder brother, one of my brothers-in-law, and one of my uncles. More than for many, being a member of the Church of England was 'in the blood'.

Furthermore, I had become passionately loyal and protective of the Church of England. When it received mockery or criticism by other Christians, I was deeply annoyed. Both my father and late father-in-law were evangelical Anglicans, and both strong advocates of the decisive shift that had taken place within this movement from the second half of the 1960s. It was at the first National Evangelical Anglican Conference, held at Keele University in 1967, that evangelical Anglicans, under the then leadership of John Stott, repented of their tendency towards separatism and committed themselves to full involvement within the Church of England. Much of this consensus among evangelicals fell away after the decision to ordain women as priests in 1992, followed by a retreat back into separatism by those unhappy at this change. But, as a keen supporter of women's full ministry within the church, I remained an ardent 'Keele evangelical', determined to remain committed to full involvement in and positivity about the Church of England.

After my ordination in 2003, I became one of the early members of Fulcrum – a group established in that year to represent this position by offering leadership to what might be called the 'evangelical centre' of the

Church of England.⁶ From 2011 to 2014, I was its chair. I was delighted about the appointment of Justin Welby as Archbishop of Canterbury in 2013. I saw this, at the time, as bringing hope for really positive change within the church.⁷ My theological commitment to what the Church of England represents, and my excitement about the fantastic opportunities that it provides for ministry and mission, remain undimmed.

What has changed, and very dramatically, is my perception of the current health of much of the Church of England and, in particular, its culture. This had been happening for several years before it crystallised as I watched the documentary about Peter Ball. What caused this awakening was my fairly constant experience of the way in which so much of church life, including its ministry and mission, was being held back by the structures of the church rather than helped by them. This was particularly true at a diocesan level. As issues of importance arose in areas of ministry involving my diocese, I realised that there was very little investment in their recognition and resolution. This led to me becoming a lot more proactive in flagging up these issues in letters and emails to bishops, archdeacons and other diocesan officers. This communication tended to receive either a minimal response or no response at all. Most of the time it was not even acknowledged. Rather than taking this as a cue to 'pipe down', the refusal to engage with my concerns made me realise the need to become more outspoken about them.

My Experience of Safeguarding in the Church of England

The most serious area of concern, and the one where the lack of engagement bothered me most, was with safeguarding. This particularly grew out of a historic case that I dealt with when I first became Priest-in-Charge (Vicar Designate) of the parish of New Malden and Coombe in 2007, having been curate in the same parish following my ordination in July 2003.⁸ It concerned a lay minister at the church called Bryn Hughes, and a matter that should have been dealt with when it first emerged several years before I came to the church.⁹ Some of the story of my experience in trying to ensure that the case was dealt with is covered in articles found online.[10] This included receiving active discouragement from pursuing the matter and significant pressure to collude with its continued suppression. I persisted, however, with the eventual result that the person accused received a criminal conviction at a trial in 2008.[11] I remain convinced that my proactivity in insisting that this matter was dealt with and facing down the considerable opposition against this, remains the most important thing that I have done in the whole of my ministry.

This was seen, however, in a very different way by my diocese. Following the conviction, I was not invited to be any part of a 'lessons-learned review' concerning the case, and I remain unsure about whether any such process occurred. Such a review, and the inclusion of everyone involved, should have been vital, particularly given the clear evidence that the matter should have been dealt with much earlier, and its significant mishandling at several stages. I would have valued the chance to reflect, in an atmosphere of mutual learning, on the ways that my own handling of the matter could have been better. With hindsight, such a review would have helped to prevent a significant failure in the case's follow-up, when no agreement was put in place at the next church attended by the convicted person. As the years went on, I realised, with increasing clarity, the reasons for this lack of engagement by my diocese, before and after that part of the case they had to be involved in. I was ministering within a church unwilling to engage with any of the crucial issues underlying its problems with safeguarding. If reviews of safeguarding failures in the Church of England took place, these were usually very limited and only fuller when significant and public scandals forced this to occur.

My first experience of wider safeguarding processes in the Church of England showed me that this culture was not restricted to my diocese. It came when a second 'Past Cases Review' (PCR2) was commissioned by the Church of England from 2019-22. It followed an earlier process that was roundly discredited because of the small number of mishandled cases from the past that it acknowledged. Within the form for PCR2 that clergy received, we had to state (in a very small box) whether any past safeguarding cases existed within our parish involving licensed ministers and whether we were happy with how these had been handled. The form said that if you were not satisfied with the response of the Diocese Safeguarding Adviser, "there will be a follow-up to the parish made through the PCR reference group". I made it clear that I was not satisfied with the response to the case in 2007-8, and I said that I was "happy to explain more about this because I don't think the lessons have ever been properly learned". I fully expected to hear back immediately but, after completing the form on 5th March 2020, I was never contacted by anyone from the PCR reference group about the matter. Whatever was said officially, the reality appeared to be that any negative feedback about the health of safeguarding in the Church of England was unwelcome.

It was my refusal to accept this culture that eventually led me into significant trouble. If the case from 2007-8 had been my only poor experience of safeguarding in my diocese, I would have been prepared to move on. Sadly, my experience of the handling of every subsequent safeguarding matter that I have been involved in had been equally unsatisfactory. Common to all of these cases was the desire by people in key positions to avoid engagement with safeguarding issues if at all possible; and if such engagement was unavoidable, to do the minimum needed to make these issues go away. Each time I experienced this, my frustration and anger mounted, leading to my increased protestation about the inadequacy of safeguarding within my diocese. For a long time, this was ignored, presumably in the hope that I would lose interest. Instead, I persisted, gradually raising the volume to the increasing annoyance of those determined to resist engagement with such questions.

The eventual result was that the Area Bishop of Kingston commissioned a 'review' of my ministry in 2020. Keen to engage with this, and initially trusting its motives, I produced a lengthy paper detailing all of my poor experience of safeguarding matters in the diocese. For four and a half months, I heard nothing in response. When I took the paper to the National Safeguarding Team of the Church of England, the response was equally inadequate. This led me to share the paper with a small group of friends and advisers, including some more national figures equally committed to improving safeguarding within the Church of England.[12]

Foolishly, I failed to redact the names of those involved in the case from 2008. While this error had no material impact, it led to a complaint under the Clergy Discipline Measure. This was brought against me by the safeguarding consultant overseeing that part of the review. This complaint not only covered the non-redaction of names in the paper, but my actions with regard to the safeguarding case in 2007-8. Initially ruled 'out of time', the latter complaint was allowed to proceed after a successful appeal by the complainant.

The result was that I was suspended from ministry by the Bishop of Southwark, for five and a half months from February to July 2021, first unofficially and then officially. No interview took place prior to my suspension. At the height of the Covid-19 pandemic, it was a very tough time. The enormous support that I received from my family, the congregation at Christ Church, New Malden (particularly the churchwardens) and friends, however, was crucial. The Christ Church members of the PCC issued a strong statement of support, asserting that the suspension was disproportionate, and that, in their opinion, safeguarding had been weaponised against me.[13] This very public support was probably significant in bringing the matter to a conclusion much earlier than might have been the case.[14] The accusation about my handling of the safeguarding case in 2007 was dropped and I received an agreed penalty for my failure to redact the names in the paper when I sent it to my advisers. This included supervision meetings three times a year with a newly appointed Diocesan Safeguarding Adviser.[15] It is worth noting that the legal costs of my defence alone, covered by the Church of England's legal aid scheme, came to over £8,000.

Back in post, I was determined to continue as Vicar of New Malden and Coombe. A large part of this was my undimmed enthusiasm for this role in an exciting and vibrant setting with the considerable challenge of 'building back' after the Covid-19 pandemic. Equally important, however, was my clarity about what the whole episode revealed about safeguarding in the Church of England and the considerable personal responsibility that came with this. I realised that if I left the parish, I would be colluding with the refusal of the institutional church to engage with its safeguarding failures and its treatment of those who 'rocked the boat' on this.

1 / DELUSIONS OF ADEQUACY

Central to this was my recognition that most of the voices challenging the terrible approach to safeguarding within the Church of England were speaking from its margins. This included immensely courageous survivors of abuse and their equally tenacious and committed advocates.[16] These people, however, were all too easily being ignored. I realised that what was also needed was a serving vicar of a lively and credible church being completely open about his abysmal experience of safeguarding in the Church of England and how every part of the church's approach to safeguarding needed to change.

The events that followed the lifting of my suspension were significant. Informed by email that I could return to ministry, there was no 'return to work' interview. It was only some twelve weeks later that the Bishop of Kingston, after an intervention from the area dean, met with me, with nothing of significance discussed. The Bishop of Southwark has never met with me since the suspension. The paper on safeguarding, written in response to a review initiated by the diocese and supposedly set up because of my concerns, has never received any response to its contents.

More disturbingly, the diocese immediately proceeded with a review of the safeguarding practices within my parish. Protesting that this investigation had no justification, the churchwardens and I refused to have anything to do with it. Our fear was that it would form a further attempt to weaponise safeguarding against me. This was vindicated when the 'report' emerged as little more than the collation of anonymous, local allegations about my supposed behaviour. Tellingly, the report was forced to admit at several points that none of the allegations against me came within the remit of safeguarding. None of the complaints were formally made and were without substance. They therefore came to nothing. But it became apparent that the strategy of at least some within my diocese was to prompt my resignation.

This became explicit when a new Bishop of Kingston arrived. It took me three months to gain an hour-long meeting with my new bishop. When it took place, he instantly signalled his acceptance of a negative narrative about me. Like his predecessor, however, the bishop was unwilling to discuss any specific examples of my alleged misconduct or even the areas in which his concerns were located. Following this, he announced to me at the start of only our second meeting in May 2023 that he wished me to leave my post as vicar. He expressed the desire for me to step out of ministry "for at least a year" while being fully paid (and presumably housed) and receiving help on "how to handle conflict more appropriately". He also made the promise that, if I showed the right progress in this regard, he would then write me "a really good reference" for a post in another diocese.

The new bishop received a polite but firm written refusal from me and also numerous letters of protest from others supporting my ministry. A general letter from 135 members of Christ Church (including all of its PCC members) expressed similar support. It urged the bishop to reconsider his "hasty and ill-informed judgment" of their vicar and suggested that he should seek to support rather than hinder my ministry.

The most significant correspondence, however, was from the churchwardens of the parish who placed their opposition to the bishop's proposal within the context of their fury at the actions of the diocese over the preceding few years. Within their letter they spoke of its demonstration of the diocese's characteristic trend of non-engagement with any of the historic material that it had received from the church, most obviously my safeguarding paper which had then been "shamelessly weaponised" against me. They further spoke about the continued deployment of a narrative asserting my poor treatment of people without substantiation, constituting the serious offence of 'gaslighting' and demanded that this cease.[17] The most devastating section was towards the end of the letter, where the churchwardens declared: "As all that has gone before has suggested, this decision is entirely and depressingly consistent with diocesan behaviour throughout the period of the review: worse, it is the culmination of it. At different times, Stephen has been faced with passive aggression, harassment and outright intimidation. It is a grim picture that reflects nothing but shame on everyone at the diocese, from the top down, who has been tainted by any kind of involvement with it. We have long suspected that the aim of the campaign against Stephen – for such it has been – has been to encourage him to throw in the towel and resign. Your deplorable suggestion of 18th May confirms that no other interpretation is possible.

Stephen's 'crime' is to have survived; his suggested removal is the desperate action of a leadership group without imagination, managerial skill or moral compass."

The result of my non-acceptance of the bishop's 'offer' was that he refused to meet with me for over two years. This had a considerable impact upon issues of ministry in the parish and was difficult to interpret as anything other than a further attempt to make my position as vicar untenable. It led to the PCC voting unanimously to make our annual pledge to the diocese only after I had had a satisfactory meeting with the bishop. This and the realisation that I wasn't going to give in, eventually appeared instrumental in changing the situation. Wider developments covered below and opportunities for me to appear on television sharing my story and commenting on the wider context of safeguarding in the Church of England, may also have been influential.[18] A meeting finally took place in June 2025 in which the bishop took a totally different approach. To his credit, he admitted that he should not have accepted the negative narrative that he had been given about me and said that he wanted an entirely fresh start. Matters were helped by the arrival of an able new archdeacon with an excellent attitude and equally committed to approaching the whole situation differently.

Wider Safeguarding Scandals in the Church of England

While these events unfolded in my personal experience, safeguarding scandals in the wider Church of England only grew in number and prominence. Earlier cases from its Anglo-Catholic tradition involving people such as Peter Ball, George Rideout, Roy Cotton and Colin Pritchard were joined by several others involving evangelicals. The most prominent of these have been the cases of Jonathan Fletcher and John Smyth from the conservative evangelical tradition, and Mike Pilavachi from the charismatic Soul Survivor network. Damning reports were eventually produced with a consistent pattern emerging in the church's inadequate response to the abuse involved.

This response has generally involved two distinct areas, often in combination. The first is people (sometimes holding significant positions of leadership within the tradition of the abuser) who have known about the abuse and yet failed to report it. The second is a failure to respond to abuse adequately by those with official responsibility within the Church of England.

The fallout from one of these scandals reached dramatic proportions in November 2024 with the resignation of the Archbishop of Canterbury, Justin Welby. This followed the publication of the Makin Review covering the horrific and sadistic actions of John Smyth over four decades and within three countries. The report also contained damning details about the cover-up of this abuse. This included its suppression by Smyth's conservative evangelical subculture, facilitating the continuation of his abuse in Zimbabwe and South Africa. It further included the case's inadequate handling by the official structures of the Church of England. While Justin Welby had close connections to the Iwerne circles that knew of Smyth's abuse, his most obvious culpability was a failure to act with proper energy and conviction when the case came to him as Archbishop of Canterbury in 2013. As soon as the Makin Review emerged, I was among the first clergy in the Church of England to call for Welby's resignation which he announced shortly afterwards.[19]

One of the reasons that I made this call was the similarities between Welby's response to John Smyth and that of the former Archbishop of Canterbury, George Carey, to Peter Ball.[20] Within *Exposed: The Church's Darkest Secret*, it was George Carey who came over most badly through his failure to pass on the key letters that he had received about Peter Ball in 1992 to the police. But when some commentators described this failure on the part of Carey as 'inexplicable', I had to disagree. Everything that I had experienced during my ordained ministry made Carey's actions entirely explicable. Whatever the former archbishop may have told himself that he considered doing, his response and the credibility that this decision held for him was heavily conditioned by the culture that he was operating within. Any official policy that existed on such matters was clearly trumped by the need to prevent the matter escalating. On a deeper level and decades apart, the actions of both archbishops exemplified the truth of the phrase, commonly attributed to the management consultant Peter Drucker, that "culture eats strategy for breakfast".[21]

Closely connected with this was my experience of what occurs when someone operating within this culture tries to resist it. Welby was criticised in the Makin Review for showing 'a lack of curiosity' over the Smyth case. Both Welby and others involved, such as the Bishop of Lincoln and former Bishop of Ely, Stephen Conway, subsequently admitted to showing 'a lack of energy' with regard to it. Both were polite ways of saying that they had sought to do the minimum possible to make the problem of Smyth's abuse, and the potential damage it might do to 'the church' go away. I was acutely conscious that in my response to the case of 2007-8, I had done 'the opposite of a Welby'. Crucially, I was also only too aware of the cost of taking such action.

The latter point is critical. Safeguarding processes and procedures within the Church of England have improved immeasurably in recent years. Following his resignation, some commented on the irony that, during his time as Archbishop of Canterbury, Justin Welby had played a significant part in their development. Some further suggested, mistakenly in my view, that the major problems with safeguarding in the Church of England only now exist at its highest levels, with safeguarding in local parishes largely in a sound condition.

The continuing error here is the failure to recognise that the establishment of safeguarding procedures only has the tiniest significance in making for a safe church. In fact, the establishment of such processes frequently makes genuine safeguarding less likely to occur, through their role in establishing what is in reality more of a 'tick-box' mentality. The cultural factors already alluded to are the crucial ones, and they lie at the heart of improving safeguarding in the Church of England. The purpose of this book is to unpack this culture further. But the point made here is that of recognising the cost that comes for those who resist this culture. Diocesan safeguarding officers frequently convey to anxious clergy that, if they follow the established safeguarding processes and regulations, all will be well. This is certainly true in terms of the *personal* safety of these clergy who, in most cases, will have adequately 'covered themselves'.

Such action, however, is not the same as insisting with tenacity that a safeguarding issue is genuinely dealt with by those it has been passed on to, rather than falling through the inevitable gaps that exist in these processes. Do this as a member of the Church of England's clergy and my experience is that your personal position becomes far from safe. Instead, you are often treated terribly, particularly if you persist in the face of resistance to safeguarding matters being properly dealt with and refuse to 'pipe down' about this. My own story and those of several others are testimony to this. From a combination of factors involving both local upset and institutional insecurity and anger, I am convinced of the truth of the observation that 'no one's life ever became easier through dealing with a safeguarding matter'. Recognition of this and honesty about the cost of being prophetic about safeguarding (unpacked further in Chapter 8 of this book) is all part of the change that is desperately needed.

The Need to Confront rather than Evade

The story of my treatment by Southwark Diocese has been included here because it reveals so much about the culture of the Church of England that has created the crisis with regard to its safeguarding processes, and how viciously those who challenge this can be treated. The contention of this book is that the appalling failures in safeguarding increasingly exposed in recent years are only the most serious outcome of a culture that handles every difficult issue badly. In the last scene of Agatha Christie's novel *Murder on the Orient Express*, every one of its major characters is found to have been involved in the murder. Through its various chapters, this book seeks to show how every aspect of the culture of the Church of England has blood on its hands when it comes to its terrible failures in regard to safeguarding.

Despite what could be read into the autobiographical elements of this chapter, and as indicated in the preface, this book is written with the very positive intention of helping the Church of England to get its house in order so that it can fulfil its calling as effectively as possible. I remain as excited and genuinely optimistic about my own calling to ministry and mission within the Church of England as when I was first ordained. The vast majority of the material that I have published has been exclusively about how the church can fulfil this calling as effectively as possible.[22] I believe that God, in spite of the problems that this book highlights, is still doing some wonderful things through the Church of England. I also believe, however, that this achievement is *despite* the prevailing culture of the Church of England rather than because of it.

While not centred upon ministry and mission, I consider this to be the most important book I have written in reference to these subjects. This is because it covers the wholesale changes that are necessary for healthy and effective ministry and mission to blossom. My contention is that, if we can establish the culture necessary for effective safeguarding, plenty of other gains will then come with it – chiefly through enabling any number of other difficult issues to be confronted rather than evaded. It is time to be honest about the many 'delusions of adequacy' that exist within the Church of England and the way these have resulted in the debacle that its safeguarding has become.

CHAPTER 2

It Takes a Village to Abuse a Child

The Inescapably Communal Nature of Abuse

The title of this chapter is risky. It has the potential to offend for at least two reasons. Firstly, because it could appear to be speaking of abuse in a casual or flippant manner. This is not the intention. The intention is instead the very serious one of highlighting an issue that is critical to safeguarding and one which, when ignored, can be devastating. Secondly, it takes a positive and much quoted phrase about the importance of community, which many are happy to affirm rather glibly, and reveals the darker and perhaps truer significance of the impact of such community upon those who are vulnerable.[1]

When examples of appalling abuse are uncovered, whether in the church or elsewhere, the tabloid newspapers in Britain know how to respond. Headlines present a strong condemnation and the language of evil is very freely used. Part of the agenda here is to leave people in no doubt about the appalling nature of abuse and the way that it destroys lives. The language used conveys a sense of the dehumanisation of those who have committed these deeds, with the revulsion seeking to draw the clearest line possible between them and 'normal' people. This revulsion obviously extends beyond individual abuse. When the 'grooming gangs' operating within Britain have been exposed, a similar language and interpretation is used about such 'sick communities'.

All of this is more than understandable. But beyond the tendency to sensationalise in cheap ways, it needs to receive an element of further critique because, at the root of this response, is a certain amount of naivety about how such abuse is enabled and facilitated by the wider communities in which it has taken place. There has been significant change in this area in recent years which can at first sight make this comment look rather out of date.

People are now very aware that large institutions, whether it be the Roman Catholic Church, the Church of England or the BBC, have often played a key role in both facilitating and failing to deal with abuse. The revelations from 2012 about the way that Jimmy Savile's prolific abuse over several decades had been facilitated by institutions as diverse as the BBC, the NHS and the Royal Family was a game-changer here. But two factors should bring caution before feeling that we have fully recognised and acknowledged the communal role in abuse.

The first of these is that it is the role of larger institutions in such abuse that people have generally woken up to. This is partly through the influence of our postmodern culture. Postmodernism is generally defined as scepticism towards the grand narratives and ideologies of the modern age, and this has very effectively prepared the way for acceptance that established national institutions and their overall leaders have had a role in allowing abuse to go unchecked. That is very different, however, from recognising and acknowledging the role of smaller communities, such as local churches, in colluding with abuse.

The second point is that recognition of the role of institutions in covering up abuse is not the same as recognising the role of a community in causing and facilitating that abuse. The whole reason for the writing of this book is to try to draw attention to the numerous ways in which Church of England churches, and the cultures within them, make safeguarding problems more likely to happen. Much attention has quite rightly been given in recent times to the scandal of 'the church' at diocesan and national levels failing to deal with revelations about abuse correctly and causing further damage to survivors in the process.[2] But my contention is that this only forms a fraction of the culpability of the church in that abuse. In fact, it could even be said that the greater attention now paid to the process by which reports of safeguarding matters are handled is the very thing that can most distract attention from the role of communities in establishing an environment where this abuse is enabled. The development of DBS (Disclosure and Barring Service) checks is very necessary but also has the potential to disguise the role of communities in safeguarding offences. This is because it encourages the idea that preventative safeguarding is essentially about finding the 'rotten apples' within an otherwise healthy 'barrel'.

It is undoubtedly very hard for 'ordinary people' to accept a communal role in safeguarding offences and abuse. It conjures up images of 'witchfinders' in the seventeenth century taking advantage of the superstition and fear of communities to prey upon their innocent victims. No one likes the idea that they might be manipulated by those who commit abuse, let alone accepting that they might have unwittingly facilitated abuse without any such manipulation taking place. But before we turn to the latter, the manipulation of communities by those committing abuse is worth examining.

The Grooming of Communities

Part of the breakthrough in thinking about safeguarding in recent years has been a greater understanding of the way in which whole communities can be groomed. However, this is yet to be fully reflected in safeguarding courses, policies or in the popular understanding of the term. Google 'grooming' and the definition most swiftly found is: "when someone builds a relationship, trust and emotional connection with a child or young person so they can manipulate, exploit and abuse them". This reflects the assumption, still held by many, that the grooming of potential victims is the major or even sole understanding of what grooming is and the one, therefore, which churches need to be most alert to. Such grooming and the prevention of it remains, of course, hugely important.

However, it is equally important to recognise that just as dangerous a form of grooming is the way in which entire communities can be groomed to make them more likely to collude with abuse. Indeed it could be argued that this is the most significant form and takes place when those who commit abuse are successful in creating a perception of themselves that disguises their threat. It is now widely recognised that the celebrity Jimmy Savile was incredibly successful in this regard, with a sophisticated mixture of factors enabling him to avoid proper scrutiny. These included, most obviously, his enormous fundraising for charities. But it also included less recognised factors such as his apparently harmless oddities, which then acted as a smokescreen, enabling him to 'hide in plain sight'. While some of this public image may well have been very consciously developed by Savile, much of his sinister agenda was probably unconscious even to him, explaining further why those around him were largely unconscious of this as well.

The Grooming of Church Communities

Something similar can occur at a more local level. In the previous chapter I spoke about the lay minister at my church who eventually received a criminal conviction. For many years, he spent a vast amount of time ministering to people in the church and helping them out in various practical ways. It is, of course, impossible to comment with certainty about the motives of others. Whatever my revulsion at the crime for which the lay minister was convicted, I do believe that most of his positive activity within the church was done out of a genuine Christian desire to serve God and others. Others might take a different view. But the *result* of this activity was that, intentionally or not, a large number of people within the church community were very effectively groomed in the general view that he was a saint. Following the conviction, there were some who admitted that, although they had no knowledge of misconduct, they had always felt slightly uncomfortable with the lay minister. It is significant, however, that some of them said that they then dismissed these thoughts because of the overall profile which he held within the church.

The effect of this public narrative was particularly apparent after the conviction when I had to announce it to the congregations at Christ Church. At the service attended by long-term members of the church, there was an audible gasp. This was completely understandable. However, almost straight away and despite the finding of the court, there was a strong element of denial that the offence could have happened, with rumours immediately developing to explain how the 'misunderstanding' had occurred. Most of these rumours imputed a role to my 'inexperience'. Rather than confront me, most of those who made this claim did so more indirectly and in a manner that kept their perspective away from challenge. Disturbingly, even some of those congregation members with a greater knowledge about the matter chose to keep quiet. While at the time I felt let down by this response, I now understand it more fully. For years they had lived within a very strong public narrative concerning this member of their church and had to suppress any thoughts that contradicted this. For many of these years, they were also living within a very conservative evangelical culture where the suppression of thoughts for fear of being seen as 'unsound' was completely normalised.

The most powerful illustration of the effect of this public narrative was when a woman in the congregation spoke to me about her upset over what had happened. Perhaps in the light of further reflection, her view has now changed. But then, in tears, she told me that she couldn't believe it wouldn't have been better for those making accusations to have kept quiet than for such a 'great man' to have been brought down in this way. At the time, I was shocked by this response. But I can now see how devastating it was to have an entire narrative that had built up around someone and everything that he represented about authentic Christianity, suddenly and violently deconstructed.

I emphasise again that I am very unsure how much of this story points to the conscious grooming of the community in order to facilitate abuse. It is, I believe, somewhat more complex. But it does, nonetheless, illustrate the huge power that comes when, for whatever reason, a very positive public narrative is allowed to develop around someone within a church community. Such a narrative, and the pressure to conform to it, has the power to neutralise the role of private and even shared suspicion. In the case of the lay minister, I was shocked to discover that the women and men who had passed through the youth group he had led, had spoken to each other for years about the alleged misconduct. Some of these comments were at the level of reporting it with an acceptance I found disturbing, while for others it contained real anger. "I'll get married anywhere but at that church" was one comment that I heard associated with its impact. But the commentary on what had happened generally remained within friendship groups, only seeping out very occasionally in the rumours that first alerted me to the issue.

A key factor in similar cases I have heard about is the role of families within local churches. If the parents of those who have suffered abuse know the abuser, an obvious impediment exists to the disclosure of what has been done. Where the abuser is seen as a 'pillar of the church', this adds a further level of complexity. In these situations, survivors get caught between their deep and continuing hurt at what has happened to them and the fear of revealing what would be a shattering blow to their parents. Many survivors of abuse become further caught between their desire to continue in a Christian faith which they know is genuine and their awareness of the wrong that one of the chief mediators of this faith did to them.

A clearer example of what I interpreted as the very deliberate grooming of a church community was connected with another safeguarding case that I had to handle. This was how I managed the association with our church of a man convicted of very serious paedophile offences. He has since died. The man was disabled, with his movement largely confined to use of a mobility scooter. I was informed by the police that his physical vulnerability was the chief reason why his convictions had not resulted in a prison sentence. But they also left me in no doubt of the high level of danger that he represented. Not only was he placed by the police in a category of being highly likely to reoffend, but in the more serious category of being likely to be reconvicted.

Without sharing many of the details about the man's offences, the police did tell me that they involved young children who had been groomed by his provision to them of sweets, cigarettes and pornography. Banned from attending Sunday services at my church, the man was allowed to attend a monthly midweek service of Holy Communion, where a very small number of people and no children were present; and also a monthly lunch, attended by a small number of older men. An agreement between him and the church was drawn up with both the diocesan safeguarding team and a special unit of the local police playing a key role in this.

While the agreement was very clear and the process involved very thorough, with an annual meeting to review the agreement, managing the situation proved extremely demanding. The overwhelming reason for this was that the man was so successful in gaining a level of support and sympathy from some members of the church. This was partly because of his very obvious physical frailty, but also through what I regarded to be a high level of grooming. Despite his lack of mobility, the man would do the shopping for an older member of the congregation and regularly chat to her and others. The conversations that he liked to have, in person as well as by phone, were extremely long-winded, with a major emphasis on affability and cheerfulness. These had the effect of largely disguising the continuing danger which he represented to children in the local area. Once again, the degree to which this was conscious or unconscious on his part is debatable. But it is also largely irrelevant. The outcome was as bad as if it had been deliberate, and it is possible that the unconscious dimension of it increased its plausibility and effectiveness.

The result of this conscious or unconscious grooming of the community was that the man felt increasingly confident to push boundaries in terms of the agreement between him and the church. Although banned from going near local schools, he would sometimes be found going past our church school, making the excuse that it was the nearest way home after delivering the shopping to an older member of the church. Fairly regularly he would also want to talk through the minutiae of the details of his agreement through the construction of hypothetical scenarios. With the highly amicable tone that he used for this came a 'wearing down' effect that required a good deal of effort and energy to resist. Conscious of what I believed was going on, I adopted a very strong response, trying hard to make my conversations with him as brief and business-like as possible. This was partly to try to offset the rapport that he was managing to establish with other members of the church and which, to my mind, was part of grooming them to regard him as harmless. But it was also because I was aware that it would be very easy for him to groom me as well.

Knowing that we both liked cricket, the man would try to engage me in amicable conversations about this. When I resisted this, it wasn't because I believed that he didn't deserve anyone being pleasant towards him. It was because I felt that the effect of such amicability would be to reduce both his and my ability to maintain clarity about the boundaries that he needed to observe. The difficulty was that he was surrounded by people who seemed unaware of this danger. Even the experienced policeman who had been assigned to monitor the man had, in my view and also in the view of some of his colleagues, been to some degree groomed by him. I also felt that our own safeguarding officer at the church was susceptible to this as well, with her nervousness about how to relate to the man perhaps playing a role here. Meetings to review the agreement would often begin in what I saw as an unhelpfully convivial manner. I would then have to speak and start the formal meeting in a more abrupt manner than I would otherwise have chosen, in order to replace the 'nice' atmosphere with one more appropriate to the gravity of the situation that we were seeking to manage.

Maintaining such boundaries and refusing to engage with behaviour that I thought could potentially groom me, brought a measure of unpopularity. The man recognised that I was refusing to allow banter to develop between us and he was upset by this. Once, when I saw him outside our church school, I spoke very firmly about his presence there being unacceptable and refused to accept the excuses that he offered for this. His response was to contact his supporters in the congregation to complain that I was mistreating him, leading some of them to then complain to me about this. I encountered further opposition when I refused to allow the older woman that he shopped for to invite the man to attend her 80th birthday party held at the church. This was because children would have been present and I saw his exclusion as both vital for their safety, and because of the mixed message that would otherwise have been sent to him. What I found tough in these situations was being presented as harsh and graceless in my attitude towards him.

Much of our mission at Christ Church is now centred upon trying to display grace as strongly as possible to those traditionally outside of the church's community. This includes people who were homeless, suffering from mental health issues or just isolated and lonely. The congregation members who supported the man were swift to claim an inconsistency in this regard. My firm response (and it sometimes had to be very firm) was to make it clear that acts of grace towards him were made *more* possible by clarity about maintaining the agreed boundaries.

Fortunately, opportunities to combine boundaries with a measure of grace did emerge. Anxious that firmness should not be my only response to the man, I arranged for him to attend a course run by The Lucy Faithfull Foundation.[3] This is a charity dedicated to tackling child sexual abuse by working to prevent abuse from happening in the first place and to prevent it from happening again, if it already has. Where I sought to show grace was in asking the PCC to pay a third of the cost for the course, while the man himself was asked to pay another third. To cover the remaining third of the cost, I approached those members of the congregation who particularly supported him. Surprised by this idea and the approach taken to its funding, the course was successful in demonstrating to the man and to others that the maintenance of clear boundaries in his management was not antithetical to showing Christian love. On this basis, I felt better able to explain as well how even the boundaries themselves were a vital application of this love.

The course achieved a measure of success in its aim of developing a greater empathy in the man towards the people that he had abused. Those who ran the programme gave a positive account of his engagement with it. As a result of this, I felt able to suggest that the agreement should be amended to allow him to attend our Sunday service at 11.00 am (where no children were present) within the parameters of a very strict set of protocols. This was all intended to form a further display of our commitment to both grace and truth in the church's relationship with the man. It was, to some degree, effective in this aim. But it is also true that some of his supporters at the church were, at points, guilty of trying to push the clear boundaries established by this protocol, giving the impression that its strictness was all rather unnecessary. Chapter 6 will look at the difficulties which many in churches have with the establishment of any boundaries regarding adult behaviour and this was another factor that I detected in those who were resistant to aspects of the management of this case.

The story of engagement with this particular person and the difficulties in maintaining the agreement have been covered in some detail because it demonstrates the extent to which the involvement of a sympathetic church can make a safeguarding situation much more difficult to handle appropriately. Whether he was fully conscious of it or not, the man's behaviour had very effectively groomed a number of people to see him as less dangerous than he was. But it was subtle and not easily recognised. It was not that any of those who knew the man denied the crimes that he had committed or the awfulness of their nature. It was more that his interaction enabled these factors to be pushed into the distant background of their day-to-day perception of him and therefore their interpretation of my relationship with him. In psychological terms, a key factor almost certainly at work here, was the difficulty of sustained engagement with the reality of what the man had done and the relative ease of letting it fade into the background.

The story of the interaction of my church with this man is one of how a community responded to the management of someone who had *already* been convicted for safeguarding offences. It is therefore highly instructive about the role of communities in colluding with such offences. If people could be so effectively groomed by someone whose paedophile offences were not in doubt, it shows how easily this can be done by someone whose offences, or potential for offences, is not yet known. The stories of both cases covered in this chapter form a strong picture of the way in which, intentionally or not on the part of the protagonist, communities can be very easily manipulated into furnishing the environment within which abuse is more likely to occur.

Grooming of a community is therefore an important factor in understanding the role of wider communities in facilitating abuse. Due to the manipulation involved, the guilt of the community here is, perhaps, somewhat mitigated. This mitigation, however, can no longer be maintained once the concept of community grooming is understood. Proper engagement with this factor should be an enduring legacy of the revelations surrounding Jimmy Savile. The foremost relevance of 'grooming' is that of communities being groomed to make them collude with abuse. It is to be hoped that church communities will push through any discomfort felt at discussing this concept and become more aware of the serious danger that it represents.

Further Ways in which Communities Collude with Abuse

Arguably more significant to the communal role in abuse, however, are those examples where communities collude with such abuse in a way less connected with the influence or manipulation of those committing it.

Once again, the worst examples of this collusion can sometimes work to disguise the existence of its more subtle and most common versions. Paedophile rings or grooming gangs are, as we are learning more and more, a horrific reality within our society. The evidence from Peter Ball's abuse shows that at least some parts of this was committed in conjunction with other clergy from within Chichester Diocese, such as Roy Cotton and Colin Pritchard, who were also actively involved in such abuse.[4] However, a more common form for the role of communities in facilitating abuse is when support is given to the one committing the abuse through the structures, cultures and agendas of the community within which this abuse takes place.

A number of elements can be seen to be operating here, and some of the deeper causes involved will be covered in greater detail in the chapters that follow. But among the most obvious factors by which church communities can facilitate abuse are the following.

The Veneration of Leaders

The full revelation of the abuse involving Peter Ball in the BBC documentary *Exposed: The Church's Darkest Secret* coincided with the emergence of allegations against Jonathan Fletcher, the former Vicar of Emmanuel Church in Wimbledon.[5] On the surface, there were considerable differences between Peter Ball and Jonathan Fletcher, most obviously in the theological traditions that they represented. Peter Ball was an Anglo-Catholic monk and Jonathan Fletcher, a conservative evangelical. The abuse by Peter Ball and the allegations against Jonathan Fletcher, however, have more in common than their widely differing church traditions might indicate.

The most obvious of these common features was the huge veneration that both men were accorded within their respective traditions. It is no exaggeration to say that they were hero-worshipped. Peter Ball was presented within his community as utterly saintly, and Jonathan Fletcher as the perfect example of a man in full submission to God's Word, with his ministry exemplifying the valiant upholding of biblical Christianity against the destructive forces of liberalism. It was this standing that then allowed Ball's and Fletcher's relationships to pass without the scrutiny that they might otherwise have received. It did this by making it very difficult for anyone to question the nature of Ball's and Fletcher's activities, least of all those who fell victim to them.

The culture of Christian celebrity is a very significant factor within almost every part of the church that is growing today. Christian festivals from the New Wine, Spring Harvest and Soul Survivor variety, all the way to the Keswick Convention, can be seen as facilitating the very type of communal adoration of preachers and worship leaders that make the abuse of this power more likely to occur. Once again, it is a very subtle process explaining how it often passes under the radar of those present. Examples of this might include leaders receiving praise and admiration for their humility about their abilities or acknowledgement of their sinfulness. The latter is usually expressed in very general terms, keeping well away from the public admission of specific weaknesses of that leader.

But the drip-drip effect of this sort of adulation is, almost always, corrupting, particularly once such leaders find themselves getting away with behaviour that they initially know should be challenged. In both the case of Peter Ball, whom I never met, and Jonathan Fletcher, whom I met on a number of occasions, I believe that it was communal adulation that played the crucial role in subverting their conscience. This conscience, it seems, was not entirely quashed. As with the lay minister in the case at my church, my explanation for why their offences did not escalate further is that the genuine Christian faith of all three, and their awareness that what they were doing was wrong (combined with fear of exposure) restrained their actions in some measure. This, I hasten to add, does not make their actions any less appalling. It simply makes the point that once the community had abdicated responsibility for holding their leaders to account, any potential checks on their activity lay with the abusers alone.

Another case with many parallels to those already mentioned emerged in 2023 with the accusations made against the founder of Soul Survivor, Canon Mike Pilavachi. Over a hundred people were reported to have come forward with allegations of emotional and physical abuse across a thirty-year period. Many of these allegations had been raised as early as 2004, but the esteem in which Mike Pilavachi was held and the celebrity culture pervading Soul Survivor and similar charismatic networks worked against these allegations being properly engaged with.[6]

When church leaders who have committed abuse are asked how they reconciled their actions with their Christian faith, they usually give one answer: they were aware that what they were doing was wrong but, because of everything that they were doing for God, they believed that he would 'understand'.[7] If anyone with a tendency towards abuse is therefore placed in a setting where adulation for their ministry becomes almost part of the community's statement of faith, it is all too easy to see how abuse is far more likely to happen.

Intense Models of 'Discipleship' and the Development of a Culture of Obedience

This factor is closely related, and it forms another aspect of church community providing an environment that makes abuse more likely to occur. It is no coincidence that the abuse committed by Peter Ball, Jonathan Fletcher, John Smyth and Mike Pilavachi, in their very different settings, took place within cultures that idealised the mentoring of younger men by those who were older and supposedly wiser.

The monastic tradition was fairly obviously the crucial influence upon the setup within Peter Ball's house, where the justification for the young men living there was their spiritual formation through his guidance and influence. Within the conservative evangelical tradition represented by Jonathan Fletcher and John Smyth, it was the biblical presentation of St Paul's relationship with Timothy which formed the major model for such influence. In both very different traditions, a highly personal bond, with almost everything of value mediated through the senior figure, has been established as the perfect form of Christian discipleship.

Another important aspect of this is its elevation to a form of privilege. Those drawn into such intense models of discipleship are normally given messages from the surrounding Christian community making it clear how fortunate they have been to be given so much time and attention by the senior partner. Particularly when the leader has any degree of 'fame', this represents a highly attractive message to almost anyone and something that it is then quite difficult for the one holding the power not to abuse.

This can be done quite easily through the giving and temporary withdrawal of approval. When I was at theological college, there was a tutor who had been immersed in the conservative evangelical tradition throughout his life and achieved a certain level of fame. He has since died, and I hasten to add that I have no reason to believe that he was ever involved in any form of criminal abuse. What was very apparent, however, was the way that he would make up his mind very swiftly each year on the value or otherwise of the new intake of ordinands. He would shower those whom he rated highly with approval and interest and make it clear that, with their gifts and talents, they had a wonderful ministry ahead of them. To those not placed in this category, he showed much less interest. As one who initially made it into the first group, I swiftly realised that neither was a good place to be. This was because the approval and affirmation that these ordinands received was completely conditional on buying into the tutor's vision for their priorities during their theological education. Sharing his vision, and not asking any searching questions about his 'wisdom' about ordained ministry was crucial to the ongoing relationship. Those who did not conform, which eventually included me, then had to cope with a scarcely concealed disappointment that they had not matched up to his earlier hopes and expectations.

Unimpressed at that stage by his behaviour, I was relieved to be relegated to his 'B' team, and I made my disapproval of his actions fairly apparent. But other ordinands found it much harder, and I am now in no doubt that his behaviour represented spiritualised abuse. Most germane to this chapter was that all of this happened within a college environment which seemed completely unable to recognise, let alone address, what was happening. The charisma and energy of the tutor in an otherwise fairly introverted setting largely allowed him to make his own rules. The experience was enough to open my eyes to a key way in which more serious abuse can be facilitated within Christian communities.

Single-Sex Subcultures

Abuse in churches can obviously take many forms, and occur across both/all genders. What seems undeniable, however, is that abuse within the church has been far more prevalent within single-sex subcultures, mainly all-male ones. The Church of England still contains many such subcultures. In a later chapter, I will be keen to draw a clear distinction between the different opinions on sexuality and accepting the impact that institutional dishonesty about sexuality in the Church of England has had upon its safeguarding. A similar distinction is needed between different opinions on the ordination of women and acceptance of the impact on safeguarding of the single-sex subcultures within the Church of England.

This is because single-sex groupings appear to lend themselves far more easily to further forms of exclusivity, be they based upon class, education or personality type. Once a grouping is exclusive enough, it can develop 'norms' of behaviour that are anything but normal to the outside world. Mixed gender groupings, even if they are exclusive in other ways, automatically subvert many of these 'norms'. It is insecurity about the prospect of such subversion that normally brings about the greatest reaction when groups that have been dominated by one gender face the prospect of becoming mixed. Normally this struggle to adjust is within the context of all-male groupings. But this is not always the case. Cultural 'norms' within primary schools can become equally challenged and subverted by the sudden appearance of male teachers into what has sometimes been an equally unhealthy female dominated subculture.

This is definitely not to say that all church groups should be mixed. I have run many church groups composed of one gender. Within youth work, in particular, there can be much value in running single-sex groups that give boys and girls the chance to take a break from all the issues that come from mixed settings. The problems appear to emerge when single-sex groupings are established as the permanent and ideal model for church groups. Again and again, across traditions as different as ultra-high Anglo-Catholicism and the most conservative forms of evangelicalism, an insistence on single-sex groupings appears to have been an all too effective means of insulating the subculture of these groupings and their 'norms' against any external critique. This then makes sense of why the most awful forms of abuse within the church have so often been committed within subcultures where a defining characteristic has been their single-sex nature.

What has been lost at this point is one of the major theological emphases made within the creation accounts of Genesis 1 and 2 – that of the goodness of the male and female, created to work together for God within that creation. The multiple aspects of this 'goodness' is something that would repay much greater thought and reflection within the Church of England. But its most obvious application in this context is the greater strength that this would bring to its preventative safeguarding.

An Unofficial Ethos of Relative Expendability

These days it is shocking enough to hear 'relative expendability' spoken about within warfare. It is within this context that the term has sometimes been used to speak of losses that had to be accepted, if other gains were to be made. The expression 'poor bloody infantry' was coined in response to the realisation that the price of such 'acceptable loss' was invariably paid by ordinary soldiers, rather than by their leaders, who were located miles behind the front line.[8]

SAFEGUARDING THE INSTITUTION

Although never stated in these terms, something similar has often been seen in the church's response to safeguarding issues. The way that survivors/victims of abuse are treated within the Church of England regularly demonstrates their relative expendability within it. This attitude is so ingrained that it appears to be uncritically adopted by those who spend any time in the church's hierarchy. These people are then shocked to hear themselves described by survivors of abuse as callous. In the previous chapter mention was made of those who described George Carey's failure to hand on letters he received about Peter Ball to the police as 'inexplicable'. However, such failure is too common an occurrence to be an inexplicable error of judgement. It is, in short, agenda-driven. The issue of institutions placing their own safety ahead of the safety of those who are meant to be within their care is central enough to this book to receive a chapter of its own. What is dealt with here are the general attitudes towards relative importance within the church that fuel this problem.

Many examples of this appear to have no connection with safeguarding. Just one of these is the treatment within the Church of England of curates. One of the greatest strengths of the Church of England model of ministry, in principle, is the concept of the curacy. This is an 'apprenticeship' model which allows someone to complete the final phase of their ministerial training by working in a parish for around three to four years with an experienced 'training incumbent'. Some curacies work out well, while others are little short of a disaster. However, with curates allocated for a whole number of reasons, regardless of the training ability of the vicar who receives them, there is a very strong incentive not to ask searching questions when a disastrous curacy occurs. This is problematic on any number of levels but particularly relevant in this context are the trite assumptions made about the 'bounce-backability' of the curates in question. Some clergy do indeed 'bounce back' from a disastrous curacy. But many do not and what seems to be at play here, whether recognised or not, is a form of 'relative expendability'.

Numerous other examples, in areas outside of those included within safeguarding, could be given. But within safeguarding they are seen again and again. In one safeguarding matter that I was involved in, I remember hearing someone declare rather tritely that they believed the young people affected "will probably be OK". This sort of wishful thinking simply represents a vague attempt to express wisdom and benevolence while abdicating responsibility. Speaking to those referred to in this instance some years later, it was manifestly not the case. Their pain was considerably increased by such callous responses.

Another example concerns the person who contributed the Foreword to this book, and who suffered persistent harassment from a senior church leader during their ordination training. As mentioned in the Foreword, this case occurred in another country within the Anglican Communion. The way that the theological college responded to the matter reflects the sorts of factors explored further in Chapter 4. The point here is that, involving the comparative importance of a senior church leader and an ordinand from overseas, this was a very clear example of 'relative expendability'.

Most disturbingly, an 'out of sight, out of mind' culture appears to be operating here. When those who have suffered abuse and have not received justice leave these churches, they can very easily receive an equivalent to the trite blessing reported in James 2.16. This New Testament verse comments on the nonsense of a Christian saying to someone, "Go, I wish you well, keep warm and well fed" while doing nothing about their physical needs. Something similar is present when wishful thinking takes place concerning those who have suffered from abuse, without providing them with support and justice. This is particularly so when concerns about the welfare of those who have committed the offences, and the institution itself, are receiving plenty of very specific and practical attention. When this happens, it is again part of the wider and all-too-common problem within church communities of a culture of relative expendability.

THE PREVALENCE OF 'CHEAP GRACE'

It was the theologian Dietrich Bonhoeffer who coined this phrase. It refers to the church's offer of grace and forgiveness without the necessary presence of factors such as confession, repentance or discipline. Most relevant here is Bonhoeffer's description of such grace being represented as "the

Church's inexhaustible treasury, from which she showers blessings with generous hands, without asking questions or fixing limits".[9]

A wider culture of 'cheap grace' is present within many churches, and it is the most common reason given for not responding to any issues that are difficult. The issue of adult misbehaviour within churches, and the tolerating of it, is once again important enough to receive its own chapter later in this book (Chapter 6). But the justification for what is presented as Christian love is usually some form of 'cheap grace'. Worse still, this cheap grace is, in reality, tacit support for the behaviour involved. If consistently poor behaviour is tolerated without any emphasis upon repentance, discipline or even the permission to ask questions within the community about this behaviour, it represents a corruption of genuine grace rather than anything reflecting its transforming reality. Despite how it may be presented, 'cheap grace' helps no one. In the context of safeguarding, it most obviously harms those who have suffered from abuse. But it also harms the abuser, who is allowed to continue in their destructive behaviour and attitudes. Its motive, however presented, is usually for the benefit of those offering such 'cheap grace' – for those who deploy it to avoid facing difficult situations. But this is ultimately harmful for their wellbeing, too. It damages their integrity and ultimately their sense of credibility and relevance.

Sadly, in almost every example of safeguarding issues receiving an inadequate response from churches, some form of 'cheap grace' is present. Whether it is more famous examples such as George Carey's 'understanding' towards Peter Ball, or more local examples such as the attitude shown by a number at my church towards both the lay minister and the man convicted of paedophile offences, 'cheap grace' is one of the most dangerous theological factors involved in safeguarding.

During my time at theological college, I remember a national expert on safeguarding coming to speak to us about these issues. He mentioned that there was one verse that he would happily see struck out of the Bible, because of the number of times he had seen it misapplied in a safeguarding context. It was 2 Corinthians 5.17. This is commonly (mis)translated: "Therefore, if anyone is in Christ, he is a new creation, the old has gone, the new has come" (NIV). The speaker said that he had lost count of the times that he had seen charismatic churches, in particular, using this verse to say that those who had become Christians (or recommitted to their faith) were now different people to those who previously committed offences and should be treated accordingly.

He then shared stories of the devastation that he had seen this attitude cause.[10] Over twenty years on, the memories of this teaching now combine with my own experience of how often trite and unthinking theology within churches facilitates their collusion with abuse. John 1.17 declares that 'grace *and truth* came through Jesus Christ' (cf. John 1.14). In Chapters 5 and 9, greater reflection will be provided on how a proper understanding of the biblical concept of grace can only become part of the solution to safeguarding when it is combined with an equally biblical emphasis upon truth.

Inadequate Reflection on the Concept of Evil

This is another theological problem which has major communal impact upon safeguarding. In his book *Evil and the Justice of God*, Tom Wright shows how the concept of evil now receives a completely inadequate response from contemporary culture in Britain. Wright argues that our culture basically denies that evil exists – until, that is, terrible events suddenly occur which make this position unsustainable. This often includes the most horrendous examples of abuse, such as the infamous murders committed by people like Fred and Rosemary West, Robert Thompson and Jon Venables, Ian Huntley or Harold Shipman. Or indeed abuse within the church, such as that committed by Peter Ball or John Smyth.

When events like this come to national prominence, the language of evil swiftly returns and is used very freely, not least by the tabloid newspapers. Wright's major point, however, is that, because our society is not used to thinking about the concept of evil with any care or sophistication, it tends then to make an immature response to these undeniable examples of its existence. Lack of serious reflection upon evil results in it being seen as an unusual problem, found within a minority of particularly wicked people. This then results in an equally simplistic approach to its solution. Examples include Tony Blair and George Bush optimistically announcing their plans to 'rid the world of evil', in the wake of the terrorist attacks on the World Trade Center in September 2001. Similarly simple solutions are implied every time the tabloid newspapers refer to the evil found (apparently exclusively) within 'paedophiles' and without reference to that which has usually colluded with their abuse.[11] Much of the superficiality of such thinking within our society is, of course, completely unrecognised.

But there is an even deeper problem when churches and Christians share in such immaturity of thought about evil. The concept of 'cheap grace' considered in the previous section could be seen as depending on a universal understanding of the prevalence of human sin. The universal plight of human beings is indeed a commonly advanced argument for such 'grace' needing to be shown in church life. However, while such an understanding might have accepted something of the breadth of sin across all human beings, it has usually engaged with little of its *depth* within them. 'Cheap grace', in short, requires a simplistic understanding of sin and evil to be sustainable. It fails to grapple with how deeply evil runs within human beings, and indeed remains active within the Christian believer, even after they are accorded the status of being forgiven and redeemed. This is the state that Martin Luther was trying to acknowledge when he described the condition of a Christian as *simul iustus et peccator*, i.e. both righteous and a sinner.[12]

Once this is accepted, we can see that churches commonly fall down on their understanding of the breadth and prevalence of evil, too. They do this, most obviously in terms of the issues tackled in this book, through their failure to recognise the presence and impact of the sort of communal factors involved in abuse that this chapter has been trying to establish. Whatever the universal understanding of human sinfulness that churches might have in theory, they can often remain largely oblivious to their collusion with evil. This is where the confession of sin that occurs near the start of most Church of England services can be rather unhelpful. However thoughtfully they are presented, such confessions, all too easily, encourage an abstract understanding of sin rather than one thoroughly incarnated through the role of Christians in perpetuating injustice and oppression. It is no coincidence that those conservative evangelical churches most comfortable talking about and acknowledging a personal state of sin are also those least inclined to engage with their congregations' wealth, power and collusion with issues of global injustice. Sin within the Bible has as much a collective understanding as an individual one. But the ease with which discussion of sin can be 'contained' is probably the key factor allowing many churches that speak about sin quite freely, to avoid engagement with any wider concept of evil.

The contention of this chapter is that whenever abuse takes place, the wider community has played a key role in facilitating and perhaps even causing this abuse, albeit usually unconsciously. This will be further recognised once we fully engage with the biblical concept of evil and the way that it runs, like a fault line, through every part of creation, most obviously through all human beings.

Like all communities, churches can be understandably resistant to the suggestion that they share culpability in the abuse of those who have been placed in their care. Understanding that their leaders might have failed in their response to the revelation of safeguarding offences is one thing. Accepting that much of church culture, in its ingrained assumptions and habitual praxis, has facilitated and colluded with such abuse is another altogether. If recognised, this can be a shattering blow and even start to deconstruct faith in the authentic nature of any of the church's ministry and mission. But this only shows how essential for the church's ministry and mission it is that this point is acknowledged. This is because, if communal collusion with abuse is addressed, many other factors that currently impede the ministry and mission of the church will be addressed at the same time. It is therefore for the benefit of every single aspect of what the church is called to do and be that it needs to engage fully with the reality and pervasiveness of evil, including the acknowledgement that 'it takes a village to abuse a child'.

CHAPTER 3

Pragmatism and Passive Aggression

How Problems are Approached in the Church of England

It is time to dig a little deeper into the collective culture of the Church of England and those factors that have contributed to the consistent role that the church and its communities continue to play in making effective safeguarding more difficult. Once again, I need to emphasise how slow I have been to recognise these factors. The emotional bias that I have felt against acknowledging them has been considerable. The more immersed that readers are within the structures of the Church of England, the more that they will struggle to see them. Defensiveness against criticism of their church is not necessarily the major factor here. It is more because, to employ a well-used expression, they are like fish that do not realise they are wet, because living in water is all that they have ever known. The response, "I simply don't recognise what you are saying" has only limited value when it is used as a critique of the content of this chapter. Indeed, it points towards its central claim.

Assertiveness and Aggression

Assertiveness is different from aggression. Or at least it should be understood as such. Being assertive is a positive term, describing the way in which a person presents their concerns in a clear and, if necessary, persistent manner. Aggression, on the other hand, is a negative term describing the forceful presentation of a person's position with no consideration for the feelings of others or the existence of alternative viewpoints. In principle, a clear differentiation should exist between these two ways of relating to other people.

In practice, of course, things are more complex. An obvious example is the way that tone of voice, choice of words, and methods of communication strongly influence how a person might categorise the words or actions of another towards them. Background and personality are also critical factors here. Both the different ways in which personalities are 'wired' and the different experiences that they have had, make a huge impact in their different ways of approaching and interpreting conflict. Most people would agree, in theory, that the extremes of both aggression and passivity are wrong as an approach to disagreement. But that still leaves considerable diversity about where the right balance should be found between these extremes, in order to create a proper and healthy assertiveness.

Such diversity is usually found within all teams that are functioning well. One person might play the role of *agent provocateur* and be the one most prepared to name and confront issues. Another within the same team might play the role of the listener and summariser of the different views present. Still another may have the role of peacemaker, through possessing the gifts needed to establish an area of compromise and then negotiate the path towards it. Most successful teams will acknowledge the role that this sort of diversity of gifting and insight plays within it. Within a Christian context, it is of course an example of St Paul's teaching in 1 Corinthians 12 about the crucial role that each part of the body of Christ has within the proper functioning of the church. Given its acknowledgement of human frailty, we may also consider it to be an equally powerful example of the teaching of Paul in 2 Corinthians about the way in which God works powerfully through human weakness.

The key factor for teams that are successful in handling conflict, however, is that there is general agreement about *the aim* of confronting and resolving such conflict. Diversity about the best way to approach this confrontation is not just possible or even just desirable. It is essential. What makes a team situation swiftly become dysfunctional, however, is when a significant part of that team refuses to cooperate in the aim of establishing an assertive culture, insisting that any attempt to resolve an issue forthrightly is by definition aggressive. There is plenty of room in teams for divergence concerning where a proper approach to assertiveness is found and, as I have indicated, nurturing this diversity is essential for finding that place. *The problems come, however, when there is an individual or even collective denial of the principle of assertiveness itself.* This is rarely an official policy or stated position on the part of those who maintain it. But this is all the more reason for why it can so easily become part of the culture that 'eats that policy for breakfast'.

During my time as a vicar at Christ Church, New Malden, I have had numerous colleagues, each with very different gifts and personalities. Some have had, like me, a fairly strong capacity for assertion, but with the accompanying danger that this can sometimes lapse into aggression. Others have possessed a strong capacity for peace-making, but with the accompanying danger that this can sometimes lapse into passivity. Still others have possessed a strong degree of wisdom and recognition of the complexities involved in many issues, but with the accompanying danger of viewing these issues as so complex that no resolution is really possible. But what my team, in its various forms, has usually agreed upon is the principle of assertiveness. In other words, that the running of a properly functioning church involves confronting issues and problems rather than avoiding them. This does not, I hasten to add, mean that every difficult issue at the church has been handled perfectly. Far from it. But I think it is fair to say that clarity over the aim of confronting and resolving problems is overwhelmingly the key thing that has made our ministry and mission effective rather than dysfunctional.

Most relevant to this context, it is also the factor which, more than any other, has provided rigour, energy and direction in our approach to safeguarding. When safeguarding issues have arisen, we have been totally clear that any approach which seeks to dodge these issues rather than to confront them is not an option. Whatever the development of safeguarding protocols and procedures might suggest, this is still far from established within the culture of the Church of England.

Relatively recently, I encountered another church where a safeguarding issue had occurred. When I asked its vicar what he had done about it and the person involved, he simply replied, "I sent him packing." Disturbingly, he didn't appear to have questioned the appropriateness of this, or any wider responsibility that he might have had for what happened

3 / PRAGMATISM AND PASSIVE AGGRESSION

next. Had the problem simply been passed on somewhere else? Examples such as this have only strengthened my resolve, and that of the team at my church, to act in the very opposite manner to this.

Clarity over confronting rather than avoiding issues was also the factor that governed the proper management at my church of the man convicted of paedophile offences, and especially the issue of community grooming covered in the previous chapter. On every safeguarding matter at Christ Church, agreement over establishing a culture of proper assertiveness has been the key factor in facilitating an appropriate response.

This has not always been the case. When I first arrived at the church as curate in 2003, the culture was almost entirely different, with discussion of difficult issues generally avoided, both within the staff team and the PCC (Parochial Church Council). Some of these issues could appear theoretical and therefore inconsequential. One example was the previous vicar's insistence that encouraging any theological discussions within the congregation was unhelpful. Within a strongly evangelical church this attitude should have been regarded as astonishing. But his rationale was that if theological discussions were encouraged, this would only result in dividing the church. The same applied to more obviously practical matters, however, and largely for the same reason – that some would not like the outcome. The overall effect was that more and more unresolved issues built up. This resulted in a deep level of frustration within the congregation and a considerable level of dysfunctionality.

The negative impact of this culture upon the church and its effectiveness was therefore serious. *But it was catastrophic when it came to safeguarding.* It didn't, to be fair, mean that the man convicted of paedophile offences wasn't managed fairly effectively. However, his existing conviction and ban from services meant that this issue was relatively self-contained and therefore a fairly simple one to respond to. But it was directly related to the issue involving the lay minister not being properly confronted when this first emerged, several years before my time at the church. An atmosphere of general aversion to conflict, combined with very specific fears about the fallout that this might bring, meant that the matter was not referred to the police or even to the diocese. It was instead dealt with 'in house', accompanied by simplistic and frankly heartless assumptions about its level of impact, unconsciously related to the concept of 'relative expendability' covered in the previous chapter. Given the suppression involved, it says everything about the wider culture of the Church of England that the only person against whom any action has been taken in regard to the case, is the person who ensured that it was eventually dealt with properly.

Changing the culture at Christ Church, New Malden into the more assertive one described earlier has been difficult, to put it mildly. A major help, however, is the relief that generally comes to a church when issues that have been evaded for years actually start to be addressed. The impact on the effectiveness of a great deal of ministry and mission is almost instant. But there will always be opposition as well. One of the hardest tasks at Christ Church has been that of addressing misbehaviour by adult members of the church, after years of this going largely unchallenged. The wider issues involved here will be explored in Chapter 6.

Significantly, those nervous about this matter being addressed have even objected to the term 'behaviour' being used at all in relation to adults. But within a leadership team containing the diversity described earlier, we have now established a general culture which ensures that difficult issues are properly named and then responded to. Plenty of discussion and disagreement still takes place on the process by which this response should then be made. Sometimes this disagreement is quite sharp! But the principle of making an assertive response to issues rather than avoiding them is now established.

Passive-Aggressive Behaviour

A culture of confronting difficult matters is one that, however carefully and thoughtfully implemented, can be impossible for some people to cope with. Those whose poor behaviour is challenged, particularly if this is a new experience, fairly obviously find it difficult. But so do those who instinctively feel that almost any challenge to the status quo is aggressive. It is common to find many people within churches, for instance, who equate aggression with someone not dropping any challenge at the first sign of discomfort in the person addressed by it. I had one colleague who couldn't cope at all with the church's transition to a more assertive culture. Presented with any level of challenge, however gentle, she would generally remain silent – but with her body language becoming more and more defensive, and then aggressive, in response to the perceived aggression that she was receiving. For a congregation member this would have been difficult but of less significance. In a central leader of the church, it caused a high level of dysfunctionality, and after several years of trying numerous ways of resolving this impasse, we had to accept that it wasn't possible. Eventually, she moved on to a position in a different church where the same challenges, for a variety of reasons, were not present.

It is this sort of response that points to the impossibility of maintaining a passive approach to conflict. Few people enjoy conflict. But for those who find it impossible to deal with, the result is always some form of passive-aggressive behaviour. This is because, as the number of unresolved issues build around them, they have to find some method of coping. Unable to deal with these issues assertively, they have to work towards their desired outcome through indirect means, such as secrecy, manipulation and deceit. The official disapproval of such behaviour in churches frequently combines with a collective fear of conflict to mean that this is rarely acknowledged and is therefore colluded with. This results in highly dysfunctional situations becoming normalised. Just one example of this is the widespread acceptance in many churches of lying as a legitimate device for evading challenge, an issue that will be examined further in Chapter 6.

The Collective Culture of the Church of England: Non-Assertion and Passive Aggression

Where these factors have their greatest impact is within those settings where, for whatever reason, they become the unchallenged culture of an entire church. This can happen in a very short time if its leader possesses such characteristics. I remember spending some time within a church where the vicar was extremely pleasant and able, but also fairly obviously vulnerable. A variety of factors were involved, all deserving of sympathy and support. Most significant, however, was the impact of this on the life of the church. It was another experienced clergyman who offered the view that almost everything that the vicar did in his running of the church was governed by his attempt to avoid further pain. This led to a timid approach to almost every problem and to the consistent avoidance of their direct confrontation. It would result in, at best, a 'tactical' approach to resolution, with an immediate withdrawal if there was any reaction.

This is sometimes known as 'the Pac-Man approach to leadership'. Pac-Man was one of the original video games from the early 1980s. Its character would make his way round a maze, trying to eliminate ghosts, but immediately changing direction every time he encountered an obstacle. More than one frustrated member of a church has described their vicar in a manner that fits with this illustration, and indeed it was one such member who provided it to me. The difficulty is that a number of people are heavily invested in this being the type of church leader they want. Characteristics within clergy such as vulnerability, caution and carefulness can, in reality, be valued less for their positive impact upon the church than because they allow those exhibiting poor behaviour or exerting undue influence within it to remain unchallenged.

One of the most insightful commentators on the Church of England in recent times has been the cartoonist Dave Walker. Several of his cartoons are hilarious in addressing the problems of dysfunctional cultures within churches and their impact.[1] One of Walker's most telling cartoons shows the true hierarchy of authority that exists in most churches, with several groupings that 'boss the vicar around' appearing way above him/her and others officially leading the church. Rather like the observations about British politics in *Yes Minister* and *Yes Prime Minister*, however, the humour within Walker's cartoons could be criticised for allowing people to laugh at such factors precisely as a way of letting themselves off the hook from dealing with them. Such humour can, whatever its intention, implicitly endorse the view that nothing about these situations can change.

This is also the reason why the greatest indicator that someone has done a good job in church leadership is often seen as the absence of conflict during their tenure. This usually needs to be supplemented by a few examples of good ministerial and missional practice, but these are not usually 'weight-bearing' in their significance. What really matters is 'keeping the show on the road' and finding clever ways of maintaining peace. The greatest praise of all can be accorded to those who find tactical ways of bringing about change that avoid a fully honest approach. I remember hearing a woman speaking glowingly of the way that her late husband, who had been a vicar, would bring about change in his churches. She spoke with pride of how he would keep his intentions largely secret and then work towards the point where other key members of the church would think that they had originated these ideas. Once again, it was seen as fine to be open about such tactics and even laugh about what they revealed about church culture. But it would have been quite a different matter if anyone taking part in this conversation had then used terms such as manipulation and passive-aggression to describe these tactics, or asked searching questions about their wider and deeper impact.

It should be clear by now why the Church of England has the senior leaders that it does. There are some exceptions, with some dynamic and imaginative clergy becoming bishops. Sadly, however, this is probably only enough to keep up appearances. The standard requirement for a bishop in the Church of England seems to be someone who is affable and pleasant, reasonably competent, but unexciting and unimaginative. Most crucially they need to have avoided upsetting anyone during their previous ministerial positions. Once again, the frequent humour used to acknowledge this can sometimes be guilty of colluding with this situation. The old joke is that when a new bishop is surrounded by other bishops at their consecration, it is because they are removing their new colleague's backbone! This, of course, is only amusing up to the point when events such as George Carey's non-actions in regard to Peter Ball reveal its humour to be rather dark in its significance.

The post of archdeacon in the Church of England in many ways exists to enable bishops to keep their hands clean from involvement in sorting out problems. In principle, it allows the bishop to concentrate upon pastoral care of the clergy and broader strategy and influence within their diocese or area. Given this brief, it might be imagined that while bishops are recruited from the more passive end of the spectrum, archdeacons would be drawn from its more assertive end. The latter is sometimes the case in both forms of appointment, particularly following the occurrence of a scandal or where there is acknowledgement that a situation has become so dysfunctional that something has to be done about it. More often, however, the characteristics most sought in an archdeacon are those of a 'fixer' – someone, in other words, who will work behind the scenes to sort things out with the minimum of conflict. Unfortunately, this can then very directly lead to manipulation and secrecy being seen as the norm for trying to resolve any problem.

Examples of Passive Aggression in Wider Church Leadership

During my ministry I have encountered such characteristics again and again. Most of the bishops and archdeacons with whom I have had to engage in a working context have been highly pleasant and affable. They have been genuinely concerned for my wellbeing and that of my family. They have been kind and broadly encouraging, if without any real interest being displayed in the detail of my ministry or the specific mission of my church. Sadly, where they have fallen down again and again is in their inability to provide a satisfactory response to anything that is in any way difficult.

If problems or issues have arisen, for which I need their help, I have usually written to the bishop and/or the archdeacon by letter or email outlining the nature of the problem and my concerns. If these problems require any level of courage, confrontation or potential challenge in their response, I generally have found that my message doesn't even receive an acknowledgement, let alone a reply. My approach has been to wait for a time and then write again, trying hard to soften the way that the continued assertiveness might be interpreted by using phrases like "can I respectfully ask…", "I would point out, with respect, that…" etc. If I am feeling brave, or if the issue is one of such importance that it must be addressed, I eventually mention the lack of acknowledgement that my messages usually receive. This normally results in some sort of reply but often one combining a measure of annoyance at my persistence with only the vaguest response, that fails to acknowledge the detail of what I have written.

Sometimes the eventual result of this correspondence is a meeting with the bishop and/or archdeacon. In my experience, however, these meetings have always been unsatisfactory. The detail of the previous emails and letters that I have sent are not engaged with, and the meeting proceeds as if the detail of these concerns has never been raised. It is usually chaired in such a way as to work towards a place of reconciliation, but only through bypassing the issues that have occasioned the meeting, rather than addressing them. This is normally justified by the desire to avoid the negatives of what has gone wrong and a more positive use of the time available (usually very limited) to agree 'a plan for moving forward'.

When I have been allowed a chance to express my concerns, the response has usually been a 'glazed' one. A key indicator of this is the absence of any questions to seek further clarification about the issues. Once I had experienced such meetings enough times, I realised the reason for their nature. An end result had already been decided at a 'pre-meeting' without me being able to influence the decision-making process.

When, on the other hand, I have been summoned to meetings with bishops or archdeacons, the following factors are normally present. No clear agenda has usually been sent, and sometimes no reason is even given for the meeting. If I request this (and this has become my more recent practice) only a fairly general and unspecific reason is given. Once the meeting is underway, however, a very clear agenda on the part of those calling the meeting becomes evident, with its intended outcome once again appearing to have been formulated in advance. The element of surprise and the heavy emphasis on affability is usually effective in ensuring that it is only after the meeting that the full extent of the manipulation involved and its outcome becomes apparent. Lack of resistance is often assumed to signal agreement to this agenda, however vague, and frustration is then expressed if my subsequent actions are not in line with it. It produces mildly threatening statements which suggest where the fault for this impasse should be located: "We've had a meeting at which there appeared to be agreement. Regrettably, however, there are clearly still problems and so further steps will be needed." It was this approach that eventually led to the 'review' of my ministry and resulting suspension covered in Chapter 1.

All of this diocesan procedure is, of course, classic passive-aggressive behaviour. In almost every aspect, it is based around trying to avoid any honest confrontation with the issues involved. In at least two ways. It is bad enough that those involved have avoided, as much as possible, honest and open engagement with those issues and problems that a member of their clergy has seen as important. But it goes further, avoiding an honest and open presentation of the agenda that its leaders are seeking to pursue as well. Rather than clearly stating the issues and problems and inviting comment and discussion about them, it has sought to bring about their desired solution by manipulation and subterfuge instead.

I have noticed similar behaviour in several other aspects of my diocese, particularly in regard to the contentious issue of churches being planted in other parishes. More than once, I have been promised by a diocesan officer that an issue will be played completely straight with me, only to later find that this has not been the case. The upset that my criticism of this has brought has eventually convinced me that some of those involved are so immersed in a culture of avoidance or dishonesty that they can no longer recognise when they are being untruthful.

None of what is reported here is exaggeration. It may, of course, not be normative. Other clergy have reported more positive experiences, with problems that they raised with their bishops and archdeacons being responded to promptly and well. This has included relatively recent experiences within my diocese. One clergyman reported two occasions when his archdeacon saw him the next day after he had flagged up serious concerns and proceeded to deal very effectively with them. Others have had similar experiences. My own father was an archdeacon within my diocese taking, I believe, a similarly active and principled response to difficult issues.

Part of my negative experience, I believe, has been caused by the expectations that I have had about problems being fully named and confronted in a clear and open manner which would seek to highlight the underlying issues involved. This appears to have generated considerable fear and, in consequence, less engagement from my bishops and archdeacons than might otherwise have been the case. Those with the most positive experiences appear to have had more limited and pragmatic goals and much less idealism about issues being dealt with in a way that would prevent their recurrence in the future.

Among most clergy I speak to, however, there is at the very least an ambivalence about their experiences and a widespread resonance with my own account of such meetings. Disturbingly, however, this is often accompanied by extremely low expectations. Several clergy, for instance, agree that few of the meetings to which they were summoned, possessed any clear agenda. But they were slow to recognise the degree to which this was problematic. In most cases, this appeared to be because they were taking a similar approach to the management of their own church, with many of the same unconscious assumptions about a passive-aggressive style being the only one available. This has been a further indication that the approach that we are now trying to take to problems at my own church is far more counter-cultural than I had realised and that this lies at the root of my frustration.

Factors Involved in Rejecting a Passive-Aggressive Approach to Church Leadership

Within Christ Church, unless confidentiality is essential, we now seek to be completely open and honest about every issue that we are trying to confront. There have been occasions where this approach has been costly. Most obviously this has been from the anger of those whose behaviour has been challenged. It has also provided ample opportunity for opposition, both within and outside the church, to cause us considerable trouble. On numerous occasions, the church has then been the victim of lies spread about us in the local community, and this has been both painful and damaging. However, the fallout from past responses to difficult situations has increased our realisation that secrecy and manipulation as a path to achieving our aims is not only wrong but actually counterproductive. Adherence to a culture of transparency and the practice of providing a full rationale for actions taken, not only transforms safeguarding but every other aspect of church life.

But the temptation always remains to act differently from this. Over the years, I have noticed the tactics that can be used by vicars to get items 'through the PCC'. This includes a deliberately opaque approach to agendas and the briefing of key members beforehand to speak up at the right moment with support. Perhaps the most 'effective' tactic is disguising the full significance of an item and then placing it very late on the meeting's agenda, preferably after a long and exhausting discussion on another item, sometimes even within 'Any Other Business'. Sadly, I noticed all of these features during my curacy and perhaps the hardest aspect of my ordained ministry was sitting as a curate through PCC meetings where I was expected to feign ignorance of what was going on. With loyalty to their training vicar often presented as the greatest virtue that a curate can possess, such situations are probably not uncommon.

But it is important to note that their effect upon a church is disastrous. Whatever short-term goals may be achieved, the long-term effects of the dysfunctionality that such tactics produce are immense. It results in frustration and a dramatic falling away of motivation in key members of the church. Indeed, a significant sign that a church has such problems can be when the most energetic and committed members lose their motivation to remain on its PCC. Another similar outcome is when the PCC is dominated for years by members who otherwise contribute very little to the practical life of the church.

For all of these reasons, such approaches to meetings have been firmly renounced at Christ Church. There is now a priority placed on crystal clear agendas going out in good time, full briefing papers attached, and a convention that when significant items are raised these will be discussed over two meetings, rather than one, before a decision is taken. Obviously there sometimes have to be exceptions to the latter. But on those occasions, it is even more crucial that there is full transparency about the reason for this and clarity over it being an exception to the norm.[2] Such an approach stands in sharp contrast to my experience of meetings with my diocese, and it explains why crossing from one culture to the other has been like stepping between two completely different worlds.

At the root of the two approaches is a completely different level of confidence about the importance of truth. In 2 Corinthians 4.2, St Paul speaks about authentic Christian ministry and says "…we have renounced secret and shameful ways; we do not use deception, nor do we distort the word of God. On the contrary, by setting forth the truth plainly, we commend ourselves to every man's conscience in the sight of God". Within this passage, Paul is only too aware of the vulnerability that this brings as the truth of the gospel held by Christians is presented as "treasure in jars of clay" (2 Corinthians 4.7). But he is also clear about how powerful this presentation of the good news of Jesus Christ then becomes. A key part of that good news is that Jesus Christ was and is full of "grace and truth" (John 1.14, 17). This message needs not only to be spoken but embodied and displayed by those who claim to be his followers. One way I have found of summarising the theological basis of this to my congregation is to suggest that God wants us to concentrate on *the means* by which we do his work and leave *the ends* to him. This doesn't mean that we never consider the consequences of what we do. But it insists that we concentrate on maintaining our integrity and making decisions that reflect the Christ-like pattern of grace and truth.

THE FALSE ECONOMY OF A PASSIVE-AGGRESSIVE APPROACH TO LEADERSHIP IN THE CHURCH

Many will perhaps accuse me of naivety at this point. For anything to get done, they will say, 'politics' is always needed. The trouble here is that the word 'politics' has become a shorthand for being devious and underhand. Christians have then devised a vocabulary to avoid acknowledging this. It's not uncommon to hear talk of 'being canny' or 'playing the long game'. Jesus' injunction to be "as wise as serpents" is also sometimes invoked, as if he was almost commanding Christians to be as crafty as the serpent in Genesis 3. The context instead is that of Jesus' followers going out into a scary and threatening world armed with both wisdom and innocence (Matthew 10.16). 'Innocence' is of course another word whose meaning has changed over the years to the point where it now reflects a sense of other-worldly naivety. But this is not its meaning. It instead represents the call to Christians to try and approach every problem and difficulty that they face with integrity. This may appear disadvantageous in the short term and even result in an apparent defeat. But even within that outcome, the kingdom of God will be advancing with frequently surprising evidence of this then appearing.

Honesty is also needed about the false nature of the apparent victories that are won when Christians act in duplicitous ways. Some of these have already been covered in my comments on the dysfunction and damaging lack of trust that is always created within church communities when such tactics are used. But the use of such tactics also has a very negative impact upon those who get used to employing them, particularly when they don't fully realise what they are doing. Those who have worked closely with bishops in the Church of England report that many of them are desperately insecure. The same goes for many parish clergy, with depression and anxiety a growing issue amongst them. A large part of this state is caused, I suggest, by the constant pressure to act in a manner that doesn't display integrity and how often this leads to a destructive path being followed.

I regularly experience this temptation. If someone had told me when I was first ordained in 2003 that the greatest issue that I would face in my ministry would be the pressure from within the church to do 'the wrong thing', I wouldn't have believed it. I now believe that a great deal of talk amongst clergy about how best to respond to difficult issues is, in reality, disingenuous. My experience is that it is relatively rare as a vicar to be in a situation where I face a genuine ethical dilemma. It is more common that I know the right thing to do but am aware of the negative consequences that will come my way if I do it.

If 'knowing the right thing to do' is ignored for long enough, it gradually becomes only an internal whisper, particularly when it is largely 'drowned out' by the surrounding culture. But that whisper is never completely silenced and its presence within Christians officially standing for integrity (while acting very differently) explains at least part of the poor mental health found in many clergy. This is the case particularly if they are aware, however dimly, of the dysfunctional and unproductive culture that they have become part of.

All of this culture has, of course, a huge impact upon safeguarding. This is why in conversations with bishops and archdeacons about the folly of their approach to process within church life, I have always taken the subject back to safeguarding. Particularly when a disingenuous approach to another aspect of church life is being defended and justified. Realising with growing anxiety the point that I am making, they usually then say that it is, of course, a different matter when it comes to safeguarding, where the approach must clearly be 'above-board'. The response that I have made, normally to deafening silence, is twofold. First, it is not always clear when a 'normal' matter of church life will grow into a safeguarding one. Second, and more significantly, a culture that is used to handling all of its problems in an underhand and passive-aggressive manner will not, and cannot, suddenly snap out of this when it comes to safeguarding. Safeguarding scandals are simply the most serious outcome of a general cultural malaise running through every part of the Church of England and one that needs to be addressed for the sake of every aspect of its ministry and mission.

The Roots of this Culture within the Church of England

In the second half of this chapter, it is perhaps helpful to reflect upon some of the causes behind the way the Church of England has developed this unhealthy culture. For obvious reasons, it cannot be exhaustive, but I start with a classic example.

An Example from the 1920s

An aspect of Stephen Neill's book *Anglicanism* that has stayed with me ever since I read it, is the section where he describes the controversy that occurred in the Church of England in 1927-8.[3] This concerned a projected new prayer book. Since 1662, *The Book of Common Prayer* had remained the only authorised form of services for the Church of England, and the more Anglo-Catholic sections of the church, growing for some time, consistently demanded liturgical change. Fearful of a dilution of Reformed doctrine and practice, evangelicals in the Church of England stood in staunch opposition to this. The revised Prayer Book was nonetheless approved by the

Convocations of the Church of England in 1927, before proceeding to Parliament for final approval. Once there, the prayer book was rejected by a Parliament still dominated by those who equated the political liberties of Britain with a firm rejection of any slide back into Catholicism. The prayer book was duly revised and passed through the Convocations again, only to be rejected by Parliament once more in 1928.

These historical details may or may not be of interest to those reading this book. But Stephen Neill's summary of the *result* of this controversy tells a huge amount about the cultural setting that still exists within the Church of England. "What was to happen next? What happened could not have happened anywhere but in England, or in connection with the affairs of any church but the Church of England. Nothing happened. The bishops decided that, in spite of the vote of Parliament, they would act as if Parliament had not voted, and that, 'The Bishops, in the exercise of that legal or administrative discretion which belongs to each Bishop in his own diocese will be guided by the proposals set forth in the Book of 1928.'"[4]

Neill was making the point that within any other country in the world these events would have then escalated into far more dramatic consequences, perhaps a full-scale separation of church and state. Church historians may have different views on the factors working against this outcome. But there is no debate over the extraordinary and peculiarly English pragmatism of the outcome. The 1928 Prayer Book was published by the Church of England, with a note at the beginning clarifying its unofficial status. The 'resolution', in other words, was a complete fudge – and one with all sides colluding in it. The 1662 *Book of Common Prayer* retained its official primacy, satisfying Parliamentarians and evangelicals, while a blind eye was turned to widespread use of the new unofficial (and not lawful) prayer book by the Anglo-Catholics. Even many evangelical clergy started to use the marriage service in the 1928 Prayer Book, which presented few problems to them in theological terms and provided an alternative to the 1662 marriage service with its off-putting talk of "men, being brute beasts"! In fact, it is interesting to reflect on how many thoroughly respectable people today were married through the use of a service that, strictly speaking, was completely unlawful.

3 / PRAGMATISM AND PASSIVE AGGRESSION

The Elizabethan Settlement

Such an approach is commonly used by the Church of England when trying to solve its problems. Its basis lies in the extraordinary breadth of traditions within it, which is arguably greater than those within any other church. For this coalition to be maintained, a spirit of pragmatism for the sake of survival has been present within the Church of England from its very beginning. Much of this was formalised in the Elizabethan Settlement of 1559, which attempted to end the religious turmoil of the previous years with a form of working compromise needed for the church to fulfil its crucial role in providing political and social stability.

Attention to the nature of the personalities involved in this process is highly instructive for understanding the Church of England's continuing nature. The historian Tracy Borman has drawn attention to the pragmatism which Elizabeth I employed in response to almost every problem she faced. Seeing the danger connected with too principled and ideological an approach to politics, Elizabeth employed all manner of passive-aggressive tactics to manage the problems that she faced. These included deliberate indecision, consistent duplicity, feigned weakness as 'a simple woman' and the sudden changes of temper which kept her counsellors unsure of where they were with her.[5] All of these factors are used to explain the political genius of Elizabeth I and her widely acknowledged status as England's greatest ruler.

But they also explain a great deal of the character of the church that Elizabeth I ruled, and the very same factors that then entered into its DNA when it came to responding to problems or issues that threatened its continuation. Much of this *via media* has commonly been regarded as 'the genius of Anglicanism', and in many ways this is probably justified. One of the things that I value most about being a member of the Church of England is the way that the different traditions within it display St Paul's model of the church in 1 Corinthians 12 as one body made up of different parts, each contributing to it in their different ways. But attention to the Elizabethan Settlement also allows a direct line to be drawn from this founding pragmatism to the widespread dysfunction within the Church of England when it comes to the delivery of effective ministry and mission. Some might argue that this spirit of pragmatism still brings more gains than losses, given its role in preserving the church. What cannot be construed positively, however, is when this has led on to a pragmatic rather than principled approach to safeguarding. It is here that the spirit of *via media* has been disastrous, with compromise, prevarication and indecision resulting in catastrophic consequences.

The Influence of Thomas Cranmer

Thomas Cranmer was another architect of Anglicanism whose personality is instructive for its impact upon the nature of the Church of England.[6] Cranmer was made Archbishop of Canterbury by Henry VIII in 1533, but his major legacy took place during the reign of Henry's son Edward VI (1547-53). During my time at theological college, I saw an essay title devised by the Oxford historian Dairmaid MacCulloch. Once again, it has always stayed with me because of the light I felt it shed on the nature of the Church of England. The title was: "'A supple conscience, a good prose style and not much else to distinguish him'. Does this adequately sum up the career of Thomas Cranmer?" Although I never wrote the essay, I have pondered its answer a good deal in the years since I first saw it. While it contains some truth in terms of Cranmer's personal frailty, I believe that in overall terms it represents a considerable underestimation of his skills and impact as a liturgist, a theologian and a politician.

What has become more apparent to me over the years, however, is how this summary does appear to describe the ideal requirements for anyone gaining 'preferment' in the Church of England today. Earlier in this chapter, I spoke about the characteristics seemingly sought by the church in its senior appointments. 'A good prose style' points to the need for a general competence when it comes to communication and organisation. More significant, however, is the 'supple' or flexible conscience that expects a pragmatic rather than principled solution to be found in response to almost every problem. The 'not much else to distinguish him' criteria for senior leaders in the Church of England is also present and will be addressed in the following chapter.

3 / Pragmatism and Passive Aggression

The Impact of Public-School Culture upon the Church of England

In tracing the development of the culture of the Church of England, the church must face the impact of the ethos of a public-school education upon generations of leaders within its ranks. When I was at theological college, there was one particular ordinand whose attitude was consistently terrible, particularly towards women. He was rude and sarcastic. But what others in the college struggled with most was the fairly constant sense of superiority that he displayed towards anyone holding a different view from his own. Several of us spoke to tutors about our struggle with his behaviour, and I remember one of them trying to explain it. "You've got to realise," the tutor said, "that, at the sort of school he went to, the very first thing you learn is how to hide your vulnerability. It's that which has produced the sense of superiority that you all find so difficult."

Significantly the college seemed much better at understanding this attitude than responding effectively to it and its impact upon others. Given the number of bishops and other senior leaders who have come from public-school backgrounds, it is important to evaluate the impact of this characteristic upon the culture and nature of the Church of England.

Perhaps the most remarkable example of this aura of confidence in the nineteenth and early twentieth centuries was the role of the Indian Civil Service in Britain's rule of India. Trained at what later became Haileybury Public School in Hertfordshire, the numerically tiny ICS managed to govern and control this huge continent with what amounted to an enormous confidence trick.[7] This British (or more specifically, English) model of leadership might appear calmly assertive and even principled. But in reality it was cover for a highly flexible and pragmatic approach to leadership with very limited aims when it came to governing the country and controlled by the central aim of 'keeping the show on the road'. With a darker side, of course, as well. No reference to the British Empire can avoid mention of the evil of colonialism and the appalling racism upon which it was based. Or the focus of much of the anger of those who have suffered directly because of this rule.

Various forms of fury at Britain's colonial history and its legacy of course exist today. These run all the way from the recent 'Black Lives Matter' movement to the scathing criticism contained in a book such as *Anyone But England: An Outsider Looks at English Cricket* by Mike Marqusee.[8] What occurs again and again in these disparate examples isn't only fury at the oppression and plundering of wealth involved. It is anger at the effortless sense of superiority and hypocrisy with which these evils have been administered. This is the reason why statues of figures associated with Britain's grandeur and prestige, as well as ones specifically associated with slavery, became a target for this rage after the murder of George Floyd in America in May 2020. As much as anything, it was an attempt to challenge the dishonesty still perpetuated about the benevolence of the British ruling class: to strip away the façade of principled and confident decency that masked a ruthless and self-seeking pragmatism.

It is important to understand how much of the legacy of this very same ethos of leadership exists within the Church of England. Christianity, of course, played a key role in nineteenth century colonialism, with much of this administered with the same effortless sense of superiority as its other components. Just as the British Army and the Civil Service today retain much of the same approach to leadership that they had in the nineteenth century, so it is with the Church of England. Meet almost any bishop in the Church of England today and the greatest impression that they will convey is that of a confident and unruffled decency; something which then justifies the apparently gentle paternalism of their leadership. This then affects and shapes a great deal of the understanding of their task.

Public appearances are especially important. The opening of new buildings, anniversaries and Confirmation services are seen as key ways of projecting the image of a benevolent episcopal leadership. Patronage is extensively used, encouraging a culture where 'being asked to take on a task by the bishop', however minor, is accorded exaggerated importance. Churchwardens are encouraged to fawn over the bishop and curates made to act as their 'chaplain' by performing servile roles that reinforce the bishop's importance. But in reality, very little of this leadership is directed into the detail of helping the ministry and mission of their churches to

3 / PRAGMATISM AND PASSIVE AGGRESSION

be effective. This is because, rather than being principled, the ethos with which most bishops conduct their role is one of day-to-day pragmatism. Preservation of the institution and its stability is seen as their major task. While archdeacons might scurry around trying to resolve the inevitable problems that then occur, the overall ethos means that this is often done in the manner of trying to 'fix' situations by using secrecy and other forms of manipulation.

The result of this is the head-shaking frustration of most effective and dynamic clergy with their bishop and diocese. Those who strongly support the bishop and the diocese are commonly those who are similarly ineffective and/or those who realise that their hope of career progression will not be helped by 'making waves'. Within this context, churches which are badly run and provide dreary and irrelevant services with little effective ministry or mission meet with little challenge. What does provoke a very strong reaction, however, is anyone questioning the basic competence of the diocese and its senior leaders. It is then that the public-school ethos is most evident. The cardinal sin of failing to be urbane has been committed, and this apparent 'rudeness' is presented as the most shocking behaviour imaginable.

The extent of collusion that takes place with this model of leadership can be remarkable. It is also telling in what it indicates about the origins of these problems. On rare occasions, when our concerns have overlapped, I have gone to meetings with bishops alongside conservative evangelical clergy. These clergy are usually in diametrically opposing positions to the bishop(s) about the issue that has occasioned the meeting. But what is extraordinary is the level of dishonesty that then takes place under the guise of politeness, usually facilitated by the majority of those present coming from a similar public-school background. Clergy driven to distraction by the behaviour of their bishop can still make statements like, "Bishop, we are extraordinarily grateful that you have so graciously given us your time because we know how incredibly busy you are." Nothing in their demeanour seems to suggest that such an approach might be duplicitous and any suggestion that it is both wrong and counter-productive meets with a nonplussed response. More than once, I have courted unpopularity by suggesting that the ethos of my diocese and conservative evangelicalism has far more in common than either side would be happy to admit.

The Impact of this Culture upon the Church of England

All of this, as indicated throughout this chapter, has a consistently negative impact on the delivery of effective work within parishes. When I have tried to talk with bishops or archdeacons about any detail of the ministry and mission of my church, it has reminded me of my time as a schoolteacher working with children for whom English was a second language.[9] This is because, within an ethos dominated by flexible pragmatism and passive aggression as the standard means of resolving problems, any talk of acting assertively in the light of principles feels like a foreign tongue.

The result of all of this – and the reason for the detail contained in this chapter – is the terrible impact of this culture of evasive pragmatism upon safeguarding. Those for whom any talk about principles is 'a foreign language', and for whom pragmatic survival is the key to approaching everything that they encounter, are constitutionally incapable of making a proper response to safeguarding. Not only will they facilitate a culture where safeguarding problems are more, rather than less, likely to happen. They will only do the minimum amount that is needed to ensure their own survival and that of the institution that they are trying to protect when such issues arise. These days, of course, safeguarding policies are a requirement in dioceses, as is the appointment of safeguarding officers. But, whether consciously or not, the safeguarding officers appointed are often those with a personality that will never 'make waves' and who have a similarly pragmatic approach, designed more to safeguard the institution than those in its care. This particular problem will be explored further in Chapter 5.

Many of us hoped that dramatic change would occur with the advent of women bishops in the Church of England from 2014. While still Chair of Fulcrum, I was an active campaigner for women bishops and was delighted when the legislation for this finally passed through General Synod. At the time, I spoke about my hope that women bishops would change the Church of England forever by challenging and then transforming its culture.[10] What I didn't expect, however, was the extent to which the women bishops then appointed would be so heavily drawn from among the wives of those already embedded within the senior structures of the church. The strongest examples of investment in the status quo within the Church of England often occur where both partners in a marriage are ordained and/or occupy senior positions within it.

Again and again when the earliest women bishops were announced, it became evident that they were married to male clergy, often occupying an existing position of influence in the Church of England.[11] Once more, the overriding characteristic of these bishops was an attractive pleasantness that gave the impression of wanting to affirm the status quo of the church rather than challenge it. Officially, this was presented as reflecting their desire to be conciliatory to those within the church who had opposed women bishops. In reality, it was a strong message of 'business as usual'. This was deeply disappointing to those of us hoping that women bishops would signal the beginning of genuine change within the Church of England. But it was also important in exposing the naivety of this assumption and revealing that the 'old boy network' had only been slightly adapted through the admittance of 'girls'.[12]

Parallels between the Culture of the Church of England and the Culture of English Cricket

A final point is needed concerning the deep level of frustration that is felt by many clergy existing within this suffocating culture, while trying to deliver effective ministry and mission. As a cricket lover, I reflect fairly often on the striking similarities between the problems and issues affecting both English cricket and the Church of England. Both have their basis in a very chequered history. Both possess a remarkable ability to employ cant ('the voluntary prolongation of genuine sentiment', see Chapter 5) to cover an essentially pragmatic approach to solving problems, where the right thing to do is normally considered, before 'good and sound reasons' for not doing so then prevail.

In cricketing terms, the D'Oliveira crisis is perhaps the worst example of this. In 1968 the cricketing world knew that the selection of Basil D'Oliveira, a 'Cape-coloured' native of South Africa, to represent the MCC/England on their forthcoming tour of South Africa would be unacceptable to the country's apartheid regime. After scoring 158 in the final Test of the summer against Australia at the Oval, and thereby contributing to a famous England victory, there was no doubt in anyone's mind that D'Oliveira deserved a place on the tour. Yet he was not selected. More recent investigation has revealed the detail of what occurred. What is particularly noteworthy in this context is the duplicity of the England captain, Colin Cowdrey.[13] Cowdrey, at the time a committed Christian and indeed lay preacher, had promised D'Oliveira that he would champion his case. But it is now clear that he did nothing of the kind. What is fascinating is the way that Cowdrey's flexible conscience enabled him to do this – a conscience shaped by his country, his public-school education and, yes, the Church of England. Other responses were similarly instructive, such as the overly generous verdict of another England cricketer, Ted Dexter, shaped by a similar culture. Dexter's comment was: "I come down on the side of honesty, a good honest piece of bungling by good honest men."[14] This was all part of the problem and points to the theme of the next chapter.

Nineteen sixty-eight may be some time ago, but very little has changed in the culture of Britain's (specifically, England's) elites since that time. The concluding part of the biographical section on the England cricketer Mike Gatting by the writer Matthew Engel on the Cricinfo website has always stayed with me because of its resonance with my experience of trying to minister within the Church of England. The article acknowledges Gatting's weaknesses before reflecting on the frustration that the player felt with his treatment by cricket's establishment and its consistent dishonesty. Engel finishes with the devastating comment that Gatting "…suffered for being a straightforward man in a game run by dissemblers."[15] Many straightforward, hardworking and devout clergy within the Church of England down the years have felt exactly the same.

CHAPTER 4

Wilful Incompetence

The Wider Culture of the Church of England

Conspiracy or Cock-Up?

The Parochial Church Council (PCC) ended in a downbeat atmosphere. Most of its members accepted that the churchwarden had not followed proper process in going ahead and purchasing a new set of hymn books for use within services. The recommendation of the worship subcommittee had been for a different hymn book.

But, rather confusingly, the subcommittee had also said that it wanted to respect the vicar's viewpoint. The minutes of the meeting reflected this lack of clarity, and the churchwarden had then felt justified in purchasing the vicar's choice of book, particularly with Christmas approaching. No one was quite sure of the extent to which the vicar himself had known about this purchase and the matter never became clear. But after some discussion, the PCC decided that, given that the books had now been bought, it was pointless to spend further time on the matter.

Some were furious at the vicar's success in pulling off yet another *fait accompli*. Others took a different perspective. "It's not great but it is understandable," one member said to another in the car park as they left the PCC that evening. "The vicar's been under a lot of pressure in the last six months with all of that dispute over the reordering and then his wife's illness. I wouldn't be surprised if the churchwarden thought that the subcommittee had agreed with the vicar's choice and didn't realise that the final decision needed to be taken by the PCC. He is, after all, fairly new to the role".

"Yes," replied the other thoughtfully. "I can't really go along with those who believe that everything that happens like this is intentional. I'm a great believer that when things go wrong in life, it's far more often a case of 'cock-up' than conspiracy."

It is easy to see why conspiracy notions are unpopular. Conspiracy theories are frequently far-fetched and, more often than not, inaccurate and wrong. They tend to be associated with obsessive personalities. More significantly, and particularly within a church setting, they are seen as deeply unattractive. Many Christians, for good reason, feel uncomfortable with the 'imputation of motive' against fellow believers that conspiracy theories usually involve. "Judge not, lest ye be judged" (Matthew 7.1, KJV) remains a very valid response when claims are made to understand, without compelling evidence, the reasons why people have taken the actions that they have.

'Cock-up' on the other hand, is far less troubling. It lends itself to the comforting notion that everyone involved in church life is trying to do the right thing. This means that recriminations and apportioning blame when things have gone wrong are then seen as pointless with any conflict that might then result from this, largely avoided. Within Christian settings, it is a more comfortable application of the doctrine of sin to suggest that, rather than it resulting in conspiracy, the fallen condition of humankind mainly works itself out in well-meaning people and organisations frequently managing to mess things up.[1]

BENEVOLENT INCOMPETENCE: CLERGY AND THE CHURCH OF ENGLAND IN POPULAR CULTURE

This is a particularly popular perception of clergy. The standard view of a Church of England vicar within popular culture remains that of a well-meaning but bumbling figure, out of touch with real life and essentially incompetent. Television vicars from down the ages have displayed this very clearly. From the numerous clergy figures portrayed by Derek Nimmo in the 1960s to the Vicar in *Dad's Army* in the 1970s and the Rector in *To the Manor Born* in the 1980s, viewers have been familiar

4 / WILFUL INCOMPETENCE

and deeply comfortable with the depiction of Church of England clergy as dim and ineffective.[2] Rowan Atkinson's portrayal of clergy in numerous films and sketches has followed a similar pattern.[3] Several ineffectual clergy appeared over the years in *Only Fools and Horses*, and it was significant that when its writer John Sullivan wanted to depict one with greater substance, he used a Roman Catholic priest instead of an Anglican vicar.[4]

A very different TV vicar emerged in the 1990s in *The Vicar of Dibley*. However, even here, the savviness and ability of Geraldine Granger could only be conveyed by presenting her as almost entirely secular in her attitudes and behaviour. Plus the genius of turning the established comic convention on its head by presenting her (alongside her initial adversary and later supporter, David Horton) as the only sane people within the entire village.[5] Order was resumed with Adam Smallbone in the 2010s comedy *Rev*, with even his name signalling a clergyman who, in almost every aspect of his ministry, was essentially weak and ineffective. Much in Britain may have changed out of sight over the last sixty years but not what television viewers were comfortable seeing in their (usually male) clergy.

Rev was also met with delight on the part of many clergy, partly because they saw their struggles and frustrations being depicted with such realism and sympathy. Like all of these TV shows, there was much that I enjoyed and found funny or moving within it. In contrast to *The Vicar of Dibley*, every episode of *Rev* saw the vulnerable Adam Smallbone saying a prayer, making a significant theological point (whether consciously or not) about God's power "made perfect in weakness". Elements of redemption also occurred within its three series. But the overall picture was bleak, with the closing of St Saviour's at the end of *Rev* essentially representing the tragic failure of the Church of England and its clergy to offer much relevance to a world that had moved on without them.[6]

EMBRACING THE IMAGE OF BENEVOLENT INCOMPETENCE

Most disturbing in the reception of *Rev* by clergy, however, was the apparent welcome of this depiction. Numerous serving clergy were consulted over its writing and, rather than being annoyed at their portrayal, *Rev* appeared to represent the way that many clergy, by the 2010s, wanted to present their ministries. In many ways this represented a much greater overturning of comedy convention than that seen in *The Vicar of Dibley*. The Church of England was appearing to give an almost official sanction to this portrayal of its hopelessness.

Part of this had its basis in wider English culture, where a historic suspicion of 'professionalism' and 'cleverness' has often developed into something approaching a full-scale romanticising of incompetence. This tradition long predated TV vicars. Many countries, for example, would have done their best to forget the disastrous Charge of the Light Brigade that took place in 1854 during the Crimean War. Within England the heroic incompetence involved in this monumental 'cock-up' was instead immortalised in the famous poem of Alfred Lord Tennyson, and then fondly remembered as an example of extraordinary gallantry. Another example, again connected with the Crimean War, is the peculiar phrase of calling someone 'too clever by half' which, it has been said, could only have originated as a negative statement in England.[7]

This long-term character trait of self-deprecation was then powerfully employed to cope with the decline in Britain's world power and influence after the disastrous Suez Crisis in 1956. From the figure of Jim Hacker in *Yes Minister* and *Yes Prime Minister* through to Hugh Grant's portrayal of a succession of charmingly diffident 'chaps' in his various romantic comedies of the 1990s and 2000s, Englishness is now consistently presented as embracing and even celebrating its own incompetence.[8]

In many ways, it remains a charming and indeed disarming characteristic. This is particularly so within Church of England clergy, where its presence is often seen as signalling kindness and approachability. Recognising this response, and grateful for any continuing sign of their relevance, many clergy then adapt to the role expected of them. This especially shows itself at baptisms and weddings. In both areas of ministry, there are often very clear expectations of the role that clergy are expected to play. A powerful, relevant and moving sermon, for instance, might well be tolerated if the member of clergy delivering it doesn't put a foot wrong in terms of its length and style. But otherwise, the right tone for clergy to set on such occasions is usually that of producing affable, inoffensive and even bumbling platitudes. "It was a lovely service, vicar" represents, more often than not, a highly dishonest collusion on the part of all sides involved. Very often, the last thing that people want to experience is the church being relevant and it can then be very easy for its clergy to collude with this.

A good example was the much-viewed wedding of Prince Harry and Meghan Markle in May 2018. The lifeless rendition of the first part of the wedding service by the Dean of Windsor passed without comment, with all of the attention focused upon the energy and passion displayed within the address that was delivered by the American Episcopal bishop, Michael Curry. Whilst Meghan Markle, and to a slightly lesser extent Prince Harry, appeared fully engaged in the bishop's address, the looks on the faces of the other members of the Royal Family reflected something approaching horror, especially its younger members. In the week that followed, many lay Christians commented with pleasure that they couldn't remember a previous time when a sermon had provoked so much conversation. But, facilitated by the address being slightly too long, there was also a great deal of criticism. If Michael Curry had been affable but slightly boring, the address would have passed without comment. However, in the eyes of many people, he had badly overstepped the mark. Sadly, this annoyance included a good number of clergy. It was not the style, still less the length of Michael Curry's address that was the problem to them. Or even its theology. It was the utterly confident presentation in a clergyman of both relevance and competence which, as such, presented an implicit challenge to the ethos of very large sections of the Church of England. He was letting the side down by revealing on an enormous stage what relevant, dynamic and exciting public Christianity both could and should be like.

The question is how we have got to a stage where anything being done well is regarded as not only threatening, but inconsistent with the Church of England? Some years ago, there was a local Baptist minister with whom I was occasionally involved when the local churches cooperated together on a project. If I expressed a conviction about the role of the church that he saw as radical, or reported something exciting happening in my church, he would usually say something like, "You're not really an Anglican, are you?" At the time, I found this rather annoying and, although we got on well, would strongly challenge its premise. In fact, I tended to go on the attack against the notion of a 'gathered church' that Baptists usually represent and how this, in contrast to the parish system of the Church of England, impedes rather than facilitates mission. But I can now see that I was defending what I wanted the Church of England to be, and what it potentially stood for, rather than its reality.

I was already aware, of course, that all was not well in the Church of England. But at that stage, I still badly wanted to believe that this was essentially down to 'cock-up'. The bishops, archdeacons and structures wanted the right things, I believed, and were working towards them but were just a little bit hopeless about how to go about this. They therefore needed help and a bit of encouragement to do better. I probably believed that similar aspirations existed among the majority of regular churchgoers. However, after around a decade of being ordained, I was forced to realise that this was not the case and I had been kidding myself.

There were major exceptions, of course, and many people in churches completely committed to the delivery of the most wonderful ministry and mission. A number of dynamic and energetic bishops and archdeacons were on the scene in the Church of England as well. When Justin Welby became Archbishop of Canterbury in 2013, after just a year as Bishop of Durham, I believed that there couldn't have been a better choice of person for that post. I said as much when I appeared on ITV's lunchtime news on the day that Welby's appointment was announced in November 2012. In April 2016, in response to the revelations about his parentage, I wrote an article for *The Sun* about his qualities which, astonishingly, they published in full.[9] Whatever my subsequent disappointments about how Welby has handled safeguarding matters, and my belief in the appropriateness of his resignation, much of his public Christian witness as Archbishop was brilliant. But none of this alters the view that the centre of gravity in the Church of England, and too much of its power, is still located with those who appear unconcerned about the effective ministry and mission of the church, and who indeed, whether consciously or not, actively undermine these things.

The Sabotage of Ministry and Mission in the Local Church

I have witnessed much of this at a local level. Throughout a good deal of its history, Christ Church, New Malden, has been a 'gathered church' and a 'preaching house' for conservative evangelicals. Reflecting a greater recognition of our post-Christendom context, the last two decades have seen the church becoming far more outward facing and missional in serving the local community. A key part of this endeavour has been trying to make our worship and other activities more accessible to those usually excluded from any priority in this regard. Specifically children and people on the margins of society have been welcomed into the church community in a dramatically new way, with exciting results.[10]

Within an evangelical setting, it is quite difficult for congregation members to object to this sort of missional shift, particularly when it is clearly explained and its biblical basis demonstrated. The result of this shift at Christ Church, however, has been an extraordinary amount of poor behaviour by those who recognise that, however much provision still exists for them within the church, it no longer revolves around their needs. This misbehaviour is made more difficult because those committing it feel completely justified in behaving this way without being able publicly to admit this justification. The issue of adult misbehaviour in church and its implications for safeguarding will be explored further in Chapter 5.

Similar dynamics probably exist in many churches. The difference is that, within many of these churches, those wanting everything to revolve around them often have greater success. I have met numerous clergy over the years, for instance, who have despaired at how many young families they might have held onto, but for the intransigence of their long-term members. Within these churches, the behaviour of such members is generally much better, precisely because it is their needs that are receiving the greatest attention. But the crucial point is this: whether it is the selfish domination of church life, or petulant behaviour because of not securing such power, both of these responses represent a very wilful failure on the part of the church. It is not that the church and its members are trying to deliver effective ministry and mission and managing to mess this up. In both cases parts of the church are actively and wilfully sabotaging this ministry and mission.

A particularly interesting aspect of this is the frequent opposition from long-term members towards any sort of progression within church life. If any significant change is mooted within a church, there is often a huge amount of resistance, usually from among its longer-term members. Interpretations of this often betray a heavy level of collusion with it. If analysis is attempted as to why such opposition is present, it remains at the level of acknowledging that 'churchgoers don't like change' – with consideration of why this might be the case being carefully avoided. If the question is pressed, answers normally point to some level of psychological discomfort on the part of those having a key part of their lives disrupted. Such explanations then proceed not only towards understanding being accorded to such feelings, but in major concessions being made as well. Or even, within many churches, the effective right of veto upon any such changes. But the real explanation for what is going on may be much more straightforward. Any change at all within churches plays havoc with existing structures of power. Within many churches, those with time on their hands and a desire to 'be someone' have carved out private 'fiefdoms' which are then threatened by almost any proposal of change.

Readers will, I am sure, be able to think of numerous examples of this in church life. It most obviously includes occasions when a strong individual or grouping has been allowed, over time, to establish almost complete sovereignty over areas such as the church kitchen, the sound system, the flower rota, or the fabric committee. Such examples might be dismissed as unimportant, but they swiftly become significant when, either directly or indirectly, they start subverting the wider ministry and mission of the church. But such 'fiefdoms' can, just as commonly, include more explicitly ministerial or missional areas of church life such as home groups, music groups, holiday clubs and children's and youth work. Particularly when such areas of church activity are valued or even prestigious, they can very easily become unaccountable, with 'interference' from anyone outside of that area of ministry resented and seen as completely unwarranted.

4 / WILFUL INCOMPETENCE

What makes this particularly difficult to deal with is when those who have established such 'fiefdoms' have been allowed to present themselves as the church's greatest servants. Often a strong level of collusion with this dishonesty is present. An apathetic majority in churches are happy to cede its major work to a few, apparently very motivated, members, who are then seen as 'saints'. Sometimes they are. But there are just as often times when a vice-like grip (in more ways than one!) has been established over the church's life which, in reality, works directly against the full development of its potential. Once again, the humour employed by those like the cartoonist Dave Walker about where the real power is located within the local church is often a way of avoiding full engagement with the damaging significance of this.

The problem is that many clergy, despite recognising such factors, are either unable or unwilling to challenge such situations. Many, therefore, avoid trying altogether. As well as allowing such problems to go unchecked, in time this also damages their self-esteem and causes them to doubt their calling. In many cases, it can go even further, causing considerable damage to their mental health and sometimes to their Christian faith. Analysis of church growth by Bob Jackson and others suggests that this is most likely to occur when incumbencies are longer rather than shorter.[11] However, facing intractable power groups within their churches is one of the main reasons why many clergy do not stay longer before moving on. It also plays heavily into the idea that the only way to avoid such problems is to plant new churches. When they are first established, church plants are often excitingly free of such problems. They therefore look like the answer. Within a decade, however, most of them face very similar difficulties.

Other clergy do attempt to deal with these problems. This, however, is very often through the passive aggressive tactics described in the previous chapter. Before I was ordained, I belonged to a church which had a very good vicar who was full of energy and vision and led the church in all sorts of dynamic approaches to ministry and mission. In this regard, he remains a hugely inspirational figure to me. But he was also fairly open about the fear that he had in challenging some areas of established power within the church, however dysfunctional their nature. He was in many ways a brilliant vicar, but unfortunately his approach to such issues was the one favoured by many clergy – seeming to tolerate 'fiefdoms' while secretly working behind the scenes to undermine them. Many clergy and churchgoers would regard such actions as a valid response, particularly because of the change they enable to happen, while avoiding outright conflict. However, using such tactics is deeply problematic. Once detected, it hands the moral high ground to those in possession of 'fiefdoms'. Most crucially, it fails to ground its case in the all-important principle of what the church is there for in the first place.

A further problem here is the role of the wider structures of the church and its officers in facilitating this situation. A major challenge is the existence of one of the most curious bodies in the Church of England – the deanery synod. Within dioceses and, where they exist episcopal areas, churches in the Church of England are grouped together in 'deaneries'. One of the more senior clergy usually serves as area dean, with some sort of responsibility for keeping an eye on the welfare of the clergy and aiding communication between them and the senior officers of the diocese. But they also chair the deanery synod, consisting of local clergy plus elected lay representatives from their churches. In theory, deanery synods should facilitate the cooperation of churches in ministry and mission and, in recent years, there has been a concerted effort to present them in this manner.

In reality, however, and helped by a lack of clarity over their status, deanery synods have largely fallen into the hands of those churchgoers least committed to a dynamic approach to church life. Partly through the lack of any clarity about their role or proper decision-making power, meetings of the deanery synod are usually extraordinarily dull. However much some area deans might try, the discussions at synod meetings often form little more than a 'pooling of ignorance' by churchgoers whose greatest motivation appears to be that of filling an empty evening whilst achieving a level of minor status. On the surface, this might appear fairly harmless, and such comments cruel and unnecessary. But in reality, dull deanery synods are highly damaging both to the credibility of the church and to its effectiveness – chiefly through their role in elevating the profile of 'churchy irrelevance' and those who represent it. This is achieved, more than anything else, by those who represent churches on the deanery synod automatically gaining places on their church's PCC. The nature of deanery synod means that places on it are rarely contested and hardly ever sought by energetic members of churches. This results in a deeply conservative phalanx being entrenched on the PCC, and it is very often these people who form the greatest obstacle to any change that will promote the ministry and mission of the church.

Similar problems afflict ecumenical Churches Together groupings. Once again, the idea behind such organisations is the commendable one of encouraging the different Christian churches within an area to work together, particularly in mission. Sometimes the results of this can be brilliant, with churches cooperating together in the production of Passion Plays, Night Shelters and projects such as Street Pastors that make a very significant impact upon the local community. Far too often, however, Churches Together groups are afflicted by much the same characteristics as deanery synods. They can even find themselves dominated by those people who have retreated into that setting because of the restrictions that have been placed upon them within their own churches. A poorly attended Churches Together annual service is often kept going without anyone asking why so few members of the affiliated churches want to come. This then has a damaging effect on the ongoing credibility and confidence of Christians in the local area.

Caught in the middle of these factors, all militating against the provision of effective ministry and mission, many Church of England clergy end up colluding with this. This is understandable, particularly when the fallout from upsetting established members of a church is so much greater than the consequences of failing to minister effectively to either newcomers or potential members. If an established couple within a church leave because they are unhappy with what is happening there, for instance, it is usually regarded as a matter of deep concern, if not scandal. If a young mother, by contrast, drifts away because of the impossibility of controlling her children within an environment totally unsuitable for them, it usually passes unnoticed. While clergy might, hopefully, be deeply grieved by such an event, there is little in structural or cultural terms to allow them to treat the needs of that young family with any equivalence to those of the older couple. In time, they therefore block out this uncomfortable reality and develop a 'supple conscience' in regard to it. But this comes at considerable cost to the effectiveness of the church, as well as their integrity and ultimately their emotional wellbeing. They begin to see their role as one of managing decline and trying to cause minimal upset to anyone in the process.

There can be a remarkable level of collusion operating here. When I attended the fourth National Evangelical Anglican Congress at Blackpool in 2003, one of the speakers was Colin Buchanan, then Bishop of Woolwich. Asked rather aggressively about his response to the problem of 'liberal unorthodoxy' among his clergy, Buchanan's response was extremely telling; but only because of a 'throwaway' comment that he made about something quite different. "When I look at the clergy in my Episcopal Area," he said, "I don't have any reason to doubt their creedal orthodoxy. I've got my doubts about how energetic quite a number of them are, but not really about their creedal orthodoxy." The fascinating thing was that at an evangelical conference (officially built around 'Fanning the Flame', not least in regard to mission), no one present seemed interested in this bishop's reservation about the ineffectiveness of many of his clergy. No one followed up on this statement with a question about how a bishop might respond to this. This is because poor performance by clergy in ministry and mission is hardly ever challenged.

Indeed it can even be rewarded, particularly if the clergy in question have successfully avoided conflict and played their role in upholding the structural status quo. In his book *Hope for the Church: Contemporary Strategies for Growth*, Bob Jackson gives a hypothetical scenario with his major target being financial approaches by dioceses that work against growth. But an accompanying 'throwaway' comment about what often happens to ineffective clergy is even more telling and made more remarkable given that it was written by a serving archdeacon.

A parish adopts good practices and its congregation grows amidst much rejoicing. A year later, it is dismayed to find its parish share has rocketed. The share is based in part or in whole on attendance that has gone up. In contrast, the sleepy next-door parish has seen its congregation dwindle but is protected from the consequences of this by its parish share being reduced. The problem for the growing church, which appears to be being taxed for its successful evangelism, is that the new people will take several years to learn to give at the rate of long-standing members. It cannot pay all its share in the next year, whereas the declining parish can. The diocese is cross with the growing church and congratulates the declining one, whose vicar becomes the next archdeacon.[12]

The final comment here was probably intended to be light-hearted and not to be taken too seriously. But its inclusion is nonetheless telling and indicates, alongside much of Jackson's analysis, how much within church culture and practice directly militates against the effectiveness of the church. After twenty-two years of ordination and eighteen years of trying to build a church entirely around the provision of effective ministry and mission, I can confirm this. Even within an evangelical setting, there are simply far more cultural and structural factors militating against the effective ministry and mission of the local church than encouraging this. Such effectiveness can certainly be found. However, it is usually reliant on extraordinary amounts of energy and commitment that somehow manage to prevail over the cultural and structural factors.

Just one of these is the difficulty of getting people to take on tasks and responsibilities within a local church, if this involves these jobs retaining any proper degree of accountability. The challenge for clergy of asking people to do such jobs 'for free' is often understood to be exclusively financial in its application. More significant, however, is the power that is often unofficially involved in this transaction. Without it ever being stated, many within churches are willing and sometimes keen to take on an area of responsibility, provided that they can turn it into the type of 'fiefdom' mentioned earlier. Shaped by the prevailing culture, many clergy are either blind to such factors or more wilfully prepared to ignore them. This is because the all-important task, dictated by the prevailing culture, has become that of 'keeping the show on the road'. It is by such means that an unofficial lack of accountability is established as the norm within many churches, with implications that go on to be very disturbing.

But before its effects on safeguarding are considered, it is important to acknowledge the impact of such factors upon general competence in the effective running of a church. When my younger brother Jon Kuhrt was Director of Liveability (formerly the Shaftesbury Society), he became so frustrated by his regular experience of the poor management of paid and voluntary staff by churches that he ran courses on how to improve this. With titles like 'Manipulation or Motivation: How to manage staff in churches', these courses majored on the liberating nature of establishing clarity about boundaries and expectations and an atmosphere of good communication and accountability. Aware of the cultural pressures at play, Jon even wrote an addition to C.S. Lewis' *Screwtape Letters* where 'Screwtape' encourages 'Wormwood' to plant the idea within churches that having such expectations of good procedure and performance is somehow 'unspiritual'.[13] However, it was in trying to implement such proper assertiveness and in the reaction that this received that I discovered how much within church culture is resistant to this. Almost every approach is preferred to the openly assertive. Challenging such a culture can be done but only at considerable cost.

If clergy do attempt to manage paid staff and volunteers, therefore, it is commonly through forms of manipulation. Some years ago, I was shocked when a member of my congregation who had previously worked for a large and well-known charismatic church in London disclosed part of what it was like to work for its famous vicar. The woman reported how frustrating it was that, having asked her to plan an event down to the minutest detail, the vicar would regularly announce, at the 'eleventh hour', that he wanted everything done differently. With a mixture of praise and uncertainty, she then suggested that this was probably because the leader was so prayerful and attentive to the prompting of the Holy Spirit. Another explanation was that he had found it to be a very effective method of managing his staff by constantly keeping them guessing about what he was going to do next. When I was a curate, I remember my training vicar saying to me that one of the ways of managing a music group and reminding them of who was in charge was to change the order of the songs shortly before the service. He then promptly did this, leaving me to witness the frustration and perplexity that resulted amongst the group. Both examples show how subtle forms of 'wilful incompetence' can be used to manage situations and respond to problems within church culture. Such approaches are always counterproductive and perpetuate or increase dysfunctionality in regard to the ministry and mission of the church, rather than address this.

I am only too aware that many of those reading this will think that the aspiration for local churches to have the effectiveness of their ministry and mission at the centre of their ethos and shaping everything else about their culture is hopelessly idealistic. If this is their view, they will probably also consider any suggestion that the problems outlined in this section can be termed 'wilful' on the part of their members and clergy is preposterous. But this shows how entrenched such attitudes and behaviour are within much of church life. It also highlights how much wilfulness is involved in the refusal by those in positions of influence to address these factors. Most disturbingly, it starts to reveal how an uncritical attitude towards such attitudes and behaviour inevitably leads to very significant problems when it comes to safeguarding.

Sabotage of Ministry and Mission at a Diocesan Level

The role of bishops and archdeacons in relation to the life of the local church has already been touched upon. But greater attention is now needed to the ways in which bishops, archdeacons and overall diocesan structures often perpetuate this problematic culture. A large part of this is through their endorsement of many of the factors creating or reflecting the problems. This is then, fairly obviously, related to their inability or unwillingness to deal with the problems that then result.

Part of this comes through the ineffectiveness of their own personal ministries. Particularly with bishops, too much emphasis is placed upon their role as a benevolent and unthreatening figurehead, with little expectation of their ability to connect Christianity with the realities of day-to-day life. Most of them are way too comfortable, for instance, in the churchy atmosphere of a boring and irrelevant deanery synod. The acid test of the relevance of a bishop, however, is whether he or she could be left for forty minutes with a group of children or young people from a church and know how to engage with them in a meaningful manner.

There are, of course, some very significant exceptions to this and ironically, as mentioned earlier, Justin Welby was one of them. It made a major impact upon my young daughter when he engaged with the children in this way at the New Wine festival. What was unusual about Welby was that he came over first as a credible Christian, second as a clergyman and only third as Archbishop of Canterbury. But, in overall terms, it is true that when most bishops visit a local church, the congregation is faced with more of the problem when it comes to credible Christianity than its solution. The heightened sense of ritual and ceremony doesn't help. Bishops' elaborate robes and mitres, curates scurrying around as their 'chaplain' and churchwardens processing with and fawning over the bishop, are all distraction exercises from a basic lack of relevance. What all of this then fosters is the sense that benevolent incompetence is somehow what Christianity, and specifically Church of England Christianity, is all about. The overall impression is given that there is something charmingly heroic in its gentle irrelevance and something deeply Christian about accepting this and not asking any searching questions about how matters could and should be different.

The point about episcopal vestments is especially significant, since a fondness for this dress can border on fetishism and increase the distance between ordinary people and the church. A strong level of dishonesty is present when bishops claim it is the congregations in their churches who wish them to dress this way. The rationale for such dress being based upon tradition is equally disingenuous. Few churchgoers realise, for example, how recently mitres were reintroduced into the Church of England with the first bishop to wear one after the Reformation being Edward King in 1885 and the first archbishop being Cosmo Lang in 1929.[14] But of course the pomposity is related to feelings of impotence. The lack of real power increases the need for show and the pretence of grandeur. The tough question which needs to be asked is what other organisation would require its leaders to wear clothes that so ostentatiously differentiate them from its other members?[15]

Another way in which the basic disconnection between episcopal ministry and relevance to real life is reinforced is through the use of diocesan staff posts. In *Blackadder Goes Forth*, a comic tension exists between

Captain Blackadder, serving in the trenches during the First World War and Captain Darling, a staff officer accompanying General Melchett.[16] Reinforced by his name, Captain Darling is portrayed as having a cosy and essentially parasitic role that has escaped front-line duty himself by feeding off the insanity and irrelevance of the army's commanders. Within most Church of England dioceses, there are numerous 'Captain Darling' posts often filled by clergy on a different track from those within parishes. These can include such roles as bishop's chaplain and canon chancellor. The effect of these posts is to reinforce a churchy subculture within the diocese that perpetuates its lack of connection to what is happening on 'the front line' within parishes. Those within such 'staff officer posts' are heavily invested in a status quo that has got them out of parish life (and sometimes enabled them to avoid it altogether) by providing them with a 'cushy number'. They all too easily, therefore, become part of a diocese perpetuating problems in regard to ministry and mission rather than working towards their resolution.

Examples of this abound within dioceses. Just one of these, mentioned already in Chapter 2 in the context of 'relative expendability', is the training of curates. One of the great strengths, in theory, of the Church of England, is the opportunity for its clergy to serve a three-to-four-year 'apprenticeship', learning how to deliver effective ministry and mission. A good curacy, supervised by a committed and competent training vicar, can lay fantastic foundations for a fulfilling and successful career. Sadly, the reality is often the precise opposite with large numbers of curacies failing to deliver any level of proper training, leaving those involved permanently scarred through the experience. Faults can be present on all sides. However, an all too common one is incompetence on the part of the 'training incumbent'. Such situations, however, are rarely met with challenge. Curates are still commonly allocated to vicars in the Church of England regardless of their training ability and largely in return for their willingness to fulfil tasks that prop up the church as an institution. These commonly include serving as area deans and ensuring that their churches continue to send large sums of money to the diocese. If a response is made to the issue of improving the training of curates, it is often to centralise such training within the diocese, leaving the vicars largely unchallenged. Those who have tried to flag up the priority of providing curates with a quality of training and experience regularly report that it is like banging their head against a brick wall.

The question of why this problem is not addressed then becomes a very interesting one. The difficulty in addressing any issue of competence in their clergy and the upset that this would cause is clearly a factor. But it would also complicate a major area of patronage that bishops and archdeacons possess and a major area of leverage that they have, particularly upon wealthier parishes. At a deeper level, establishing a culture of general competence poses a considerable threat to those who recognise that they would probably not be in their jobs if such a culture were to prevail.

This also explains why actual performance by clergy within ministry, let alone mission, plays so little role in their supervision. During two decades of ordained ministry, I have had many annual reviews. These reviews have taken various forms and, on the surface, have a certain amount of professionalism. Preparation before the review is required and involves completion of paperwork on the part of the person being reviewed, including critical reflection upon their ministry. But the options contained within this paperwork mean that any critical questions about the effectiveness of this ministry can normally be avoided. When it comes to the interview part of the review process, I have found in every case that any conversation about actual ministry or mission is always prompted by me. This is normally with very little engagement or interest from the reviewers, who have always been much more comfortable limiting the conversation to my personal wellbeing. This focus is always kind, thoughtful and not without value. But, once again, it does seem that nervousness about the establishment of any culture of competence is a major factor here. The result is that poor performance by clergy within their parishes is rarely challenged and good performance rarely encouraged. The impression given is that ministry and mission are too nebulous to be analysed or their effectiveness assessed. I am assured that ministry and mission are regularly discussed at bishops' staff meetings. But my experience suggests that such discussion is kept at the level of future possible appointments, rather than being based upon any concrete analysis of what is happening 'on the ground'. Annual 'statistics for mission' might be requested and collated but any tough questions about productivity or effectiveness appear to be completely avoided.

It is important to recognise the agenda contained within this refusal to confront specific issues. Part of this is demonstrated in the refusal to engage with church discipline, unless it becomes impossible not to do so. This important issue will be examined in Chapter 6. In the previous chapter, I spoke about the difficulty I have had in getting emails acknowledged, let alone responded to by bishops and archdeacons. I also mentioned the problematic approach taken to meetings with agendas kept unclear and relevant communication often ignored. In both cases, a natural disorganisation and lack of confidence and/or ability is usually at play. But if such incompetence consistently works in favour of those displaying it, it must become legitimate to consider it wilful. This is where, however, the emphasis on a very English pleasantness and urbanity (covered in the previous chapter) becomes a crucial part of the defence strategy. When acknowledgement is made near the start of a meeting that 'things could have been done a little better', busyness is cited as the reason and an apology is made, it then becomes seen as 'rude' not to accept this and move on. The significant advantage gained for those who have operated this poor process, however, remains. As with all passive-aggressive tactics such 'gains' always represent a 'pyrrhic victory'.[17] The frustration and resentment that result mean that a structure that is meant to be supporting the ministry and mission of churches becomes more dysfunctional.

Wilful Incompetence and its Impact on Safeguarding

When it comes to the Church of England and its problems therefore, the dichotomy often presented between conspiracy and 'cock-up' turns out to be a false one. A more accurate paradigm for understanding the prevailing culture within the institution could be said to be that of 'wilful incompetence'. A natural lack of confidence and therefore widespread incompetence in the delivery of ministry and mission is endemic, not only among large numbers of the bishops and clergy but within the institution and structures of the church itself. This is the strong element of truth within the 'cock-up' diagnosis. But, crucially, this incompetence is not agenda-free. In fact, in many cases within the Church of England, it even resembles policy. A church that is naturally and structurally incompetent has discovered that, in many cases, this tendency serves a purpose in managing the institution. It therefore becomes heavily invested in not acknowledging, let alone challenging and addressing this situation.

Sadly, this general approach to church life is then inevitably and very directly related to its safeguarding. This is partly because, while safeguarding is a relatively recent concept within church life, the culture and general tendencies shaping the approaches taken towards it, have existed and gone largely unchallenged for much longer. Back in Chapters 1 and 2, a number of examples of poor safeguarding practice were given. All of these can now be seen to very directly relate to the wider culture of wilful incompetence that exists in the Church of England.

The most basic of these is the ingrained habit of inertia and the 'policy' of managing problems by refusing to manage them. This characteristic, while fairly disastrous in terms of providing and facilitating effective ministry and mission within the Church of England, has been found to be an 'effective' one for avoiding conflict and keeping the institution of the church going. But it also explains the evasive and uncertain response that safeguarding issues have received when survivors or others have approached those in authority. It further explains the duplicity involved in the promise of action being taken, when none then occurs. It explains, as well, the resolute commitment to non-communication that appears to have accompanied almost every safeguarding scandal that has occurred within the Church of England. Finally, it explains the tendency of the church, if at all possible, to do absolutely nothing in the face of safeguarding concerns and then continue acting as if none of these issues had ever been raised. Sadly, none of these long-standing tendencies within the church and its leaders can be suddenly re-programmed when safeguarding issues arise. They have, instead, governed and directed the whole approach that is taken to safeguarding, with all of the consequences that have become so tragically familiar.

It would be more comfortable if we could see the transfer of this culture of incompetence into safeguarding as something that is largely unconscious rather than wilful. Unfortunately, much of the evidence suggests otherwise. Evasive and uncertain responses when people first raise safeguarding issues are not agenda-free but have the aim of making it harder for such allegations to be sustained; particularly given the courage that it has usually taken for these allegations to be made in the first place. An example already cited was when the Bishop at Lambeth said, "What do you expect me to do?" to those bringing information to him about Peter Ball. Pushing the issue back in this manner represented an attempt to take the energy out of the attempt of these people to get justice, by making them feel more vulnerable and uncertain.

I have seen the same at a local level. There is a world of difference between someone saying, "If you choose to take this further, I am going to support you every step of the way" and "If you choose to take this further, I do have to warn you that this process will be, in all likelihood, very painful and difficult." The latter approach is, of course, easily justified on the basis of care and concern for those who have been affected by abuse and the desire for them to be fully aware of what they are getting into. It could also be claimed that those using such approaches are largely unaware of psychology and the power of 'suggestion' when used in this way. In reality though, however much natural incompetence and lack of understanding is involved, it can represent an instinctive and wilful attempt to use such tools to close matters down and ensure that allegations are less likely to be sustained.

Much the same goes for the long delays that are often involved in responding to almost anything involving safeguarding. Once again, this is easily justified on the basis of the complexities involved, the danger of hasty responses, and the care that is consequently required. But there is very little excuse for the poor communication that usually accompanies these delays and piles up stress and uncertainty upon those who have made allegations. Both approaches have the effect of making survivors feel completely unsure of 'what is going on' when they deserve to be given as much support and security as possible. When apologies are given for these factors, 'cock-up' is usually invoked as the reason for what has happened. But in reality, this incompetence is often far more wilful and agenda-driven than is being admitted. It represents an attempt to take the momentum and energy out of the allegations being made and perhaps result in them being dropped altogether.

Such tactics can be thwarted through the resilience and persistence of survivors and the support they are given by friends and family. But they are still a considerable scandal and the cause of as much pain as the abuse itself. One of the most tragic aspects of the Peter Ball documentary was seeing Cliff James, one of the survivors of the Bishop's abuse, saying that he had more problems with the church than with Ball. This was because, while he recognised Peter Ball as a twisted and damaged man, he saw the church's inadequate response to Ball as something far more wilful.[18]

Another tragic aspect of the Peter Ball documentary was hearing another survivor, Phil Johnson, describing at the end of the programme what it was like to be part of the National Safeguarding Panel for the Church of England. While acknowledging that much greater efforts are now being made in regard to safeguarding by the church, Johnson then said, "…sometimes I still think they'd rather I wasn't there, they'd rather I go away."[19] Those to whom Johnson is referring would probably claim that this impression is not intended. As has been said already, it is impossible to discern fully the motives of others and probably a fair amount of incompetence is involved in their failure to relate to Johnson and his concerns properly. But when this has the effect of deflating someone with key experience and damaging their motivation to make sure that safeguarding in the church is properly responded to, it is legitimate to regard this incompetence as agenda-driven. It displays the continuing desire to do as little as possible in regard to safeguarding and the instinctive impulse to close down any attempts to bring about 'root and branch' change.

In one of the episodes of the BBC sitcom *Yes Minister*, Jim Hacker visits a brand new, state-of-the-art hospital which has no actual patients. When he tries to draw attention to this fact, those involved in the hospital instead highlight all the wonderful aspects of its equipment and provision.[20] Obviously this scenario is exaggerated farce. But it does point to how it is perfectly possible to have wonderful policies and procedures established in regard to safeguarding and still be completely and wilfully incompetent in the way that it is handled.

In some ways, the Church of England is now at a more dangerous stage than ever in regard to safeguarding. This is because it has many of the policies and procedures that are needed but not the iron determination to make these policies and procedures work. It is rather like David Brent in the television 'mockumentary' *The Office*, knowing that he shouldn't appear racist or sexist but constantly displaying such attitudes because he has no deeper understanding beneath his platitudes.[21]

The only solution to the wilful incompetence that currently characterises the approach of the Church of England to safeguarding is for a decisive conversion to take place which will hold achieving justice and vindication for those who are abused, as the most important thing that the church can ever do. If this takes place, the competence will follow. This will not only transform the way that safeguarding allegations are then handled but also lead to the establishment of a culture that works much harder to prevent safeguarding issues from arising in the first place.

'Carry On Church of England'?

Several references have been made in this chapter to popular culture and the light it sheds on the very British (or more accurately, English) nature of the Church of England. These are not intended to be flippant but to point to the frequent flippancy of the organisation itself in relation to safeguarding. But perhaps the fullest insight into the character of the Church of England is provided by the *Carry On* films. These films, which had their heyday during the 1960s, are best known for their bawdy humour. But they also represented a post-Suez attempt to cope with Britain's decline as a world power by presenting a nation able to 'carry on' through a uniquely British ability to accept and laugh at the more ridiculous aspects of our society.[22] The series never went anywhere near the then dangerous territory of parodying the church. But years after it finished, it is striking how many parallels to the *Carry On* characters and their roles still exist within the

Church of England. Like all satire, what follows is an exaggerated rather than false version of reality.

Insecure about their abilities, overly conscious of their status and apt to use passive aggression to solve any problems they face, many of the church's bishops represent Kenneth Williams or Kenneth Connor type characters. Aware of their weaknesses, these bishops are frequently assisted by formidable 'matrons', who act as their enforcers and uncannily resemble Hattie Jacques or Joan Sims. Meanwhile, many ordinary clergy represent the accident-prone Jim Dale, the kind-but-dim Bernard Bresslaw or the hapless Charles Hawtrey, doing their best to cope in the middle of all the chaos and generally failing to do so. Others take on the Sid James role, standing at the side and either shaking their heads in frustration or raucously laughing at the nonsense they are witnessing. In recent years, the Church of England has even found some Barbara Windsor figures, willing to add a bit of glamour to the overall sense of farce.

'Carry on Church of England' represents a very popular and enduring British comedy for all of these reasons. Most of the general public want to see it this way and the church has very often gone along for the ride, coping with the blow to its self-esteem by telling itself that its self-effacement is probably rather appealing. The humour soon disappears, however, once we recognise the darker consequences of this rather lazy celebration of the church's incompetence.

CHAPTER 5

Captivity to Fear

Getting it Wrong About Safety in the Church

At some point in the 2010s, Southwark Diocese produced a safeguarding policy. Attractively presented and clearly set out, this policy contained over a hundred pages and a great deal of material. Much of this was excellent and very useful, concerning good practice and procedure in regard to safeguarding. It remains a very helpful guide for parishes who are required to keep it in a prominent position in their churches. There was just one major problem with the document – its name. The policy was entitled 'A Safe Church'.[1] Through its title, the policy thus confused and conflated two very different things: *the church keeping people safe and the church keeping itself safe*. The huge problem, clearly unrecognised by those responsible for devising and formulating the policy, is that this piece of confusion lies at the heart of pretty much every case of mishandling of safeguarding by the church.

One of the most noticeable aspects of the Peter Ball case was the way that the church's response, at almost every step, was guided by a concern to protect Ball himself. The emphasis was placed on the wonderful nature of the man and his ministry and this acted as the major control upon the way that the allegations against him were then interpreted and responded to. Again and again, it was Ball's 'safety', rather than that of the people affected by his actions, that appeared to be the central concern of those holding power in the decision-making process.[2]

Rather than being simply based upon personal charity, the support extended to Ball by the other bishops conveyed a strong sense of collegiality.

This suggests that the safety of the church as a whole was also seen as somehow being at stake in the way that the allegations against Peter Ball were handled. Trying to understand the psychology involved here is inevitably speculative. But it does appear that entertaining any doubt about the ministry of someone seen as a pillar of the Church of England and its episcopal ministry, brought a level of insecurity that couldn't be coped with. Peter Ball was not only a bishop but a significantly influential figure, meaning that less charismatic bishops such as Carey and others, appear to have seen their own credibility as somehow bound up with that of their colleague. But it went deeper than this. A fear of confronting difficult truths about the institution that provided almost all of their identity was also instrumental in these bishops (and others within the church) allowing themselves to ignore the information that they received about Ball.

The giveaway here is the way in which other members of the established elites within Britain also fell over themselves in their efforts to support Peter Ball. All sorts of powerful and influential figures, including the then Prince Charles, cabinet ministers and members of the judiciary, intervened on Ball's behalf and were almost certainly a critical influence on the investigation of 1992-3 resulting in him merely receiving a police caution. The refusal among the privileged classes to countenance any questioning of Peter Ball's propriety appears to have been based upon something very similar to the collegiality accorded to him within the church. This immediately casts doubt on whether the support that Ball received from his colleagues in the Church of England had its basis in anything distinctively Christian. In reality, the widespread support that Ball received from its numerous sources, was all about preserving and protecting the status quo.

Examples of the safeguarding of institutions taking priority over the safeguarding of people occur in many areas beyond the church. It can also reach the most extraordinary proportions. One of the most shocking revelations in recent times, already mentioned in this book, was the prolific abuse committed by the celebrity Jimmy Savile over several decades, in multiple contexts and with countless numbers of victims. As so often in such cases, the public only became aware of this shortly after Savile's death in 2011. Scarcely less shocking than the abuse, however, was the extent to which the threat posed by Savile and the question marks that existed for a long time about his conduct were ignored, and perhaps even suppressed, by significant sections of two of the country's most venerated institutions in the BBC and the NHS. In each case, the overriding concern of those who knew about or suspected Savile's crimes was safeguarding the wellbeing of these institutions and, more crucially, their vested interest in them. The evil involved in the abuse, in other words, went far beyond Jimmy Savile. Protecting the wellbeing of institutions had spectacularly triumphed over protecting the wellbeing of the very people that these institutions were established to serve.

Another case came to prominence in January 2024 through an ITV drama called *Mr Bates versus the Post Office*. The events depicted in the drama involved a series of miscarriages of justice as more than 900 sub-postmasters/mistresses were prosecuted by the Post Office between 1999 and 2015 for theft, false accounting, and fraud due to errors caused by the Horizon accounting software.[3] Once again, the public were deeply shocked by the revelations about the way that those in positions of power had closed ranks to protect their vested interests in the Post Office and its reputation. This involved widespread deceit and corruption, with many regarding Paula Vennells, the CEO of the Post Office during the most critical period, as the most culpable person involved. The fact that Vennells was an ordained minister, highly regarded by Justin Welby and apparently shortlisted to become Bishop of London, was telling in what it indicated about the correlation between this scandal and events in the Church of England.

The Primacy Given to Protecting the Church as an Institution

Sadly, this misguided priority lies at the heart of every safeguarding case that the Church of England has mishandled. When the details of these safeguarding failures are examined, the consistent pattern that emerges is one where protecting the institutional status quo has governed all of the decisions taken.

This is why perpetrators of abuse are treated so much better than those people who have been abused, particularly when the latter seek justice. The logic here is terrifyingly simple. Those who commit abuse are exploiting the status quo of the church and, on this basis, are usually heavily invested in the institution. In most cases, they are more than willing to attend boring deanery synod and chapter meetings and sit on diocesan committees. They seek to be as friendly as possible to their bishop, regularly inviting him or her to their church. They ensure a good amount of Parish Share (a financial contribution to the wider church) is paid by their church to their diocese. Investment in the institution is vital for such abusers, since it is this institution that is providing the environment for their abuse to be able to happen. This explains why those equally invested in the institution – most obviously bishops and archdeacons – are instinctively sympathetic to them. Far more than these leaders realise, they are 'batting on the same side' as abusers because both are invested in the institutional status quo.

Such factors explain why Stephen Cottrell, when Bishop of Chelmsford, did nothing to stop the abuser David Tudor from being reappointed as an area dean and later becoming an Honorary Canon of Chelmsford Cathedral. Much about Tudor's abuse was already known to Cottrell at the time that these appointments took place. Any concern about this on the part of the future Archbishop of York, however, was outweighed by his instinctive desire to build up the institution of the Church of England. This left little room for questioning the significance of rewarding someone like David Tudor, whose more sinister agenda involved being equally invested in the institution.[4]

Even apparent exceptions turn out to be more aligned to these dynamics than is commonly realised. On the surface, Jonathan Fletcher was the opposite of an institutional clergyman, reflecting few of the obvious ways that abusers invest in the structures of the Church of England. In reality, however, Fletcher fully exploited the semi-autonomous nature of Emmanuel Wimbledon as a Proprietary Chapel and its niche position within the status quo of Southwark Diocese.[5] It is significant that he was later revealed to be a member of 'Nobody's Friends' – an exclusive dining club for socially well-connected Anglicans, regularly meeting at Lambeth Palace.[6] Most of those who commit abuse within the Church of England turn out to have a very significant investment in the institution which, sometimes in subtle and hidden ways that it doesn't even recognise, becomes equally invested in them.

Those demanding justice for the abuse that they have suffered, on the other hand, represent the precise opposite of all of this: namely, a very clear and present threat to the institutional status quo. This is because such people create considerable instability through calling the Church of England to account and expecting it to show the characteristics that it consistently tries to avoid: courage, clarity and principle. This is the reason for their shabby treatment and why it is difficult to find any survivors of abuse in the Church of England who are happy with the treatment that they have received from the organisation, its hierarchy and its safeguarding officers. To everyone with a vested interest in the status quo, survivors of abuse represent a serious threat to the institution and its credibility and one which therefore needs to be neutralised as swiftly as possible.

A number of points need to be noted here. Complaints from survivors of abuse about their treatment by the church are sometimes explained away as if they are unavoidable. Dressed up as pastoral insight, the claim being made is that the damage caused by their abuse has been so profound that survivors will always be angry with the church, however their case is dealt with. This is nonsense, and a further example of the additional abuse at the hands of the church that survivors often refer to. My experience is the very opposite, with survivors of abuse often embarrassingly grateful when they receive genuine compassion, a listening ear and the justice and vindication they deserve. Sadly, while I have received such gratitude and affirmation from survivors on whose behalf I have acted, there are very few examples of this being shown to senior leaders in the Church of England, for obvious reasons.

Another important point concerns the feedback that clergy give about safeguarding in their diocese. During the writing of this book, I asked a number of clergy about their experience in this regard. Some responded negatively, but a number replied by saying that their experience of safeguarding was 'extremely good'. Further questioning, however, revealed that the overwhelming reason for these positive responses was not because these clergy had seen justice or vindication received by victims/survivors of abuse. Often, they had only the sketchiest knowledge of the outcome of these cases. The reason for their positive feedback was because their diocese and its safeguarding officers had taken the matter out of their hands, meaning that it was no longer their responsibility. On diocesan safeguarding courses, a consistent message is now given about the importance of parish clergy passing responsibility upwards. This is a definite improvement on the previous unofficial message that clergy should be 'defusing' such problems themselves. The resulting danger, however, is that timid clergy are only too ready to breathe a sigh of relief at being able to 'kick the problem upstairs' to their diocesan safeguarding team, thereby ceasing to have any responsibility for it. Such a process often has deeply unsatisfactory results for survivors of abuse, with defence of it by clergy becoming yet another example of the priority of the institutional status quo shaping the heartless response of the church to their treatment.

Deeper theological thinking should challenge all of this fear and institutionalism. Firstly, by calling out a weak understanding of the nature of the church and its calling and, secondly and more significantly, by calling out Christians over their fear and lack of confidence about truth-telling.

Seeing the Church as an Organisation rather than the Body of Christ

This lies at the root of the confusion displayed in terms such as 'a safe church'. The New Testament uses several images for the church. But the one with most relevance here is that of the church as the body of Christ. Indwelt by the Holy Spirit, the church represents the body of Christ on earth, called to implement God's loving rule over the world through modelling the community of self-giving love that exists at the centre of God's being. Drift into seeing the church merely as an organisation or institution and many of the important implications of this understanding of the church drop by the wayside.

This has several implications, but one of the most critical is understanding of the importance of the church's members. Within human organisations and institutions, hierarchies of status are always present.

A heavy amount of 'spin' is sometimes used to disguise this, and Christian-adjacent language can even be appropriated for this purpose, such as the decision by the department store John Lewis to designate all of its employees as 'partners'.[7] But whatever the stated aim and even intention, greater importance is typically accorded to the wellbeing of those in possession of the greatest status or position within human institutions. This is because the whole of their collective health and wellbeing is seen as depending on such hierarchies being carefully maintained.

The most powerful example of a human institution in the early years of Christianity was the Roman Empire. Officially Rome included everyone, with *Pax Romana* and Caesar as 'saviour' among the slogans used to promote its universal blessings. But, in reality, and behind the image generated by its impressive buildings and provision of 'bread and circuses', it was a deeply hierarchical system based from top to bottom on patronage and clientage. It was also built upon cruelty and slavery. The New Testament book of Revelation is exposing the evil reality behind the 'spin' when it reaches for its apocalyptic imagery to describe 'the beast' and 'great prostitute' (Revelation 17).

One of the advances in biblical scholarship in recent years has been the realisation that the New Testament presents Jesus Christ and the church as the *reality* to which Caesar and Rome were the parody.[8] To the surprise (and in some cases horror) of his scholarly peers, the historian Tom Holland has made a very similar case.[9] Rather than being mere 'background', the mention of Caesar Augustus at the start of Chapter 2 of Luke's Gospel is the vital prelude to imperial terms previously associated with Caesar, such as 'lord', 'saviour' and 'bringer of peace', being deliberately given instead to the tiny, vulnerable baby in the Bethlehem manger.[10] A similarly deliberate reappropriation to Jesus of imperial titles and concepts is seen in St Paul's letters, with major implications for his followers.[11] While the New Testament is clear that church leaders are to be respected (1 Timothy 5.17; Hebrews 13.7), any sense of hierarchy and/or segregation is abolished in favour of the genuine community and partnership summed up by its frequent use of the term *koinonia*. It is not only in reaction to the infamous Jewish prayer thanking God for the intercessor's 'superiority', but also to the hierarchy of the Roman Empire, that Paul declares: "There is neither Jew nor Greek, slave nor free, male nor female for you are all one in Christ Jesus" (Galatians 3.28).

The other crucial aspect of this ecclesiology is that the whole purpose of this sacred community is to reflect God's loving rule of the world, with particular emphasis on seeing Christ within those who are vulnerable (Matthew 25.31-46). Debates continue as to whether Jesus just refers in this vision to those who are vulnerable within the church or with a wider reference to those in similar jeopardy within the world. But, like other aspects of Jesus' teaching (e.g. Mark 10.35-45; Luke 22.24-30), there should be little debate about his counter-cultural agenda within a surrounding society that believed that 'might was right'. In story after story throughout the gospels, we see Jesus focusing his care on the most vulnerable in society and demonstrating their priority within the kingdom of God.

The distinction between understanding the church in this manner and understanding it as a purely 'human organisation' is therefore a crucial one for safeguarding. When the church is understood as the body of Christ, every single member of that body matters. In fact, according to St Paul's teaching in 1 Corinthians 12, if any member of the body of Christ suffers then so does the entire body. This means that it becomes unthinkable to envisage a situation where one member or potential member should be treated badly or their rights set aside for 'the sake of the church'. Especially the more vulnerable ones. Members of the body might choose to give up their rights or freedoms for the sake of that body (1 Corinthians 8-10), but this will never be imposed on them. Drift into seeing 'the church' as an organisation or institution, however, and this swiftly leads to a much less relational and less egalitarian understanding of it. Individual members recede in their significance in the light of 'the whole' and a hierarchy of value in terms of its members swiftly emerges. This is where the 'relative expendability' discussed in Chapter 2 comes in. The conscience of those in positions of power might, of course, continue to play a role in the treatment of individual members. In ecclesiological terms, however, there is little to provide a check on their dispensability.

This is not because there is any confusion about this matter within the services by which clergy and bishops are ordained. Within the ordinal, both *clergy and bishops are unambiguously instructed to care for those people entrusted to them rather than an organisation.*[12] The language used in these services is very relational and should leave no room at all for bishops or clergy to believe that their commitment to 'the church' should ever be in tension with their call to care for and protect actual people. Indeed the most striking part of the commission of bishops, already used as the title for another book on safeguarding, is "to heal and not to hurt".[13] The calling to proclaim God's love by caring for people and placing this ahead of every other priority, could not be more explicit.

Confusion also reigns when justification for not acting in response to safeguarding allegations is based upon concern for 'the church' and its reputation. In this case, a sort of Christianised version of utilitarianism ('the greatest good for the greatest number') is being invoked (cf. John 11.50). As well as being wrong for the reasons already mentioned, those who use their concern for 'the church' as a reason for not acting well in regard to safeguarding matters are usually kidding themselves. More often than not, even this supposed motive is serving as a mask for more selfish concerns. A leader might tell themselves that the reason for their inaction is concern for the church's reputation or its ministry and mission. In reality, though, it may be because this will then become another difficult thing he or she will have to deal with, risk becoming unpopular over, or result in their being seen as disloyal. As already mentioned, no one's life has ever become easier through dealing with a safeguarding issue. The dishonesty contained within the non-action that results, points to another important theological deficit normally involved in the church's poor handling of safeguarding.

Fear and Lack of Confidence about Truth

As we have noted, propaganda was a major weapon in the armoury of the Roman Empire. 'Fake news' is far from a modern invention. It formed a vital part of the propping up of this institution and its hold over those in its power. Back in Chapter 3, we saw how the British Empire during the nineteenth and twentieth centuries employed similar tactics. A critical moment in the passion narrative of John's Gospel is when this imperial perspective comes face-to-face with Jesus. Jesus speaks to Pontius Pilate about being a king who "came into the world to testify to the truth." He adds, "Everyone on the side of truth listens to me." Soaked in the culture of an institution constantly parading its glitz and power while covered with the blood of its victims, Pilate can only respond with the cynical riposte, "What is truth?" (John 18.37-8).

Central to Christianity, by contrast, is a full confidence about the existence of truth. One of Jesus' most famous statements is: "If you hold to my teaching, you are really my disciples. Then you will know the truth, and *the truth will set you free*" (John 8.31-2). Later in John's Gospel, Jesus describes himself as "the way, the truth and the life" (John 14.6). The salvation brought by Jesus – in contrast to the fake versions of salvation offered by the Roman Empire – is completely based upon truth. This emphasis continues in the rest of the New Testament, with Paul urging the early Christian churches to be completely confident about the liberating power of truth and constantly making use of the metaphor of light to speak of its importance:

"For you were once darkness, but now you are light in the Lord. Live as children of light (for the fruit of the light consists in all goodness, righteousness and truth) and find out what pleases the Lord. Have nothing to do with the fruitless deeds of darkness, but rather expose them. It is shameful even to mention what the disobedient do in secret. But everything exposed by the light becomes visible—and everything that is illuminated becomes a light. This is why it is said: "Wake up, sleeper, rise from the dead, and Christ will shine on you." (Ephesians 5.8-14; see also Philippians 2.14-15)

None of this confidence about truth has been displayed in the numerous safeguarding scandals that have taken place in the Church of England. The constant examples of evasion, cover-up and non-action cited in this book instead display a complete fear about truth and an attempt to limit the dangers associated with it. The problem, as ever, is the wider culture within the Church of England and aspects of this culture that have escaped challenge for too long.

'COVER-UPS' IN NON-SAFEGUARDING SITUATIONS AND THE DAMAGE THEY CREATE

Anyone who runs any type of organisation cares about its reputation and recognises the fallout that occurs when that reputation is damaged. This is often the basis for cover-ups within the church. When these occur outside of safeguarding, they are frequently pardoned. But this approach never delivers genuine wellbeing to any organisation. In 1974, the famous Watergate scandal in America brought about the resignation of its President, Richard Nixon. Since then, it has become common to hear political commentators saying that it is always the cover-up, rather than the original offence, that brings the greatest damage. Cover-ups of various kinds are endemic within the Church of England and the excuse given for them is always that of protecting 'the church', or that part of the church involved. Such thinking is never right because, whatever their intention, cover-ups always bring far more harm than good.

An example which springs immediately to mind is the controversies that regularly affect theological colleges and how the fallout from this is often handled. For some reason, it is fairly common for serious controversies to afflict the theological colleges that the Church of England uses to train many of its ordinands. At the root of these controversies is usually a serious breakdown in relationships between key figures within the leadership and/or governance at the college. Time after time, these controversies are 'resolved' through leaders suddenly leaving the college, amid a secrecy that turns out to have been formalised through the signing of a Non-Disclosure Agreement (NDA). The reason given for this is always to protect the wellbeing of the college and, by implication, the wider church. The problem is that such approaches neither bring the resolution they seek nor protect the college and church. The secrecy involved in the use of NDAs breeds suspicion and rumours about what has happened and simply makes the circumstances appear more suspect. This has the impact of lessening trust in both the college and the church as a whole. It also has a damaging impact upon the integrity of those people who know more than most about the details of what has occurred but then feel that they have to collude with the secrecy through their silence. What appeared to be a relatively easy, short-term solution comes with a longer-term price tag.

Similar things happen at a more local level. The previous chapter started with a fictional scenario at a PCC where due process had been abused and proper discussion of the matter was completely avoided. Sadly, this is not uncommon. When anything unpleasant or difficult takes place in churches, the collective instinct to 'move on' is very powerful, particularly if further investigation will involve conflict and/or digging down into aspects of the culture that have caused the problem. Once again, the official reason given is to protect the church, but the result is usually the precise opposite.

Many years ago, I was a member of a church where a charismatic and able vicar had persuaded the PCC to lease a property on a busy main road in the parish to use as an 'alternative worship centre'. It was in the earliest days of 'Fresh Expressions of Church' and the vision was an exciting and attractive one. However, partly due to a lack of critical process on the part of the PCC, the project was rather ill-founded and failed to last. As a result, a large amount of money was lost. By this stage the vicar who had initiated the project had left to take up a more senior role. But in the aftermath of the centre's closure, the leadership of the church was successful in closing down any proper discussion of what had gone wrong. It was difficult to get openness about the amount of money that had been lost, and there was an implicit message given to PCC members that it was somehow unkind and destructive to ask searching questions about the venture and its failure. The message was one of 'moving on in Christian love'.

Aware of the weaknesses in this approach and in response to questioning, the churchwardens did assure members of the PCC that 'lessons had been learned'. However, given that none of these lessons were shared or made public, this appeared to be merely a tactic to close down further discussion. In the conscious thought of those taking this approach, it represented a proper and responsible attempt at damage limitation for their church. In their unconscious thought, however, they appeared heavily invested in avoiding any uncomfortable truths about those aspects of the church's culture of which they were part, and the role their weaknesses may have played in the episode. Furthermore, this approach, while more comfortable in the short-term for those involved, had negative consequences for the church. These included an erosion of trust in its leadership and a damaging degree of suspicion about Fresh Expressions. Worse still, it gave legitimacy to the idea that truth was something that those in positions of responsibility had to control and limit, if the church was to continue to function.

I have had similar experiences in meetings with officers from my diocese over the years. Various techniques are employed to cover up things that have gone wrong and to avoid the uncomfortable questions that any proper discussion will expose. The most common of these techniques is for the person chairing the meeting to allow a limited discussion to take place before advancing the view that 'while we could look back, it's perhaps more positive and better use of our time to instead look forward and to agree how we move on from this point'. Once such a 'suggestion' is made, it immediately becomes seen as unreasonable to do anything other than acquiesce and collude with this agenda. But all this does is to bury the deeper issues that have created the problem, allowing them to continue and to go on creating further problems.

Another non-safeguarding area where such an approach is often taken, concerns clergy conduct. Particularly when it comes to sexual affairs involving clergy, the general 'wisdom' appears to be to keep what has happened and its consequences as secret as possible. In terms of reducing hurt to those involved, this is completely understandable. But another motive was revealed in an instance where a bishop, on being asked about transparency over discipline in the Church of England, declared, "Why should the church be responsible for giving the tabloids their headlines?" This response was a telling one, suggesting that for those outside of the church to become aware of frailty within it could only be a bad thing. Once again, an unwillingness to go through the difficult task of engaging with what has happened and helping the affected church to grow through the experience, is a bigger factor than is usually acknowledged. But the lack of openness in such scenarios, whilst appearing to make things easier, is always damaging.

I can think of one church where some of its members colluded with the misconduct of its vicar in a manner that then affected the whole atmosphere of the church after he had moved on. The fact that he was promoted to a more senior position and was influential at a national level within the Church of England made matters worse. A subsequent vicar realised that the only way for the church to move on was for a greater openness to take place about what had happened, including repentance on the part of the members who had colluded through their silence with what the former vicar had done.

To be clear, the chief motive operating in terms of the secrecy involved in these examples is usually that of trying to avoid personal discomfort. What makes responding to this complex, however, is that this motive is hardly ever acknowledged. Instead, the façade is maintained that this approach has its basis in wisdom and experience and is being adopted for 'the good of the church'. As we saw with the content of the previous chapter, these same tendencies then have devastating implications for the church's safeguarding. This is because a mindset that is used to hushing up failures in the church is not easily changed. When I have advanced this view to bishops and archdeacons, they have looked anxious, before expressing the hope that the seriousness of safeguarding should lead to a different and more transparent approach. But this is wishful thinking, designed to protect themselves in the face of a challenging question. If efforts are consistently made to prevent difficult truth from being spoken to the church, then safeguarding disasters will simply be the worst possible outcome of this policy.

The Role of 'Cant'

Cant is a particularly English type of untruthfulness and has been described as sanctimonious talk, typically of a moral or religious nature. Rather than full-blown hypocrisy, it usually represents 'the voluntary over-charging or prolongation of genuine sentiment'.[14] This was mentioned at the end of Chapter 3, where parallels were drawn between the culture of the Church of England and that of English cricket.

Through its role in safeguarding institutions, cant often plays a significant function in marking out and giving status to 'insiders'. The most obvious form of cant is the repetition of values so often and so mechanically that these expressions become empty of meaning and simply preserve the legitimacy of the institution on behalf of which they are being invoked. Within cultures where cant has become the norm and is closely associated with being pleasant, urbane and supportive, those employing it can often become oblivious to its role in helping untruthfulness to become normalised.

Examples of cant abound in the church. The giveaway is often the use of the language of 'reality' when excessive claims are being made. Bishops will be heard referring to 'the very real opportunities' or 'the very real potential' present in projects that they are keen to endorse. Clergy then reciprocate by taking to social media to announce how 'deeply proud' they are to be a member of their diocese because of the 'very real commitment to ministry and mission that it displays'. Another prominent example of cant can be seen in the Church of England press releases, commonly used to announce senior appointments. Usually full of over-the-top assertions about the 'outstanding ministry' of those appointed, such press releases are 'singing to the gallery' and rely upon a widespread and dishonest collusion that ensures that anyone who questions the truth of these statements can be presented as negative and unkind.

Sadly, cant has been deployed a great deal in recent times in reference to the church's safeguarding. Only too aware of the growing scandals around safeguarding in the Church of England, bishops have got used to expressing 'shame' about this and the determination to see 'very real and lasting change occurring'. Unless such words are accompanied by swift and practical action, they represent meaningless cant of the kind condemned in James 2.16.

Confidence about the Importance and Power of Truth

At the basis of all of this, as we have noted, is a lack of confidence about the liberating power of truth. Those involved in the episodes and examples set out in this chapter are instead deeply fearful about truth and believe that it needs to be controlled and restricted, if danger is to be avoided. This stance is rarely stated openly and, instead of this, its proponents tend to hide behind the importance of protecting 'the church', and specifically their own responsibility for this. This leads directly to the penchant for passive-aggression examined in Chapter 3. Ironically, it is when complete openness is shown, and organisations are prepared to risk looking bad in the process that the greatest respect for them is sometimes achieved. A theological explanation of this is that in these cases, churches are concentrating on doing the right thing and leaving the consequences of these actions in the hands of God. It takes a strong degree of courage for churches and their leaders to focus on 'the means' in terms of their actions while leaving 'the ends' to God. This could be seen, however, as a definition of what practical Christian faith is all about.

One example of the difference made by confidence about truth concerns the funerals of those who have taken their own life. Like many clergy, conducting funerals is an important part of my ministry. Most of these funerals are of people I have never met, and sadly, these have included a number of suicides. In such situations, there is a very strong temptation for the circumstances of the person's death to go unmentioned during the service, and I am told that this is often what happens at such funerals. The family's wishes are obviously a very important factor here and should always have the final say on the matter. However, a less acknowledged and more significant element often at play is the wish of clergy to avoid any mention of suicide as well. While this might be justified on the basis of pastoral sensitivity towards the family, its primary reason is often a lack of confidence on the part of these clergy about how to handle and speak into this difficult truth.

In every such funeral that I have taken, I have placed a great priority upon being completely open about the circumstances of the death. In each case, the family has understood the reasons that I have given for wanting to do this and have agreed with this approach. The importance of this is twofold. First, it avoids a situation where everyone at the funeral, or at least a large number present, is aware that the major cause of pain and anguish is being avoided. Second, once the suicide is acknowledged, it enables the funeral service to speak into the full horror of this event. It may sound an exaggerated claim but, paradoxically, the more awful the circumstances of a funeral, the more genuinely confident I feel about the power of the message that will be delivered at it. The reason for this is because, at such funerals, the only thing that can make any possible difference is the gospel message of God's love being more powerful than evil. People are desperate for a message that evil will not be allowed to have the final word and are usually as receptive as any grouping that I have spoken to. Pointing to their own acts of love towards the bereaved as an act of defiance towards evil and refusing to allow it to win, facilitates an explanation of what the love of God in Jesus Christ is all about. Much the same applies to the funerals of children that I have taken, as well as the two involving murder. The result of having the courage to deliver such a message is often startling, with those present realising that God's light is still present in the darkness and that "the darkness has not overcome it" (John 1.5).

However, none of this is possible if the full truth about the darkness is not stated first. If the horror of what has happened is ignored or downplayed in the funeral of a victim of suicide, it means that the power of the gospel to speak into the tragedy is negated as well. I hasten to add that, as soon as I have said that the person took their own life, I mention those factors that are crucial to a proper sensitivity being shown. This includes, most obviously, the advances in how we now understand mental health and what these reveal about how badly the church often responded to suicide in the past. But the pastoral impact of such funerals means that they are easily the most important ones that I have taken and, at the core of their approach, has been confidence about the importance and liberating power of truth.

On a wider stage, the most outstanding example of this in recent times has been the truth and reconciliation process in South Africa, following the end of apartheid. This was based on the conviction that genuine reconciliation could only take place when it was preceded by complete truthfulness. This enabled the most horrific crimes to be admitted before the most astonishing acts of forgiveness were then extended to those who had committed them.[15]

My brother Jon Kuhrt has demonstrated how this principle equally applies to making an effective response to difficult issues in Britain, such as homelessness.[16] Far too often, Christians responding to homelessness have preferred to lay the sole emphasis upon displaying God's grace to those in need of help. John's Gospel, however, describes Jesus as being "full of grace and truth" (John 1.14, 17), and it is only through an emphasis on both of these virtues that help can be brought to people in a way that is truly life-changing for them.

Examples of the importance of truth replacing falsehood in church life even extends to areas that could be seen as trivial. This includes the 'urban myths' that easily develop in churches. One of my predecessors as vicar at Christ Church was struck down by viral encephalitis in the late 1980s, a disease from which he nearly died. It was a desperately worrying time for his family and traumatic for the church and, thankfully, after several months of illness, he survived. But part of the narrative that then developed around the episode was that the vicar had contracted this encephalitis during an earlier sabbatical that he took in Africa. Many years later, I invited the vicar's widow and other family members back to Christ Church to open a new entrance and see a bench that had been established in his memory. It was a moving occasion but one of its most interesting aspects was the concern of the vicar's wife to tell me that the story about her husband contracting encephalitis in Africa was completely false. Some might have argued that it should not have mattered to her, but it clearly did. This was probably because an over-dramatisation of what had occurred was irritating, but also because of the basic principle that truth matters – and within church life more than anywhere.

Lies and falsehood – including those which might seem completely trivial – are damaging to the life of the church. This is because smaller lies can easily beget bigger ones and help foster a culture where truth doesn't really matter, particularly if this reinforces a popular or convenient narrative. Such an approach, if it continues unchecked, can bring a great deal of darkness to a church, luring it away from the light of reality and therefore relevance to the world around them. Truth, in short, matters at every level in church life.

Liberation Brought by Truth and Openness in Regard to Safeguarding

If the power and importance of truth applies to every part of church life, this is especially the case in regard to safeguarding. Some restrictions on openness must of course apply in safeguarding situations, particularly where information emerging too swiftly about a case would prejudice the outcome of action being taken over it. Or in some matters of confidentiality. A clear distinction should be made, however, between acknowledging temporary requirements for discretion and the general principle and aim of openness and transparency. This will be achieved if, at every stage of the process, safeguarding in churches is approached with a full confidence in the ability of Christianity to handle and cope with truth.

This confidence about truth will, in the first place, shape and guide investigations into safeguarding offences. Rather than simply responding to the issues that have to be dealt with, those with responsibility in the church will seek to shine the light of truth on as wide an area as possible. In secular institutions, such wide-ranging investigations will often only take place after the emergence of a major scandal that demands a change of approach. This happened with Operation Yewtree and investigations into historical abuse by celebrities after the revelations emerged about Jimmy Savile in 2012. Within the church, however, a confidence about the importance of truth should mean that proactive investigations are more readily embraced. Clergy and other church leaders should be doing this on the principle that everything should be exposed to the light and that, without this approach, the church will never be able to function properly.

This was my firm belief in terms of the episode regarding the lay minister mentioned in Chapter 1. Part of the anger that I incurred from various directions was for digging up an issue that had occurred before my time at Christ Church and which was seen as an unnecessary disturbance of things that belonged in the past. I was always clear that my major motivation was the thoroughly biblical one of bringing justice and vindication to those who had been abused. Protection of any future potential victims was obviously extremely important, too. But another part of my motivation was the belief that Christ Church would not be able to move on until the matter had been properly dealt with. This was only in part because of the anger felt by those who had been affected by the matter and the perplexity of those who knew that it had not been dealt with properly. Both were relatively small groups, and their concerns could have been approached pragmatically. What made all the difference, certainly to my motivation, was a theological conviction about the healing and transforming power of truth. I firmly believed that a spiritual blockage was present at Christ Church through the cover-up of what had occurred and the inadequacy of the church's response. I also believed that it was only the whole matter being brought into the light that could remove this obstruction and allow the church to move on.

But confidence about truth will also affect how much openness there is concerning safeguarding issues once these have been dealt with. This is vital for a number of reasons. One of these is its potential in enabling others who have been similarly affected to come forward. This is because they become aware of the outcome and are encouraged by the way that justice has been seen to be done. Equally vital is the way such openness enables churches to address things about their culture that need to change in the light of what has happened. All sorts of reasons can be given for believing 'the less said, the better' and that, after such events, everyone should seek to move on as quickly as possible. Confidence about the power of truth, however, brings a very different approach; and one that is, ultimately, far healthier for the church.

I faced this situation in the aftermath of the episode regarding the lay minister and his conviction. I had just become vicar of Christ Church after four years of being curate there and central to the vision for the church going forward was creating a service as accessible as possible for children and young families. I have written about this elsewhere.[17] But the key point here is that, having established a 'Sssh Free Church' and being full of enthusiasm and expectation about how this was going to work out, I was only too aware that the last thing the launch of this service needed was to coincide with revelations about a safeguarding scandal at Christ Church. However, it was also very clear to me that this was a moment when I had to do the right thing and be completely open about what had happened, regardless of the consequences. I realised that the new service and its potential for success could very easily be destroyed through the local community becoming aware of what had happened. But I also believed that, if this occurred, it would be no less than we as a church deserved for our shameful role in responding so badly to the case when it first emerged.

In the event, the emergence of the case and its coverage in the local press did not damage the new child-friendly service at all. In fact, openness about what had happened and a willingness to speak about its previous mishandling, was something that appeared to develop a greater degree of confidence in the ministry that we were seeking to provide. New congregation members were, if anything, too understanding about the ways in which many churches have mishandled safeguarding matters. But the most crucial part of their response was their recognition that complete openness about what had happened, regardless of the reputation of the church, was a strong indication that their children were now in safe hands.

Some years later, I had the chance to reinforce this. Over a decade had passed since the court case involving the lay minister and its coverage in the press, and most newcomers at the church were unaware of its occurrence. A large new building had been constructed at the church entirely for ministry towards children and young people, with purpose-built rooms and a number of large corridors. I decided to use these corridors to establish an extensive exhibition of the history of Christ Church. This included those events that we could look back on with pride but also those that reflected badly on the church. The latter included a huge and divisive row in 1870 that resulted in a breakaway church in New Malden, terrible attitudes taken at points towards Roman Catholics, and the public endorsement of Freemasonry by the then vicar of the church in 1961. But foremost in this regard was honesty about the previous mishandling of safeguarding. Placed near the entrance to our Scramblers Room (our group for age 3-5s) and where parents collected their children, was a section of the exhibition referring to this.

There were some members of the church who were worried about this being included in the exhibition. I argued that for any presentation of the church's history to have integrity, it had to present this history 'warts and all'.[18] This, to my mind, was the most important factor involved. But a revealing aspect of this part of the exhibition was the impact that it had on parents new to the church, who observed it. Some expressed surprise that the church had chosen to 'out itself' in this manner. But this was swiftly followed by the recognition that it showed how seriously we took the care of their children and how determined we were to be transparent. Being completely unconcerned about the safety of the church's reputation was, paradoxically, what served this reputation most, because it made clear that being a safe church was entirely about the safety of those entrusted to our care. By this stage, the church was also obliged to display notices about safeguarding in other prominent positions around the building. But I was in no doubt that this section of the Christ Church exhibition was the most powerful and relevant way in which we were displaying the importance that genuine safeguarding now has for us.

Gaining Clarity About the Relationship Between Truth and Safety

This chapter began by stating the widespread confusion about safety in a church context: whether it refers to the safety of the people within the church and to whom it ministers, or the safety of the church as an institution. But, at a deeper level, this confusion extends to what safety itself represents. If truth is regarded as dangerous, it will always be included in those things that the church needs to be protected and kept safe from. If, on the other hand, truth is regarded as 'a friend', it will be seen as vital to genuine safety and welcomed into every aspect of church life.

A major problem here is the deep insecurity among many bishops and clergy about their effectiveness and performance. One of the greatest frustrations during my curacy was the unwillingness of my training vicar to ever allow discussions to go back to first principles and question why we were 'doing church' in the form that we were. It was only later that I realised that for someone insecure about their ministry, the question "why are we doing this?" is the most terrifying one that can be asked.

Most of the meetings that I have had with bishops and archdeacons have been similar in their unwillingness to discuss matters of principle and truth. If such discussions take place, they are normally kept at an abstract level rather than allowed to become incarnate in concrete ministerial and missional practice. I remember one diocesan meeting where I was asked to speak to a group of academically-minded clergy about my theological understanding of the death of Jesus. I spoke about this and the group listened with interest to my thoughts. But when I progressed to how this theological thinking might be implemented in practical ministry (not least in regard to the funeral ministry referred to earlier), their faces glazed over with relatively little interest shown. Theological truth, it seemed, could be debated but only in an abstract manner, with the view that it was almost being profaned through extending this discussion to how it should be implemented 'on the ground'.

This is the reason for the yawning gap that exists between the world of academic theology and that of practical ministry. Most of what I have previously written has been an attempt to bridge these two worlds and demonstrate how theological truth can be transformative when it is accompanied by a commitment to implement it within ministry and mission.[19] But it took me some while to recognise that the separation of these worlds is not accidental or simply the result of a lack of ability in this regard. It is agenda-driven and the result of a desire, on both sides of the divide, to keep church practice safely away from any discussion about theological truth. Such integrated discussions are 'unsafe' because they carry the possibility of having to review the way that church is being done in the light of fresh insights derived from greater reflection upon the gospel. When this occurs, theological truth is being regarded as something that needs to be contained and controlled, rather than received as the liberating force that should be part of setting the church and its people free.

When it comes to safeguarding in the church, listening to the stories and concerns of survivors is paramount. What appears time and again in their statements is a desire for truth. In virtually every case, the terrible hurt that survivors have endured is made far worse by the truth being suppressed about the factors involved in their abuse and especially the church's collusion. These survivors are not, for the most part, out for any sort of revenge on the church, or even those directly responsible for their abuse. What they want instead, and indeed demand, is *vindication*. Revenge and vindication are different. Revenge is commonly defined as 'the action of hurting or harming someone in return for an injury or wrong suffered at their hands'. Vindication, on the other hand, refers to someone being publicly declared to be in the right and/or the recipient of an injustice that is now being clearly and openly revealed and condemned.

Truth, fairly obviously, lies at the heart of such vindication, and once this truth is allowed to be spoken, it is remarkable what then becomes possible – particularly in terms of the most amazing acts of forgiveness. But this only forms the practical outworking of what lies at the heart of the Christian faith that churches profess to believe in and live by. It is about believing what the Bible says when it declares that "grace and truth came through Jesus Christ" (John 1.17 cf 1.14) and also that "perfect love drives out fear" (1 John 4.18).

A charming if somewhat bawdy film that speaks powerfully of the transforming power of truth is *Liar Liar*.[20] In the film, Jim Carrey plays Fletcher Reede, a gifted but crooked lawyer for whom the use of lies and deceit has become a way of life. This brings him a certain measure of success within his professional career but also a great deal of hurt to his five-year-old son, Max. On being let down by his father yet again, Max makes a wish when blowing out the candles on his birthday cake that his dad will go a whole day without being able to lie. This wish then comes true. Fletcher not only cannot lie but every time he attempts to lie, he instead speaks the truth. Depending on the taste of the viewer, most of the consequences of Fletcher's subsequent behaviour are either hilarious or downright rude. But the message of the film is ultimately the hugely positive one about the healing and restoration brought about by truth. Removed for just one day from a mindset where deceit and duplicity are part of the fabric of everyday life, Fletcher is forced to confront the nature of what he has become and the effect of this on others. The film therefore represents a considerable rebuke to the way that so much of Western society is built upon duplicity that it cannot even recognise this. But it also applies to the church, which should be equally stung by its realisation of the harm done to those it should be protecting, when it sits lightly to valuing and speaking the truth.

C.S. Lewis is perhaps a more reassuring figure to quote as this chapter ends. Safeguarding is an important term to continue using because of the sacred calling that the church is given to keep vulnerable people safe from harm. But in other ways 'safety' is a problematic concept for the church because of the overtone of caution that often accompanies it. When it comes to protecting those who are vulnerable, the church should be totally risk averse, with every possible caution displayed about their care. Paradoxically, however, such care for the vulnerable will only be achieved when the church becomes far less concerned about its own safety as an institution because of its reliance upon Jesus Christ.

This is displayed in C.S. Lewis' *The Lion, the Witch and the Wardrobe* when Susan and Lucy first hear from Mr and Mrs Beaver about Aslan. Mr Beaver describes Aslan as a great lion who is the son of the great Emperor-beyond-the-Sea, King of Beasts. Mrs Beaver adds that 'if there's anyone who can appear before Aslan without their knees knocking, they're either braver than most or just silly'. Susan and Lucy are intrigued at the sound of Aslan but also rather nervous about him, with each of them inquiring about whether he is 'safe'. The response that they receive from Mr Beaver is instructive and worth reflecting on: '"Safe?", said Mr Beaver; "don't you hear what Mrs Beaver tells you? Who said anything about safe? 'Course he isn't safe. But he's good. He's the King, I tell you"'.[21]

CHAPTER 6

Seen and Not Heard

Inconsistent Attitudes Towards Behaviour in the Church

As mentioned already, the whole of my childhood and teenage years were spent growing up in churches. Happy enough to be a clergy child, this experience was an overwhelmingly positive one. Engaging and relevant services, kind and interested adults and wonderfully committed leaders of the children's and youth groups that I attended were stand-out features of these years. There was, however, one aspect of all the churches that I belonged to in these years that really annoyed me. One that I felt strongly enough about to vow that I would never collude with when I was older. This was the completely different standards of behaviour expected of children compared to adults.

THE BACKGROUND OF CHILDREN IN CHURCH

Expectations of children in church owe a great deal to the legacy of the past. It is only relatively recently that they have been welcomed into services at all. Going back a hundred years in Britain, church services were for adults. While some upper-class children might attend these services with their parents or governess, concessions for these children were neither expected nor given. Christian provision for working-class children was chiefly provided by the Sunday School movement, which had its peak from the mid-Victorian era through to the 1950s. Unlike today, these Sunday schools were kept separate from church services and usually held on Sunday afternoons. Within particularly pioneering churches, this started to be supplemented by children's services, essentially replicating the style of adult services but with a simpler approach taken to the sermon. Worship for adults and children, however, still remained separate until the start of 'family services' from around the late 1940s and 1950s. These were generally evening services provided for 'twicers' and their children, rather than representing any change to the 'main service' held in the morning.

Generally speaking, it was during the 1970s that the great merger took place of adult worship and provision for children. Much of this was driven by necessity. In terms of numbers attracted, the Sunday School movement was well past its peak and it became more common for such groups to be held during Sunday morning services. Within evangelical Anglican churches, 'family services' generally moved to Sunday mornings, often taking place on a monthly basis in place of the 'normal' services. Within non-evangelical Anglican churches, such provision was less common, and Sunday schools struggled to survive. In such churches, choirs often represented the largest engagement with children and young people, and a certain amount of youth work was sometimes built upon this.

The effect of greater entertainment for children and young people in the surrounding culture from the 1980s was double-edged. Influenced by this and encouraged by organisations like CPAS (the Church Pastoral Aid Society) and Scripture Union, provision for children and young people in some churches became steadily more imaginative and attractive. In far more churches, however, the growth of secular attractions and having fewer 'churched' parents, accelerated the dropping away of children and young people.

The situation today in terms of provision by churches for children and young people is fairly bleak. Within many, perhaps most, Church of England churches, there is hardly any provision at all for children and none for young people. Church choirs can still attract children, but nothing like the numbers of the past. Within many evangelical churches, children's work can still attract good numbers and appear quite healthy. Even here, however, the fall-off has become younger and younger, influenced by the growth in children's sport and other activities on Sunday mornings. Even within the most dynamic evangelical churches, attracting and retaining teenagers has also become much more difficult. It is in response to these developments that some of the more imaginative approaches to current provision for children and young people within churches have developed.

'Messy Church', aiming beyond provision simply for children, is perhaps the most outstanding example of this, as is the growth of churches employing youth ministers to build relationships and community with 'unchurched' young people in their locality.[1] Significantly, however, rather than increasing 'child-friendly' church, these developments have essentially represented a move back to the separation of church provision for children and adults.

Behaviour Expected of Children in Churches

Against this background, it is not surprising that if children are present within churches today, they are generally expected to behave in ways more natural to adults. Welcome a group of schoolchildren on a midweek trip to church and it is still common to hear their teachers telling them they must be quiet and avoid giving off any energy at all as they enter the 'holy' building. Much the same attitude is taken to their presence on Sundays. Even if the welcome to children in churches is warm and genuine, there is still the widespread assumption that their expectations and therefore behaviour should conform to those of the adults.

Exceptions, of course, exist. There are some churches where parents are so consumed by their own experience of the worship that they are scarcely aware of their children's behaviour. Rather than being positive, this approach demonstrates a neglect of children and is often as damaging to their experience and perception of Christianity as an atmosphere where they are expected to be 'seen and not heard'. In overall terms, however, it is true to say that in most Church of England churches there is a norm expected for children's behaviour. If children are present they are expected to restrain their natural impulses and show respect – ostensibly to God but, in reality, more for the sake of his adult followers. Parents are largely aware of this and expected to be its chief enforcers.

Children learning to behave properly within church, or anywhere else, is of course both right and necessary. But the expectations of this behaviour must be realistic, age-appropriate and also conscious of any more specific differences on the part of the child. They should also be accompanied by an equal commitment to their Christian teaching and nurture. Many passages in the Bible are relevant here, pointing to the importance of providing both discipline and proper instruction for children (Deuteronomy 5.16; 6.6-9; Joshua 4.20-24; Proverbs 3.12; 13.24; 19.18; 22.6, 15; 23.13-14; 29.15; Ephesians 6.1-4; 2 Timothy 3.15; Hebrews 12.7-11). I have written elsewhere of the conviction that for churches to practise infant baptism with integrity, it must be accompanied by placing absolute priority upon the holistic Christian nurture of these children.[2]

Parenting courses are becoming more common and some of the best of these are provided by churches. The one provided by Nicky and Sila Lee presents a parenting quadrant created by a vertical scale representing discipline and a horizontal scale representing warmth. This quadrant then contains four parenting styles. An approach to parenting that is strong on discipline but weak on warmth is *authoritarian*. One that is strong on warmth but weak on discipline is *indulgent*. One that is weak on both discipline and warmth is *neglectful*. All three of these approaches to parenting have fairly obvious problems, meaning that the approach most likely to produce happy and secure children is one that is strong on both discipline and warmth. This style is termed *authoritative*. Parents who place an equal emphasis on the priorities of both warmth and discipline are showing genuine love for their children and are more likely, therefore, to make progress in the tricky business of parenting.[3]

Something similar should surely guide the approach taken to children by churches. Expectations of appropriate behaviour by children in church are important but this should always be in the context of a huge amount of warmth being shown towards them. The overall leaders of a church play a crucial role here, often setting the tone by their example. The behaviour of some children is very challenging but usually with understandable reasons that require both patience on the part of the church and careful thought about how best to respond to them.

Even this can be seen as wonderfully positive. Within my own church we have noticed that many of our most regular junior-aged children are those who struggle to fit into other forms of Sunday morning provision in the outside world. From seeing challenging behaviour in the group simply as a problem, this has helped us to see it instead as a wonderful opportunity that God has given us to show his love to those who need it most.

Most children in church, including those whose behaviour is more challenging, recognise when an effort is being made for them. This is especially when this effort is displayed by the vicar, greeting them by name on arrival with a large and affirming smile. If children in church do receive warmth, realistic expectations and anything approaching appropriate provision for their needs, their behaviour is often fine. The fascinating thing – and it should probably be stated in stronger and more negative terms – is how rarely this can be said for many adult members of churches.

Adult Behaviour in Churches

The vast majority of adults within the churches that I have belonged to during my life have been wonderful. They include most of the closest friends that I have had and some of the most outstanding examples of godliness and kindness possible. During the twenty-two years that I have been ordained, I have been fortunate to have a succession of incredibly committed and faithful churchwardens and congregations full of people of all ages displaying faith, humour and often immense courage in the face of difficult and demanding circumstances.

However, it is also the case that I have experienced some truly terrible behaviour by adult members of these churches – behaviour going well beyond anything that I have seen from children or young people. Furthermore, the worst examples of such behaviour have not come from those peripheral to church life or irregular in their attendance, or those with obvious medical or psychological needs. The most consistently poor behaviour has been shown by established, long-term members who would see themselves, and are generally seen by others, as very committed Christians.

The overwhelming cause of this poor behaviour is when these people have not got their way over an aspect of church life. We have already seen in Chapter 4 how some established churchgoers believe that, if they feel strongly enough about something, they should then have a right of veto in regard to it. This is especially the case if it involves any change being made to the status quo and is perceived as a threat to their comfort or position. Even, or particularly, if they represent a minority viewpoint.

The most common responses have ranged from outright aggression to the kinds of passive-aggressive behaviour covered in Chapter 3. Aggressive responses have included shouting out at meetings, storming out of services and considerable displays of anger. Passive-aggressive behaviour has included sulking, refusing to agree to meet up to resolve matters and, above all, taking other opportunities to 'punish' those who have upset them – most commonly by mounting an irrational and seemingly senseless opposition to a completely different area of church life. One of the easiest ways to do this is when any sort of building project takes place. The nature of church building projects, with their complexities and the various permissions they require, means that they can provide almost endless opportunities for anyone intent on causing trouble. But there are plenty of other opportunities as well. One of my churchwardens summed it up well when he said that church life provides some with a 'playground' in which they can indulge almost every destructive impulse that they possess.

Other examples of poor behaviour in churches are more subtle. Sometimes it grows out of a situation where a person has taken on excessive jobs and responsibilities in a church as part of an attempt to make themselves indispensable. The underlying causes of this are complex but it can represent an attempt by such people to gain recognition or status in response to unmet emotional needs. More basic but often related, is the instinct fill their lives with busyness to keep painful thoughts and memories at bay. Approaching membership of a church in this manner, however, never achieves these goals and often leads instead to such people becoming more and more frustrated as all of their hard work fails to bring what they are hoping to gain from it. In the worst cases, this results in extraordinary levels of exasperation, rudeness and bossiness towards those working less hard for the church and failing to appreciate 'all they are doing'.

At this point some readers might be reacting to this picture and feeling that the duty of the church is to bear with such people, with understanding, love and care being the answer to their needs. In pastoral terms, this is completely agreed. Reflecting the command of Jesus that willingness to forgive should be endless (Matthew 18.21-35), such people's needs and the underlying hurt involved should indeed be met with continuing love and patience. The major problem, however, is that those who behave in this manner are rarely prepared to receive pastoral care. Any acknowledgement that pastoral issues are involved in their behaviour is normally hotly denied. Unfortunately, this means that any action taken in regard to the impact of their behaviour can easily be made to look uncaring and thoroughly unpastoral.

But unwillingness on the part of church leadership to respond to such behaviour is itself a pastoral failure – in terms of their commitment to the whole church and its other members. The agenda of those adults who cause the most trouble within church life is usually the desire to have a greater degree of power over others. Any responsible church leadership will combine never giving up on such people in pastoral terms with the refusal to allow power to be seized in this way. This involves setting clear boundaries in terms of behaviour and responding to their breach.

Sadly, within many churches this does not happen, with long-standing members in particular, able to behave as they wish. The scandal is that poor behaviour of a similar nature by children would never be tolerated. I can think of one situation that summed this up well. A number of years ago, I asked my two new curates to organise a service for Maundy Thursday. Poorly attended in the past, they organised a very different and highly imaginative service. Effective publicity meant that an unusually good number then came, including a number of young people. The approach taken to the service was fresh but not offensively radical, and yet the behaviour of some of the longer-term members of the church in response was terrible. Rather than being happy that so many had come, we had supposed pillars of the church refusing to engage with the service and making loudly negative statements about it. The most telling comment in response came from one of our young people who said: "If a teenager behaved like that in church, people would say, 'How typical!'"

Collusion with Adult Misbehaviour in Churches

This is common for a number of reasons. Clergy are generally timid in their response to such behaviour and feel that doing nothing is the best or only option. This is usually because they would not receive proper support if they were to act. Despite the importance of their office, churchwardens can be reluctant to get involved and the same goes for most church members. Rather than taking responsibility for responding to this important issue, the culture within many churches is utterly resistant to dealing with adult misbehaviour.

The most popular explanation for this is people's dislike of conflict, plus the desire to express the love and understanding that they associate with the Christian message. An honest assessment would also identify the strong investment that members of churches have in the status quo. In the same way that any change within churches represents a threat to this status quo, so does any challenge to the behaviour of adults. Even if they find the behaviour of some within their church upsetting and annoying, the majority of church members prefer an atmosphere where this is never confronted. Where the behaviour results from someone taking on excessive roles and responsibilities in church life, this can be because clergy and other congregation members are so relieved that these responsibilities have been taken on, that they tolerate and then collude with the poor behaviour that comes with this. The major root of this, however, is the desire for church to remain a place of peace and comfort rather than challenge.

This is the reason why some evangelical churches can combine 'challenging' preaching with a remarkable tolerance of poor behaviour by their members. When this is the case, the preaching in question usually turns out to be challenging those on the periphery of the church (or even those not present) rather than its committed members. It is also usually focused on doctrinal conformity rather than personal or collective conduct towards others. Such an approach to preaching can unwittingly endorse poor behaviour. This is because it reinforces the idea that, if a Christian feels strongly enough about something, it is fine and even admirable to mount a forceful objection to it. Sometimes this is right and important.

More often, however, and particularly when the result is uncontrolled expressions of anger, this represents the response of those who sense their position is being threatened. In such churches, the lack of challenge to this type of behaviour can result in it becoming completely normalised. One person from such a context commented that poor behaviour had been tolerated in her church for so long that those most guilty of this were no longer aware they were acting badly.

Similar factors can operate in very different contexts. Within some churches, for instance, music has a centrality which can lead to those most invested in it behaving extremely poorly. This can equally occur within churches with a choral tradition or those where worship is led by a band. It is usually brought about by a personality or grouping determined to get their way and this can result in the most remarkable degrees of feuding and pettiness. Clergy being beholden to their musicians for the provision of worship is often a key factor in allowing such behaviour to go unchallenged. But so is the tendency of some church leaders to manage this kind of situation through versions of 'divide and rule'. This is most commonly through refusing to manage such a scenario, thus allowing the more difficult musicians to cancel one another out. Like all passive-aggressive behaviour, any short-term 'advantages' that come with such tactics are then outweighed by the greater level of dysfunctionality they create in church life.

The result of all of this is that challenging poor behaviour in churches is often seen as much less acceptable than the poor behaviour itself. Perhaps the best example of this is the attitude in many churches towards lying. This was touched on in Chapter 3. It may be shocking to state it so boldly, but within many churches it is more or less acceptable for Christians to lie, particularly if the person is upset or angry about something that has happened in church life. Examples extend all the way from massive and wilful exaggeration, to stating things that are completely false. To suggest that the person doing this is lying, however, is usually seen as completely unacceptable. This is because, within a passive-aggressive mindset, lying is a legitimate way of solving problems and any restriction of this 'necessary tool' is seen as deeply threatening. Anxiety about avoiding conflict means that the acceptance of this state of affairs in churches often goes far beyond those who would behave this way.

The problem is that such a culture plays directly into the hands of those prepared to use poor behaviour to prevent the church from changing in any way they find uncomfortable. For some years, I had a colleague who would regularly respond to any challenge to the status quo in church life by making statements that no one else believed were true. Another colleague eventually observed that this forced a choice between dropping the point of challenge or calling out the lie. What made the tactic so effective in closing down discussion, was everyone's knowledge that the surrounding culture had made the latter completely unacceptable.

Collusion with Adult Misbehaviour by the Wider Structures of the Church

The lack of support for clergy in such situations, and the consequent pressure to do nothing in response, is not just something that comes from congregations. Very often it comes directly from their superiors, too. Clergy without apparent trouble in their churches are perceived as wise and reliable, while those where there is conflict are seen as the opposite. The thought that this might be because the former are evading difficult issues and the latter trying to grapple with them is not usually considered or acknowledged.

Another effect of this general culture (and here we start to get closer to the subject of safeguarding) is that any genuine attempt at discipline in the Church of England is largely absent for the vast majority of its members. The Clergy Discipline Measure has existed since 2003 and carries a certain amount of compulsion in the responses that it requires from bishops and archdeacons for the behaviour and conduct of their clergy. No equivalent, however, yet exists for lay members of churches.[4] This puts clergy in an invidious position when it comes to trying to deal with misbehaviour in their churches. The problem, however, is more cultural than structural. It lies in the deep reluctance, mentioned throughout this book, of most bishops and archdeacons to get involved in resolving anything that is difficult.

Refusal to Use Available Means of Discipline

An example of this was when my churchwardens and I tried to gain the assistance of our bishop in response to the consistently damaging behaviour of a member of the church. The behaviour was persistent and distressing, not least through the amount of time and emotional energy that was required to deal with it.

Founded upon complete consensus within the leadership team, we eventually wrote to our area bishop about the matter. In the letter, we reported that the behaviour had now reached a level where formal discipline was needed. We therefore requested that the bishop consider barring the person involved from receiving Holy Communion. This request was not one that we took lightly, and one I cannot imagine having to take again. But we believed that it was the only thing that might communicate the seriousness of the disruption being caused to the church and its community, ministry and mission.

Such is the misunderstanding surrounding it, that some comment is needed at this point about excommunication. Despite what is commonly believed, barring someone from receiving Holy Communion is not about pronouncing that they are no longer a Christian and casting them into 'outer darkness'. This would rightly be seen as a contravention of Jesus' instructions in Matthew 7.1ff. Excommunication, instead, represents the attempt, when all else has failed, to give sacramental significance to the rupture in church relationships caused by a member's conduct. Matthew 18.15-17 describes the process which commonly leads up to such action, which should only be taken when every other attempt at collective resolution has failed.

The logic of excommunication is that the sacraments are powerful symbols which can speak with a strength which goes beyond that of words alone. For a Christian believer, however obdurate and intransigent they may seem to have become, such a denial of the sacrament can bring home to them the serious and damaging consequences of their actions upon both the community and their place within it.

The problem is that, within the culture prevailing in the Church of England today, people are unwilling to see excommunication in this manner. Grim images of the Spanish Inquisition or Calvin's Geneva tend to be invoked when people reject any idea of excommunication. They see it as an appalling example of a barbaric approach to Christianity that we have now, thankfully, moved beyond. However, the misuse of something should not be an argument against its use at all. Instead, it points to the paramount importance of its proper, appropriate and careful use.

Excommunication should only be considered after every other approach has failed and the person's behaviour is considered unacceptable, not only by the church's leadership but by the church as a whole. The key point is that it is temporary and restorative in its aim rather than permanent. While the person is placed, sacramentally, outside of full membership of the community, they are still allowed to attend services, because the aim of the process is their repentance and restoration. It therefore represents another attempt to incarnate the principles of truth and reconciliation. In this particular case, I was fairly sure that it represented our best chance of finally getting through to the person concerned and to them recognising the unacceptable nature of their behaviour and its impact.

The bishop, however, was unwilling to engage with our request. Rather than replying by letter, he phoned me to say that any such action 'would not be wise'. When I asked why this was the case, he had very little answer and clearly wanted me to let the whole matter drop. Instead, I asked him whether there could ever be a situation where he used his authority to bar someone from receiving Holy Communion. His answer was very revealing: "Well, obviously I would if I discovered that someone had three wives". "So even bigamy isn't a problem, unless it comes in extreme forms?", I rather testily replied.

Those at the church from a non-Anglican background were particularly taken aback by the bishop's response. No one was in favour of a reactionary approach to such matters, but the request had been made after years of catastrophic disruption. The idea of barring the member from receiving Holy Communion may have had problems that we had failed to foresee, and a better alternative may well have existed. But the critical point is that the bishop was completely uninterested in coming up with any alternative discipline. Worse still, he appeared to be indifferent to the effect that the behaviour was having upon the church. He showed minimal interest, and never asked for an update about the matter. Left to deal with it ourselves, our response as a church leadership team was to bar the member from reading the Bible or leading prayers within services. This seemed fairly inadequate, but it was the closest that we could get to exercising any measure of church discipline in the matter. The behaviour continued and, at the time of writing, is ongoing.

Interestingly, it was another member of the church who provided the most effective response. This member was extremely earnest and kindhearted and was deeply perplexed by the behaviour of someone whom he saw as a fellow brother in Christ and the damage that he believed this was doing. He was a member of the same 'home group' as the person but announced that he was unable to attend the group until the conduct ceased.[5] This action represented an application of many of the principles involved in excommunication set out above. He was seeking to give symbolic weight to his message about how unacceptable the behaviour was. It was clear that his response did make a level of impact upon the protagonist, particularly given that it was taken by a friend who was not one of the leaders of the church. I was extremely grateful that he had acted with such courage and responsibility, and if he had been joined by others it would probably have been enough to change the situation.

Undermining Attempts to Respond to Adult Misbehaviour

Another case was somewhat more complicated because it involved someone whose ministerial role was closely connected to the misconduct of someone else. For several years, the situation remained unresolved, with all of the church's leaders aware of the sensitivities and potential distress involved in trying to deal with it. Eventually, however, the behaviour reached a level where we knew it was irresponsible not to respond to the factors involved. Steps were taken to flag up the issue in a manner that sought to balance grace and truth. We were determined to be both sensitive and realistic about what was possible, while not avoiding a matter that was having a significant effect upon the life of the church.

It was a difficult situation, made more complex by unwillingness on the part of the person concerned to acknowledge the problem, let alone discuss it. What made it much worse, however, was the involvement of the archdeacon. An annual interview with me as vicar was necessary for the ministry to continue and, ahead of this, I made it clear that the issue would need to be discussed. The archdeacon, however, was then approached and agreed to conduct the annual interview instead. He was new in post and someone that I had not yet met. His intervention was intended to remain secret and without reference to me, and I only discovered about it when others who knew about it felt that it was important to inform me. The archdeacon was both aggrieved and evasive when I tried to speak to him about the matter. He refused constant requests to explain what he had done and why he hadn't spoken to me about it. What he did make clear was his belief that I was the one being unreasonable – both for refusing to accept the situation and in response to his actions. The result, sadly, was worse for the person concerned than if the archdeacon hadn't intervened, with their ministry at the church coming to an end.

With hindsight but without exaggeration, I can now see how this second case was in many ways paradigmatic for the Church of England. In my challenge to someone who was playing a role in making behaviour unaccountable, I was challenging the entire culture that they represented. The annoyance that I experienced from the archdeacon was because he, rightly, saw my insistence that the issue be confronted as a wider challenge to the institution itself. This was because any suggestion that someone should be held to account for the reasons involved represented a dangerous challenge to the status quo. Especially if they were 'respectable', committed to the institution, and possessed an authorised role within it. Challenging the archdeacon's own conduct was a further indication of the unacceptable nature of my position. The whole episode demonstrated, with very worrying implications for safeguarding, that if a conflict arose between challenging misconduct and preserving the fundamental status quo within the Church of England, it was the latter that had to be upheld.

Further Inconsistencies in the Approach Taken by Churches to Misbehaviour

Mention of 'respectability' and 'position' points to another worrying truth about behaviour in the Church of England. So far, the major contrast made in this chapter has been between the different expectations of behaviour that exist in most churches for children and adults. These inconsistencies, however, only form part of a broader problem of one standard of behaviour existing for established members of a church and another for those located further from its centre of power. This is often related to social distinctions and, once recognised, its implications for the church's failures in safeguarding are obvious.

Paradoxically, such inconsistencies can occur most when an effort is being made to reach beyond the normal social class attending the church. Some years ago, I was part of a church that established a 'Welcome Club' for marginalised people in the local area. The aim of the club, and much of the practice associated with it, was very good. But one of the things that marred it was the element of 'ungrace' that was allowed to enter into its set-up. One member of the church successfully argued that those attending should pay a nominal amount and should eventually be turned away if they failed to bring this. It was not that the cost of the lunch was large or that the church needed the money. The reason given was 'to make sure the club was valued'. This formed part of a not-so-subtle message to those coming about the behaviour that was expected of them. This was largely caused by nervousness and was, to a degree, understandable. But it also represented a fair amount of prejudice that stood in sharp contrast to the relaxed welcome that greeted middle-class people when they came to the church. To have made acceptable standards of behaviour clear to these people when they first arrived would have been regarded as outrageous.

The experience of this was influential in shaping the lunch club that we eventually established at Christ Church called Grapevine.[6] The aim was to reach those often excluded from the church, and community more generally, with God's love in Jesus Christ. Those of us who launched the club were clear that we wanted grace displayed through every part of it, starting with making no charge to those coming but giving them a fulsome welcome instead. We tried to make sure that 'behaviour' was only approached in the same manner that it would be with anyone else coming to the church i.e. with an assumption that it would be good. An atmosphere of welcome and equality appears to be the major reason that the club has become so successful. In the years that we have been running Grapevine there have been some moments when we have had to be firm about behaviour. But these have been rare, probably because of the strong and confident atmosphere of grace that is present and the 'buy-in' to the club's values that this appears to encourage.

Significantly, an episode that tested this was when we attempted to integrate our communities by including members of Grapevine within a church trip to Littlehampton. Some members of Christ Church were uncomfortable with the presence of Grapevine members on a church outing and made these feelings clear. The trip was, nonetheless, a great success, fulfilling its aim of displaying the unity that can and should exist across social and cultural boundaries through people belonging to Jesus Christ. Most members of the church rose to the occasion and went out of their way to mix with members of the lunch club. But seemingly in reaction to its aim, the event was also marred by some vague and unsubstantiated accusations made afterwards about the behaviour of members of Grapevine. These allegations were made by middle-class members of the church with the expectation that I would accept them and abandon further plans for integration. Since the allegations lacked any sort of evidence or even clarity, I was unwilling to do this, receiving a fair degree of annoyance in response.

The episode revealed a great deal about social prejudice in churches and how vicars can be expected to reinforce this. The very opposite, of course, is needed from leaders of churches. Honesty compels me to say that, during the eighteen years that the church has been running Grapevine, all of the significant poor behaviour at Christ Church has been committed by (a small minority of) regular, long-term, adult members of the church.

When an effort was made to respond to this by establishing a policy for behaviour at the church, however, it encountered a good deal of resistance. A telling comment made at the PCC was that having such a policy would give the impression that adults were going to be treated in the same way as children. The unfairness contained in this statement was challenged and the point made that, generally speaking, the behaviour of the children at Christ Church was much better than that of the adults.

Some objected to the word 'behaviour' being used at all in the context of adults. Once again, however, the crucial factor was a social prejudice that wanted to pretend that poor behaviour is not an issue among middle-class people. During the discussion, the point was made that it is becoming increasingly common to see notices in places like stations, shops and banks making it clear that zero tolerance will be shown to misbehaviour against those working there. This exposed that the real problem lay with the type of people whose behaviour we were trying to address.

An additional factor appeared to be at work. This was that members of the church could 'smell' that greater accountability was 'in the air' and didn't like it. This was not because the PCC was full of people who wanted to misbehave. It was because a number of its members were nervous about the status quo being challenged and didn't want to take responsibility for responding to a tricky issue. This was not unjustified because the worst behaviour that takes place in church is often when those behaving poorly are challenged, however gently, about this. The reaction can be so extreme that even the bravest and most proactive vicars and churchwardens avoid doing it again! This is usually part of the intention of those making such a response to their behaviour being challenged. It points to the need for the clear standards and expectations that a well-written policy about behaviour in church life is seeking to establish and communicate.

The Impact upon Clergy of the Church's Failure to Respond to Poor Behaviour

As well as its other negative effects, it's important to recognise the demoralising impact that lack of accountability for poor behaviour in churches can have upon clergy and their wellbeing. Obviously, clergy themselves are far from perfect. This book contains plenty of examples of this! But the existence of a discipline measure for clergy, with no equivalent for the members of their churches, contributes very significantly to the 'siege mentality' that many vicars fall into.

The sitcom *Rev* sought to reflect this. In one sense, its portrayal of the archdeacon as a sinister, shadowy figure suddenly appearing to call Adam Smallbone to account in the back of taxis was ridiculous.[7] But it nonetheless caught something of the angst and even paranoia that clergy can develop about the impossible odds stacked against them and the lack of support from the structures of the church as they face these challenges. One of the things that can most demoralise clergy is when they start to believe that they are simply running an inward-looking club for selfish and unaccountable people. "Is this really what I got ordained for?" is the regular and tragic question that results.

Worst of all is the way that the lack of accountability for the behaviour of lay members of churches can justify the passive-aggressive tactics mentioned earlier and developed by many clergy to cope with such scenarios. This, to repeat, only serves to make matters worse. A proper structure for lay accountability and discipline would give clergy much greater confidence to act properly in such situations. They would feel empowered to challenge poor behaviour, rather than feeling that the only alternatives are to 'go with the flow' or act equally badly in their efforts to contain it.

The Implications of the Church's Approach to Behaviour for its Safeguarding

By this stage, it will hopefully be obvious why an extended discussion of behaviour in church life has formed the content of this chapter. The failure to respond appropriately to poor behaviour in churches, particularly when this behaviour comes from long-term and 'committed' members, is a direct contributor to making these churches unsafe.

This is partly because, when poor behaviour becomes normalised, it leads to an unaccountable culture which soon facilitates even worse conduct. Church leaders who have not been challenged for bullying people or using other means of coercive control, for instance, steadily lose more of their moral compass and start to see even darker forms of behaviour as acceptable. This is why the worst forms of abuse in church life have often been committed by 'larger than life' characters with considerable ability, energy and charisma. All of these attributes should be entirely positive in a Christian leader. When they become combined with a lack of accountability, however, and a culture where poor behaviour has become normalised, they all too easily become toxic. Failure to recognise that this can happen to the most inspirational and dynamic of Christian leaders is connected to the inadequate reflection on the depth of evil covered in Chapter 2. The breadth of this evil includes those unwilling to challenge poor behaviour because of their investment in the status quo and who thus become another contributor to the appalling abuse that such behaviour can grow into.

But another impact of the normalisation of poor behaviour in churches is that they become seen as 'a soft touch' by those with predatory intent. Seeing poor behaviour remaining unchallenged, encourages those with more sinister intentions to pursue them, knowing that they are likely to remain unchallenged as well. Ironically, a culture where obviously poor behaviour is tolerated can allow those with overtly better behaviour but even worse intentions, to 'fly under the radar'. Back in Chapter 2 we examined the subject of grooming and saw that its primary and most dangerous form comes through abusers or potential abusers grooming an entire community to see them as harmless. In a church where poor behaviour has become normalised, it can appear wonderful to find someone who will work hard and be committed to the church without similar problems of conduct. It is the normalisation of poor behaviour in other parts of church life that contributes to those regular scenarios, following the emergence of abuse scandals, where people are shocked that someone 'who everyone found so nice and helpful' is involved.

The other significant relationship between failures in behaviour management in churches and their safeguarding, concerns the inconsistency that has been a large theme of this chapter. The normalisation of wildly inconsistent standards of behaviour within the church reinforces the impact of many of the negative factors for safeguarding examined earlier in this book, such as elitism, arrogance, dishonesty and relative expendability. It is children and disadvantaged adults who are the major victims of this inconsistency. We shouldn't be surprised, therefore, that the Church of England has a major problem with the safeguarding of these very same people.

Once again, the Peter Ball case is instructive here. One of the most distressing aspects of this case was the huge imbalance between the support given to Peter Ball and that received by those he had abused. Scores of letters and phone calls supporting Ball were received by those handling his case in 1992-3 and these were clearly instrumental in the leniency then shown to him.[8] Central to this were the stark differences in social background between Ball and the young men he abused, and the assumptions that accompanied this.

It was not Ball's saintly character that was the major reason for the favour that he received over Neil Todd. It was the relative value that each of them already held within a culture consistently unfair in the way it accorded such value. Ball was regarded as a pillar of the establishment, who had quite possibly had a regrettable lapse. Neil Todd, by contrast, was assumed to be, at best, a deeply troubled young man and, at worst, a shameful troublemaker. Ball had taken the trouble to invest in such young men, only for their damaged backgrounds to cause them to abuse his generosity and kindness.

This attitude continued to be taken right up to the point where it was impossible to maintain it any longer. It was instinctive snobbery which caused the then Prince Charles to write to Ball after his resignation, lamenting the 'monstrous injustice', and ensuring that he was provided with a 'grace and favour' property through the Duchy of Cornwall. This contrasted with the Prince's reference to Todd as 'this dreadful man'.[9] Prince Charles' protestations after Ball's conviction in 2012 that he had been duped by the bishop, was at most a half-truth and showed the weakness and pride involved. The future king should have admitted that everything about the culture that he lived in and represented had conditioned him to show an extreme bias towards Peter Ball and against Neil Todd. As with other instances cited in this book, Ball's friends realised that the accusations against him challenged the whole system upon which their own position and structural privilege was based. Sadly, there appears to have been hardly any difference in this episode between the examples of this attitude found inside and outside of the church.

Interestingly, Ball's saintliness was not something that was universally acknowledged. A number of those who worked or lived around him reported that they found him arrogant, high-handed and only interested in those from exclusive backgrounds. Significantly, those who made this critique filled positions such as gardeners at Gloucester Cathedral rather than people with influence or power. It is with hindsight that Ball's appearance on the chat show *Wogan*, during the late 1980s, makes uncomfortable viewing. As with Jimmy Savile, however, questions now need to be asked about how the cultural setting in which Peter Ball was located allowed his fairly obvious vanity to be interpreted so uncritically.

A Watershed Moment for the Church

The Suez Crisis of 1956 has already been mentioned a couple of times in this book. Another key event in post-war Britain was the Profumo scandal in 1963. This involved the resignation of the Minister of War, John Profumo, after he admitted that he had lied to Parliament about his relationship with a young woman called Christine Keeler. At the height of the Cold War, Keeler had also been having an affair with a Russian naval attaché. The significance of the Profumo scandal, which contributed to the fall of the Conservative government the following year, was in ending the age of deference. Up to that point, the elites in Britain had been able to maintain their standing as the natural leaders of society through their effortless sense of superiority (discussed in Chapter 3). The exposure of their behaviour through the Profumo scandal thus brought with it a much greater scrutiny of those who, up to that point, had managed to escape this.

The recent safeguarding scandals that have rocked the Church of England need to become a similar watershed moment. The abuse committed by Peter Ball, Colin Pritchard, Roy Cotton, George Rideout, Jonathan Fletcher, John Smyth and David Tudor was all built upon a deeply unhealthy structural privilege embedded within the Church of England. Each of these figures possessed, much like celebrities such as Jimmy

Savile and Rolf Harris, an appallingly arrogant sense of entitlement. But further attention is needed to the culture of the Church of England and the particular traditions that provided the fertile soil for such attitudes to grow and make the tragic impact that they did. Each of these men existed for years within a church culture accepting wildly inconsistent standards of behaviour. Such was their privilege within this cultural set-up that they were able to escape any proper accountability for the power that they possessed. It was this that led to the inevitable abuse of that power. Urgent attention is needed to the wider approach to behaviour in the Church of England that brought this about.

CHAPTER 7

What Has Sex Got to Do With It?

The Impact of Dishonesty About Sex in the Church

This has been, by some way, the most difficult chapter to write in this book. This is primarily because I am aware of its potential to be immediately misunderstood by many of its readers, leading to its arguments being dismissed before they are properly heard and engaged with. Many of those who have agreed with much of the book so far and applauded its agenda, will find this chapter the most uncomfortable one to wrestle with. This is because it inevitably touches upon the subject of sexuality within the church. Obviously, hugely different perspectives on this issue exist within the Church of England, and some may be furious that it is even mentioned within a book about safeguarding. But I believe that, if its case can be heard, there is an important point being made in this chapter that can be accepted by those on both sides of this debate. It may be that those on either side will want to use it to advance their cause, but the point that I want to make is that *the widespread and institutional dishonesty within the Church of England about sex is a major factor affecting its frequently disastrous approach to safeguarding.*

Historical Developments within the Church regarding Sexuality

Clerical celibacy became fully established within the Catholic Church from the tenth century onwards. Scholars disagree about the key factors involved in the maintenance of this aspect of the church and the relative

7 / WHAT HAS SEX GOT TO DO WITH IT?

importance within this of tradition, theology and factors such as its implications for the inheritance of property. The degree to which it resulted in genuine celibacy on the part of the clergy is, of course, difficult to establish. There is no reason to doubt that a number of clergy and those within religious orders took their calling to celibacy with great seriousness and were successful in maintaining it. But it appears that many others saw clerical celibacy as a symbol needing to be officially upheld, rather than something needing to be strictly practised. This produced the fairly common situation in the medieval world where marriage was the norm for the laity and various forms of concubinage for the clergy.[1]

It could be argued that this planted an institutional dishonesty about sex within the Western Church that it has never fully moved beyond. It is even more difficult to comment on homosexuality within the Medieval Church due to its totally forbidden status. It was undoubtedly a reality but would have been even more suppressed within a church refusing to acknowledge any expression of sexuality on the part of its clergy.

The Reformation dramatically changed the picture in heterosexual terms with a rejection of clerical celibacy becoming a core element within its identity. Key reformers such as Martin Luther, Huldrych Zwingli, John Calvin and Thomas Cranmer all demonstrated this in their own practice, making strong and eventually very public displays of contented married life. For a good few hundred years, as England became a firmly Protestant country, celibacy, while not completely disappearing from the Church of England, lost any sense of being an ideal status for its clergy. It is significant that when Cosmo Gordon Lang became Archbishop of Canterbury in 1928, he was the first bachelor to hold this post in 150 years. The standard view, reflected within the literature of Jane Austen, Charlotte Brontë and Anthony Trollope, was that of Church of England clergy either possessing or being 'in want of a wife'. In the days before women's ordination was seriously entertained, it was clergy wives who often represented women's service to the church most fully. Lechery and sexual exploitation on the part of clergy undoubtedly continued to exist. But the expression of clergy sexuality was understood, fairly unambiguously, within a robust and confident understanding of the goodness of the male and female partnership within Christian marriage.

As with so much in the Church of England, it was the rise of Anglo-Catholicism from the mid-nineteenth century, and its dominance in the first half of the twentieth century, that eventually changed this picture. While diversity existed among the Tractarians and the Oxford Movement with regard to clerical celibacy, the revival of Catholic doctrines and practices and the example of key figures such as John Henry Newman inevitably brought a return of the idealisation associated with this state. Whilst the majority of Anglo-Catholic clergy continued to be married, it became seen as respectable, and in some ways rather superior, to remain 'a celibate'.

Overtly separate from this tradition, developments within evangelicalism showed a level of similarity to this, particularly from the 1940s onwards, with prominent figures such as Eric Nash, John Stott, Dick Lucas and Jonathan Fletcher representing the growth of an idealisation associated with evangelical celibacy. Within evangelical circles, more weight started to be given to St Paul's personal position on marriage (1 Corinthians 7), with the application that those who were really committed to the ministry of the Word would forgo marriage out of devotion to this calling.

Throughout all of this time, of course, homosexuality remained "the love that dare not speak its name".[2] From being publicly regarded as unthinkable during the Victorian era, the early years of the twentieth century saw a certain loosening of attitudes towards it. For the most part, however, this change was exclusively contained within the upper classes, extremely discreet and heavily influenced by the role within that culture of boarding schools and all-male universities. It was from within the upper classes, however, that many of the clergy within the Church of England were drawn, and with its re-embracing of celibacy, it could be argued that the church enabled those who were gay to find a life that gave a public respectability to their decision not to get married and have children.

Over the following years many gay people found a (largely non-sexual) fulfilment in the close, mentoring relationships practised across the various theological traditions of the Church of England. For evangelicals, summer camps of the Iwerne Minster kind, provided an idyllic, all-male setting, away from the outside world. Of course, most of those who flourished in this environment were not gay, but settings like these allowed and indeed encouraged an intensity of same-sex relationship which relieved some of the inevitable loneliness of those who were. The illegality of homosexuality at the time and the consensus within the church about its official status as an 'abomination' meant that, paradoxically, little critique was given to these relationships. Disparity in the age and power of those within these close relationships received little scrutiny as well. Some of those who were gay did choose to get married, sometimes receiving a level of 'understanding' from their wives and at other times feeling the need to keep their orientation to themselves. In overall terms, however, this appeared to be the state in which many gay Christians were content for the situation to remain.

But outside of the church, of course, the world moved on. The 'sexual revolution' of the 1960s included the decriminalisation in 1967 of 'homosexual acts' for those over the age of 21 and within a few decades, clergy were living within a world which had dramatically changed in its views of sex and relationships. Personal choice gained sovereignty in terms of all matters concerning relationships and the physical expression of sexuality eventually became viewed as essential to emotional and spiritual wellbeing. The culture in Britain changed from a society still happy to openly mock gay people in the 1970s and 1980s to one where this was unacceptable. By the 1990s, 'coming out' had come to be understood as an act of courage and integrity and, increasingly, a responsibility on the part of those who were gay.

Changes in Regard to Sexuality in the Church of England

Against the background of other significant changes in the Church of England, most obviously the decision to ordain women as priests in 1992, many began to believe that it was now right for the church to accept the full expression of homosexuality and the removal of any restrictions upon gay clergy. Changing Attitude and Inclusive Church were two groups that formed with the intention of bringing about full gay emancipation within the church. Rapid support for this programme then developed, initially within the more liberal and liberal-catholic sections of the Church of England. A particular spokesman for this perspective was Jeffrey John in his 1993 book *Permanent, Faithful, Stable: Christian Same-Sex Partnerships*.[3] Opposition from those opposed to this, most obviously conservative evangelicals, was central to the eventual non-appointment of Jeffrey John after he was announced as Bishop of Reading in 2003. Such controversies served to strengthen the competing convictions about sexuality and the resolve to campaign on either side of this argument.

A more recent development has been greater support for official change coming from the evangelical sections of the Church of England. While it is probably true to say that the majority of evangelical clergy in the Church of England remain conservative on homosexuality, large numbers are now changing in regard to this.[4] This is particularly the case among the ordinands and younger clergy that the Church of England is now committed to recruiting. Some influential churches believe that it is damaging to their mission to take a strong position either way on this issue. Within many evangelical and charismatic congregations, many younger members appear to have decisively shifted on the issue of sexuality, now regarding any denial of full equality to those who are gay as incompatible with Christianity.

Strong opposition to this, however, has continued. A significantly new aspect, in recent years, has been the openness of a number of conservative evangelical clergy about being 'same-sex attracted'. This included Vaughan Roberts, the prominent, conservative evangelical Rector of St Ebbe's in Oxford. This group remains convinced that sexual expression should be restricted to lifelong marriage between a man and a woman, with those who are 'same-sex attracted' called to a life of celibacy.[5] These clergy also resist using the word 'gay' or 'homosexual' about themselves on the basis that their identity is not defined by this aspect of their life experience. Within a wider culture increasingly convinced that sexuality is core to people's identity, this approach met with a large amount of derision from some within the church committed to the greater emancipation of those who are gay.

While all of these various debates and controversies have taken place, the situation 'on the ground' has also changed very significantly. Many churches within the Church of England contain members who are openly gay, and in plenty of these churches this is regarded as completely uncontroversial. Numerous clergy also now live with their same-sex partners with varying degrees of discretion and openness. Many diocesan posts are filled by those in this situation, possibly because of the greater privacy facilitated by such roles. However, it is also true to say that there are now an increasing number of parish clergy in openly gay relationships with the full support of their congregations. If a poll was taken amongst regular churchgoers about the Church of England giving full equality to those who are gay, the result would probably be a landslide vote in favour.

Against this background and without any formal change to its doctrine of marriage, a measure of change has occurred within the Church of England, partly in response to developments brought about by Parliamentary legislation. When Civil Partnerships were introduced by Tony Blair's Labour government in 2004, the House of Bishops declared that it did "…not regard entering into a civil partnership as intrinsically incompatible with holy orders, provided the person concerned is willing to give assurances to his or her bishop that the relationship is consistent with the standards for the clergy."[6] When same-sex marriage was introduced by David Cameron's Conservative government in 2014, the Church of England produced a less equivocal response which sought to combine a respect and love for people who were gay with the clear assertion of its continuing belief that marriage exclusively represented the union of a man and a woman.

A more significant change within the Church of England occurred in February 2023 when its General Synod voted in favour of introducing blessings for people in same-sex relationships. This decision, supported by both archbishops, followed a lengthy process of discussion about sexuality throughout the Church of England called 'Living in Love and Faith'. The Synod also voted to 'lament and repent' of the failure of the Church to welcome LGBTQIA+ people and for the harm that these people have experienced – and continue to experience – in churches. This development was accompanied by the assertion that the doctrine of marriage within the Church of England had not changed.

The result of this was unhappiness on both sides of the debate. Those who were conservative on sexuality saw the decision as a significant step towards the erosion of the clear biblical principle that sex exclusively belonged within marriage between a man and a woman. Many in favour of full gay emancipation were equally critical of the decision, calling the measure 'a tiny step forward' at best and making it clear that nothing other than the church's progress towards a full endorsement of 'equal marriage' was acceptable. The overall leaders of the Church of England presented it as an honourable and indeed biblical compromise similar to the response made to the issue of Gentiles and the Jewish Law in Acts 15.[7] Both wings of the sexuality debate, on the other hand, appeared to agree that the decision by the General Synod was a highly unsatisfactory 'fudge' that deliberately avoided making a clear decision or giving a clear answer to the pressing issue of the church's response to gay relationships.[8]

How Homosexuality is Currently Managed in the Church of England

The overwhelming support for equal/same-sex marriage within Britain, and increasingly within the church, prompts the question of why it has not yet been endorsed by the Church of England. It is true that change can be very slow within the church. It was only in 2000, after years of discussion and debate, that the Church of England changed its official stance on offering remarriage, under certain conditions, to those with a former spouse still living. The decisions to ordain women as deacons in 1987, as priests in 1992 and finally as bishops in 2014, occurred after a similarly long process. Many believe that it is only a matter of time before similar change takes place in the church's full acceptance of homosexuality.

There are, however, a number of factors militating against this. Compared to the other significant changes made by the Church of England in recent years, making a biblical case for the church's acceptance of homosexuality has proved difficult. Attempts have been made to do this and have persuaded many that the biblical injunctions against same-sex relationships are not targeting anything resembling the faithful, same-sex marriage being advocated today.[9] On the other hand, advocates of gay marriage have struggled to make a positive biblical case for this, in the face of the Bible's consistent message that marriage represents a covenant relationship between a man and a woman.

A more significant factor appears to be concern for the unity of the church, both in terms of the Church of England and the Anglican Communion. For a number of years, movements such as GAFCON and the Anglican Mission in England (AMiE) have already sought to provide alternative structures for those unhappy with developments in the Church of England. With the acceptance of same-sex blessings by its General Synod in 2023, the momentum behind these structures may already be unstoppable. A large part of the aim behind the accompanying assertions that the church's doctrine of marriage had not changed was to keep enough of those who were conservative on sexuality within the church. A key factor here appeared to be recognition of how much of the existing finances and credibility of the Church of England depends on its large and lively evangelical congregations.

Another crucial factor in this ongoing situation of compromise/fudge, however, needs to be acknowledged. It is one that can appear similar to concern for the unity of the church, but is actually very different. *This is the large degree of investment that exists in the current status quo of the Church of England maintaining one position on homosexuality in official terms and another in practice.* The reason that this goes unrecognised is partly because greatest attention in the sexuality debate is given to those campaigning for and against radical change. But it is also because the agenda of preserving as much of the existing status quo on sexuality as possible is a largely surreptitious one, heavily conditioned by the preference of many gay clergy about how their personal situations should be handled.

Part of this can be traced back to the historical conditions described at the beginning of this chapter. The more catholic parts of the Church of England, in particular, have a long tradition of avoiding anything official in their engagement with sexuality. The wider context is the deep appeal for many clergy in the Church of England of being largely left to their own devices rather than being closely supervised or accountable. The result of this is that, instead of stridently demanding their rights, many gay clergy prefer the expression of their sexuality to remain completely private, rather than open to debate or discussion. Many would claim that this reticence is the legacy of a homophobic society and the ongoing impact of this. Others would suggest that it reflects an ongoing personal ambivalence on the part of these clergy about their sexuality and the resulting development of what psychologists would call an 'approach-avoidance conflict'.[10] These factors are not, of course, mutually exclusive. But whatever the cause, the result of this combination of freedom and secrecy is a complete lack of accountability among large swathes of clergy about how their sexuality is expressed.

A further layer of investment in this status quo is then provided by the bishops of the Church of England. Some of these bishops share similar characteristics to those just outlined, producing a collective sympathy for those who wish the expression of their sexuality to remain a purely private matter. A greater factor, as noted in Chapter 3, is the tendency of the church's bishops to approach every problem or difficulty with a pragmatism aimed at 'keeping the show on the road', rather than attempting to achieve its proper resolution. Resolving anything difficult brings a measure of conflict which those with a passive-aggressive personality will avoid for as long as possible and then seek to manage secretly, rather than openly. Such a mindset is deeply uncomfortable, and indeed fearful, about issues of truth and being honest about problems. It prefers to let any situation 'rumble on', only getting involved in responding to the further problems that this creates when it becomes absolutely necessary. The prevailing ethos within the Church of England is thus one that is very comfortable with ambiguity, and with a significant distance existing between official policy and actual practice. Keeping this gap fairly wide allows bishops to avoid the implementation of policy when, for whatever reason, things become uncomfortable and appears to justify their belief that the wisest thing to do in any tricky situation is nothing.

Back in Chapter 3, mention was made of the controversy over the new Church of England Prayer Book in 1927/28 and the extraordinary nature of its 'only in England' outcome. In his description of this event, Stephen Neill wrote in 1965: "Any clergyman in England who uses any part of the 1928 Prayer Book is breaking the law. Yet such illegalities are committed every day and have become almost a normal part of the practice of the Church. It is an impossible, intolerable and humiliating situation. But it has lasted for thirty-six years, and seems likely to last for many years yet."[11]

As it turned out, the limbo over the 1928 Prayer Book lasted around fifty years, until the experimental alternative services introduced from the mid-1970s. The reason the situation lasted for so long was a lack of investment in its resolution and a collective happiness on the part of the Church of England to 'rumble on' with a pragmatic working compromise, however unsatisfactory it was in terms of clarity and truth. This was all aided by a hefty dose of elitist English arrogance, with its tendency to believe that 'rules are made for the obedience of fools and the guidance of wise men'.[12]

Through the combination of factors discussed in this chapter, a similar situation currently exists in the Church of England with regard to the sexual behaviour of its clergy. Despite the recent measure regarding same-sex blessings, the official position of the Church of England on marriage remains unchanged with its clergy therefore expected to be married to a husband or wife of the opposite sex or remain celibate. The *unofficial policy* is that clergy are given the discretion, particularly if they are gay, to act in accordance with their own conscience. Various ways are found of squaring these two things, all of which involve the need for 'a supple conscience' when it comes to the truth. Clergy applying for posts who are known to be gay are often warned in advance to say as little as possible about their domestic situations and are only asked in the most abstract terms about whether they are prepared to live in accordance with "the standards expected of clergy within the Church of England".

With these standards left deliberately unstated and ambiguous, the message is given that the expression of their sexuality by clergy is a purely private matter. When bishops are approached by others to question the living situations of gay clergy and the inconsistency of this with the position of the Church of England, they have a standard response that enables the question to be completely avoided. The first part of their response is usually to affirm their support for the position of the Church of England regarding sexuality. The second is to refuse to discuss any specific people in regard to this.

The situation that this produces is as frustrating for those favouring full gay emancipation within the church as those who are conservative about homosexuality. In the autumn of 1994, ten Church of England bishops were 'outed' as being closet homosexuals outside Church House in Westminster by the gay pressure group OutRage. The group specifically claimed that they did this to expose the dishonesty involved in the Church of England's approach to homosexuality and the damage caused by this. A good deal of hurt and dismay was felt about this action within the church, particularly on behalf of Mervyn Stockwood, the former Bishop of Southwark, who died just a few weeks later. In many ways, however, the reaction about the 'improper' nature of what they had done reinforced the very point that OutRage was seeking to make.

Colin Coward of Changing Attitude has been just as critical as conservative evangelicals of the difference between the official policy of the church and its practice on homosexuality, arguing that it is deeply hypocritical. Recent criticism of the Church of England's approach came from the late Bishop of Buckingham, Alan Wilson, who took his fellow bishops to task over their lack of honesty and transparency. Wilson was referring in several cases to bishops' lack of openness about their own sexuality and relationships. His main target, however, was their lack of honesty in ordaining and appointing actively gay clergy, while publicly avoiding any clarity over this reality.[13]

As I hope is now clear, a major theme of this book is that however 'successful' such dishonesty might appear as a means of managing the church, it is deeply damaging to its ministry and mission. The stress for bishops involved in maintaining the church's position on sexuality and its inconsistencies has a number of effects upon them. The duplicity works to erode their general confidence about any matters of truth and, in particular, their ability to integrate theology with practice. It is thus a direct contributor to their blandness and the general inability of these bishops to present relevant and credible Christianity to the clergy that they are meant to be leading, to the congregations within their churches and to the general public.

In the worst cases, this situation leads to an episcopal defensiveness that is unable to cope with questions to which they don't have a convincing answer, and petulance when these questions continue to be pressed. This leads to many bishops surrounding themselves with people who will defer to them and/or act as their enforcers. It results in episcopal authority moving to the centre of their theology contributing to further insecurity as they realise that their position relies on factors extrinsic to anything of value that they actually do. All of this creates desperate weaknesses for ministry and mission in the Church of England. But the most disastrous and least acknowledged effect of the Church of England's approach to sexuality, is how this dynamic influences its handling of safeguarding.

Implications of the Church's Approach to Sexuality for its Safeguarding

As indicated at the start of this chapter, the different opinions within the church in regard to homosexuality make any discussion of how it relates to safeguarding fraught with danger. But, to repeat the point already made, concern at the serious implications for safeguarding of the church's approach to sexuality can and should include those on both sides of this debate. In fact, up to this point, the greatest honesty and outspokenness about the effect of the church's policy on sexuality upon its safeguarding has come from those who champion full gay emancipation, such as Bishop Alan Wilson.

Discussion of this needs to begin with honesty about the nature of what appears to be the majority of the sexual abuse that takes place in the Church of England. In wider society, sexual abuse is committed by both men and women, who target victims of either the same or the opposite gender. An abuser may not discriminate when it comes to gender, and instead choose their victims based on their level of vulnerability and opportunity. Within the Church of England, however, we see a different picture. Full statistical evidence, for the most part, is not available. But based on the cases that have come to light publicly, the vast majority of sexual abuse in the Church of England appears to have been committed by older men against younger men or boys. This is a point that needs to be expressed with great care if it is not to be misunderstood.

The point being made is emphatically not that people who are gay are more likely to commit abuse than those who are heterosexual. Evidence from wider society shows that this is definitely not the case. Nor is it even the case within other churches that sexual abuse is predominantly committed by older men against younger men or boys. Within the Protestant churches in North America, for instance, there have been numerous abuse scandals in recent times with virtually all of these cases involving offences committed by men against women. The point being made here is a far more specific one regarding the Church of England: *that a definite link appears to exist between the confusion that the Church of England has in its approach to homosexuality and the problems that it has in reference to safeguarding.*

This has had a number of effects. Some of them are specific to the gay subcultures that exist within the Church of England, while others impact upon the effectiveness of safeguarding across the whole of the church.

The Lack of Accountability for Non-Heterosexual Clergy in the Church of England

This has several causes, starting with the most obvious one that, officially, practising gay clergy do not exist within the Church of England. In reality, of course, they do exist, with the majority of bishops deeply sympathetic to and supportive of them. The combination of these two factors, however, has then resulted in a situation where almost any form of accountability for the sexual expression of clergy outside of an obviously heterosexual setting, has become impossible.

This stands in some contrast to heterosexual clergy. The process involved in clergy selection within the Church of England is a lengthy and careful one which includes a great many questions being put to potential ordinands. These rightly include questions of a very personal nature because of the impact that such matters may have upon the exercise of pastoral ministry. Those who are married are commonly asked about the condition of their marriages and whether their conduct within them is consistent with the standards required of clergy.

These questions can be very specific. I remember the DDO (Diocesan Director of Ordinands) for my diocese asking me about this when I was going through the clergy selection process in 1999. First he spoke generally about the standards of personal morality that the Church of England required of its clergy and the importance of my life conforming to these standards. He then sharpened the specific application of this by saying: "In short, I'm asking whether you are faithful to your wife?" All but the most liberal of viewpoints would probably regard this as a perfectly valid question to ask of someone who is married wanting to enter ordained ministry.

Making such a question specific in its application is more complex (but still possible) when it is put to someone who is single. Given the current approach of the Church of England to homosexuality, however, it is practically impossible to put to someone who is gay. An equivalent of the general introduction that the DDO used with me is still possible and is probably commonly used with all potential ordinands. But the supplementary practical question that followed was the really important one. Embarrassment, fear of appearing homophobic and uncertainty about the actual position of the Church of England, all combine to mean that those whom DDOs know or believe to be gay are able to avoid anything like the same scrutiny.

It bears repeating that criticism of this situation can and has been made by those on both sides of the sexuality debate. Many on the revisionist side of the argument would agree that this lack of accountability is a problem and, indeed, would use it as part of their argument for why fully gay emancipation within the Church of England is urgently needed.

The Impact of Complexities in the Positions on Sexuality within the Church

This needs further honesty. One of the biggest myths in public perception of the Church of England is that those who are conservative or liberal on

SAFEGUARDING THE INSTITUTION

sexuality will have a corresponding view on the ordination of women. The common assumption, uncritically reflected in both *The Vicar of Dibley* and *Rev*, is that those who support or oppose women's ministry will maintain a similar support or opposition to gay emancipation and vice versa. In many cases this is true, and it is understandable why groups such as Inclusive Church, on the liberal/progressive side of these debates, and Reform and Church Society on the conservative/traditionalist side, have wanted to present these issues as essentially belonging together.

However, this is certainly *not* the case for those many evangelical Anglicans who combine a conservative position on sexuality with a strong support for the full ministry of women within the church.[14] For many years, this represented my own position, based upon the application to both issues of the male/female partnership outlined in the early chapters of Genesis as displaying the image of God and leading to its unique fruitfulness. Most obvious in terms of procreation, the fruitfulness of this union can be seen to apply beyond this to every aspect of life including the ministry and mission of the church.

It is also true that there are other sections of the church which combine the strongest opposition to women's ministry with a significant gay subculture. Such groupings tend to escape scrutiny for at least two reasons. The first, already mentioned, is the common perception that being anti-women within the church always means being anti-gay as well and vice versa. The second and more significant factor is that such groups are not usually interested in any *official* change when it comes to gay rights and indeed would present their position as opposed to this. In practice, however, the aversion of these groupings to women's ministry is intrinsically linked to a pervasive all-male culture which includes a vast amount of homosexuality, both suppressed and expressed, within it. They are invested in the church's current status quo in regard to sexuality precisely because of the lack of accountability that this brings with it.

Forward in Faith is a conservative Catholic group within the Church of England committed to maintaining the faith "as traditionally received" and opposing innovation. Unfortunately part of the tradition that such groups appear committed to preserving is a lack of earthly accountability for its members in the expression of their sexuality. This is reinforced by a tendency to see 'modern' things such as safeguarding as another unwelcome, worldly intrusion from the world of 'secular management' into a sacred community accountable to God rather than people.

It should now be clear why abuse within the Church of England is so regularly committed by those coming from its 'conservative' Anglo-Catholic tradition. In general terms, such abuse is not uncovered within groupings committed to full and open gay emancipation within the church, such as members of Inclusive Church. Instead it is overwhelmingly from those sections of the church committed to the preservation within it of an unaccountable, all-male enclave. This provides the link to the problematic role of single-sex cultures discussed in Chapter 2 and also the arrogance discussed later in this chapter. Much of the bitterness towards the inclusion of women in any capacity within the church is because of the threat that their presence alone brings to such cultures and their desire to remain unaccountable.

This sheds further light upon the abuse committed by evangelical clergy and lay leaders within the Church of England, which has also tended to be committed by older men towards younger men. This has also usually come from the conservative wing of the movement that is completely opposed to women's ordination. Within conservative evangelicalism, active homosexuality is more taboo than anything else. However, the respect given to singleness within conservative evangelicalism has also provided an opportunity for some who are secretly gay to find refuge within it. This may well include refuge from their own discomfort about their sexuality, suggesting that at least some of their anger about gay emancipation within the church is a projection of their personal insecurity in this regard. This may apply to other expressions of anger as well.

It is repressed homosexuality that provides the best explanation for the terrible sadomasochistic abuse committed by John Smyth upon dozens of young men over four decades from the 1970s onwards.[15] It also explains the activities of Jonathan Fletcher during his thirty-year ministry at Emmanuel Wimbledon which, whatever its other causes, bore many of the hallmarks of an 'approach/avoidance conflict' when it came to sexuality. In both cases, it further explains the inability of the conservative evangelical tradition to handle what had occurred, particularly in the case of Smyth, and the facilitation by the conservative Titus Trust of his move from Britain to South Africa.

It needs to be repeated that none of this represents an argument that gay people are more likely to commit abuse or that any sort of organic connection exists between homosexuality and the abuse of others. It is instead making the very specific argument that the way in which the Church of England has approached homosexuality has increased the likelihood of same-sex abuse being committed within it. Those who argue for complete gay emancipation within the church would point to this as one of the greatest reasons for its necessity. Conservatives need to acknowledge that 'the gay lobby' could be right about this and it certainly points to the urgent need for the Church of England to come down on 'one side of the fence' on this issue.

The reason why such resolution has not occurred is not just down to the Church of England's desire for unity. Nor is it due to its anxious instinct for survival, resulting in an avoidance of clarity in response to every problem that it faces. A situation currently exists with regard to sexuality within the Church of England where, to put it crudely, the conservatives (despite the introduction of same-sex blessings) still hold 'the theory', while the revisionists hold 'the practice'. This situation has existed for some time with, if truth be told, a great deal of acceptance of this status quo and the major concern on both sides being that of any significant 'slippage' from the ground they currently hold.

In many ways the two sides resemble Russia and Austria-Hungary facing off against each other in the Balkans prior to the First World War. Both crumbling and insecure, these former superpowers could just about cope with the delicate status quo but were terrified at the prospect of any development that would strengthen their opponent and further their diminishment. And just as neither power was concerned about the Slav peoples caught in the middle of their insecure rivalries, so the opposing wings within the Church of England seem just as indifferent to those suffering abuse as a direct result of the church's present unsatisfactory status quo in regard to sexuality.

7 / WHAT HAS SEX GOT TO DO WITH IT?

THE WIDER IMPACT OF THE CHURCH'S APPROACH TO SEXUALITY ON SAFEGUARDING

The most important point here concerns how the dishonesty of the Church of England in relation to sexuality facilitates abuse. The willingness of the church to perpetuate a situation where it says one thing on sexuality in official terms and permits the precise opposite in practice has fostered a number of general attitudes among its clergy that could not be more corrosive when it comes to effective safeguarding.

The most serious of these attitudes is that which believes that truth and integrity don't matter when it comes to sex. We have seen already in Chapter 5 that the failure of the Church of England to deal with fear means that truth is commonly seen as something dangerous rather than liberating. Whatever its cause (and undoubtedly the prevalence of homophobia has played a role in this), the Church of England has actively encouraged a culture of secrecy and dishonesty when it comes to sex. Clergy, in particular, have been given the message that a legitimate space exists between what they are expected to subscribe to in theory and what, in practice, is left to their own discretion. This leads to a sense that it is fundamentally out of order to seek any sense of truthfulness or accountability from clergy or others for any matters of sexual conduct. As a result, clergy and other church leaders feel justified in making up their own rules about sexual conduct, because it appears that responsibility has been delegated to them in this area.

A connected factor here is the fostering of arrogance that springs from this. This plays a key role in facilitating abuse, because clergy are emboldened to think that their calling, wisdom and service to God entitles them to be the judge of what is appropriate conduct on their part. Arrogance is often a potent factor in abuse. One of the most chilling aspects of the trials of celebrities such as Rolf Harris and Max Clifford in the wake of Operation Yewtree was seeing the brazen sense of superiority that they displayed as they arrived at court. Peter Ball, when asked if he had a message for his victims as he arrived at his trial, did say that he was "very sorry". However, through most of the interviews that the police conducted with him, Ball displayed an arrogance summed up by his repeated use of the phrase, "You wouldn't understand".[16] He also used spiritual explanations for his actions such as being "naked before God" that he knew would make no sense to those questioning him. At the root of all of Ball's justifications for his conduct was the belief that he possessed a spiritual discernment not revealed to others about such matters.

Whether Ball's conscience remained untroubled when he committed his abuse is, of course, difficult to know, particularly now that he has died. Mention has already been made of clergy guilty of abuse admitting that they knew what they were doing was wrong, but also believing that, because of everything that they were doing for him, God would 'understand'. Such attitudes are much easier to form if a clergyman has received the implicit message that, because of his office, he is only accountable to God for his actions. Within Anglo-Catholic circles, this is reinforced by two particular features of their spiritual formation. One of these is the strong emphasis upon the priest as the one who grants absolution to sinners through the process of confession, absolution and penance. In theory, such priests should confess their own sins to another priest. In practice, it is all too easy for priests, used to dispensing forgiveness, to forgive themselves for abuse they have committed, accompanied by an act of self-nominated penance to 'make up for this'. The other contributing factor is the heavy emphasis in Anglo-Catholicism upon the ontological change brought to a person through ordination. This, of course, should bring an increased sense of fearful responsibility and loving service to those in their charge. In reality, however, it easily fosters the arrogance of belonging to a superior caste which feels justified in then making its own rules of self-accountability in regard to conduct.

Such attitudes are by no means restricted to Anglo-Catholics. Evangelicals can easily develop approaches that are very similar. While there is much less emphasis within evangelicalism upon the priest/vicar being the dispenser of forgiveness, the opposite emphasis can cause similar problems. This is because when confession does not have to involve anyone other than God, the individual sinner can easily forgive themselves. Another key factor within conservative evangelicalism is its strong emphasis upon the movement representing a 'righteous remnant' within a church that has badly lost its way. With praise heaped upon those leaders who represent this most strongly, it is almost impossible for such people not to become arrogant, and then to see their personal failures as 'understandable' given the overall courage that they are showing for God.

Both of these tendencies within Anglo-Catholicism and evangelicalism tend to be fostered within their particular networks, rather than through the official authority encountered within the church. However, it is within the general context of a church unwilling to be honest and open about sexuality that these churchmanship factors have their greatest impact. The saying that 'nature abhors a vacuum' is relevant here. In the absence of honesty and openness about the church's position in regard to sexuality, and any desire on the part of the bishops of the Church of England to resolve its inconsistency, this space is filled by clergy becoming self-governing on the issue. If the impact of this was limited to facilitating the personal decision on the part of clergy to have a gay partner, most members of the Church of England would probably not object to such an approach.

But as this chapter has sought to show, its impact goes way beyond this. In almost every case of abuse committed by clergy and other leaders in the church, their activities have been set within a context where accountability about their sexual conduct was virtually non-existent. Disturbingly, where awareness of their actions has been present, they appear to have received a level of 'understanding' from those in authority that is very similar to that received by a member of clergy with a gay partner. Whilst there is clearly a massive difference between these two situations, such a distinction appears to be far from clear to the leaders of a church that is institutionally unclear and muddled over sex.

It is very tempting for those sympathetic to the Church of England to put this collusion with abuse down to 'incompetence' rather than 'conspiracy'. But once again it is 'wilful incompetence' that provides the most convincing explanation for this. A church that is naturally fearful, muddled and duplicitous in its approach to sexuality has discovered that this approach works relatively well for maintaining the status quo within the church and avoiding difficult questions and decisions. It therefore possesses no motivation to resolve these issues, despite their devastating impact upon the ministry and mission of the church.

A critique that could be mounted against the contents of this chapter is its almost exclusive focus upon the sexual conduct of clergy. While many of the greatest abuse scandals within the Church of England in recent years have involved members of clergy, there are plenty of other examples involving lay people. The critical factor here, however, is the way in which the lack of accountability for the sexual conduct of its clergy has so heavily set the tone for large sections of the Church of England. Lay ministers, choirmasters, youth workers and others who have committed abuse have done so within an organisation where clergy have overwhelmingly created the cultural norms that have both facilitated this abuse and refused to respond to both its threat and its occurrence with any seriousness.

It is now time for the Church of England to recognise the catastrophic impact of its policy in regard to sexuality upon its safeguarding. Sexuality is, very obviously, a hugely controversial issue within the church and one where the avoidance of proper confrontation appears understandable. Until, that is, the implications for its safeguarding are recognised. Consensus may never be possible on homosexuality within the church and the aim of this chapter has not been to persuade people either way on this issue. Some will use its contents to make the case for full gay emancipation in the church and others for the precise opposite. But it is time for everyone, of whatever perspective on sexuality, to wake up to the fact that the current situation cannot be allowed to continue. Until dramatic change occurs, members of churches will continue to be abused and pay the price for the wilful confusion created by the Church of England's duplicitous policy on sexuality, which its leaders seem committed to preserving.

CHAPTER 8

Prophets and Whistleblowers

The Courage Needed to Rock the Boat in Churches

It is nearly time to finish the critique and present a positive vision of the changes which, if made, will address the problems within the culture of the Church of England that create and perpetuate its problems with regard to safeguarding. None of this will be possible, however, without courage. Back in Chapter 5, we looked at fear and its role in both preventing safeguarding issues from being dealt with and in creating these issues in the first place. We now need to look at the crucial role of courage in addressing safeguarding, and we need to be equally honest about the obstacles that stand in its way and the sacrifice that it entails. But before that, a story…

Amos and Miriam

Amos was slightly late home that evening. It was the season when the ripe figs were ready to be picked meaning that his work as a shepherd was supplemented by extra labour amongst the sycamore trees of Tekoa. Once he was back inside his little hut, Amos could tell from the atmosphere that something was wrong. Normally smiley and cheerful, his wife Miriam was a good deal quieter than usual. The plates were put down on the table with more of a clatter than was necessary and little eye contact was made as the couple ate their meal. Amos tried to think what he had done wrong. All the while their two-year-old son Enoch continued to play on the floor with the toy sheep that his daddy had made for him. Eventually Miriam snapped and revealed the cause of the tension. "In case you're wondering",

SAFEGUARDING THE INSTITUTION

she declared, "I discovered today what is in those oracles that you've been so busy writing. Yes, I've read them, Amos!" "Oh," replied Amos, drawing breath as he spoke. "Well, Yahweh has been revealing them to me, Miriam, and so I have to write them down". "Yes, but it's what you're going to do with them that worries me," his wife replied. "What do you mean?" Amos responded nervously. "You know precisely what I mean!" Miriam spat back. "Yahweh doesn't reveal messages like that without expecting his prophets to deliver them. Sheep and fig trees will soon be a thing of the past for you! He'll be wanting you proclaiming those messages! And then what's going to happen?"

There was a pause as Amos summoned the courage to speak. "Well now you've mentioned it, Miriam," Amos said slowly, "I'm going up north to Bethel tomorrow." "Bethel," his wife repeated, trying to retain her composure. "The King of Israel's shrine? Where Amaziah is priest? Why would you want to go there?" "Because, Miriam, that's the place where Yahweh has told me to speak his word." There was a pause, and for a moment Amos thought he was going to get away with it. But instead Miriam exploded with tears: "So you're going to Bethel, and you're going to speak all that stuff you've been writing about Israel's worship not being worth one jot to God whilst Israel is so full of injustice? All that stuff about God hating their noisy songs, all that stuff about the evil of their bribery and exploiting of the poor, all that stuff about Yahweh's judgement soon coming upon Israel, all that stuff about him wanting instead for justice to flow like a river and righteousness like an ever-flowing stream?" "Oh you read that bit," Amos said trying to sound positive, "I was rather pleased with that." "I've read the lot!" thundered Miriam. "Do you think that for one minute Amaziah and King Jeroboam are going to put up with any of those things being said?" "I don't know," Amos replied, "but God has given me these words and he expects me to speak them. It is all true, Miriam. You know it is." "I know full well it's true," replied Miriam, biting back the tears as she picked up little Enoch and cradled him in her arms.

"But think, Amos, think! What good is it going to do, proclaiming that message? It may be true but they won't listen if you just stride into Bethel and say it like this. You'll simply put their backs up. They'll hate it.

And they'll hate you! And what will happen then? Think of little Enoch… and me. Think of all the other things Yahweh wants to do through you. It's surely important to play the long game on all this justice stuff? Why don't we read those oracles through this evening and tone them down a bit? Keep the challenge but put it more positively. Set a wonderful vision of future restoration and leave out all of that stuff about the terrible state of Israel at the moment. Perhaps you could play up a bit more those oracles you include early on about the transgressions of all the surrounding nations like Moab, Edom and Ammon? They're the really evil ones, after all." "I'll think about it" was Amos' only response as they turned in for the night.

In the morning Miriam awoke to find herself alone. Enoch was still sleeping soundly, but Amos had gone. A brief message of his love was written on some of the parchment he had used to write the oracles that Miriam had read the day before. As she looked out of the doorway and saw the sun starting to come up over the hills of Tekoa, Miriam imagined Amos appearing at the king's shrine at Bethel and proclaiming his message. She thought back to the times when he was just a shepherd and tender of fig trees and what life was like before Yahweh had taken him from tending flocks and told him to go and prophesy to Israel. Both those sheep and Amos' family needed tending and surely that too was a divine calling? What would happen to all of them if his message received the response she was sure that it would? As she looked down at little Enoch, she wondered whether her husband was showing the most amazing courage and faith in Yahweh… or the most stupid and irresponsible folly.

The Nature of Courage and its Place within the Prophetic Commission

The command to be courageous occurs throughout the Bible (Deuteronomy 31.6-9; Joshua 1.9; Psalm 31.24). So does the command not to be afraid (Psalm 27.1; Mark 5.36; Luke 1.30; John 14.27). Courage, however, is not the absence of fear. It is the act of coping with that fear and refusing to allow it to control one's actions. Another definition of courage is the ability to do something that is frightening. It is significant that these biblical commands occur almost exclusively within God's calling or commissioning of people to do his work.

Part of this was through the prophets. Numerous prophets appear throughout the Old Testament. But significantly, the prophetic movement appears to have particularly grown around the same time as the institution of Israel's monarchy. 1 Samuel makes it clear that the manner in which Israel's monarchy was established was an act of rebellion against God. Part of God's response to this new situation was to raise up prophets to speak his word to a people increasingly out of touch with him. Prophecy itself then became corrupted, with many prophets only too happy to deliver the messages that those in power wanted to hear (e.g. 1 Kings 22; Jeremiah 28). The message of these false prophets was normally to assure them of God's blessing. The genuine prophets, however, were much less reassuring, usually delivering highly uncomfortable messages that neither the people nor their kings wanted to hear. They were essentially 'whistleblowers' about Israel's sin.

This calling meant that the prophets were rather solitary figures as well. While they did receive some support and on occasion needed to be reminded that they were not alone (e.g. 1 Kings 19), they were given a very lonely calling. Elijah and Jeremiah are perhaps the most obvious examples of this. Much debate has taken place over the precise identity of the servant referred to in Isaiah 40-55, but these passages nonetheless make clear that the proclamation of God's word and the suffering of his servant belong together.[1] The New Testament writers, of course, see this prophetic calling supremely fulfilled in Jesus Christ as both 'the word made flesh' (John 1.14) and the one called to suffer and die as God's answer to a sinful world.

But after the coming of the Holy Spirit, prophecy very much continues within the church. Paul lists prophecy within all four of his lists of the gifts that the Holy Spirit gives to the church (Romans 12.6; 1 Corinthians 12.10, 28; Ephesians 4.11). The book of Revelation is an example of such prophecy. A Christian prophet called Agabus is also mentioned twice in the book of Acts. In the first instance, Agabus prophesies about an upcoming great famine which led the Christians at Antioch to recognise the need to support their fellow believers in Jerusalem (Acts 11.27-28). In the second, Agabus reappears at Caesarea to speak of the suffering awaiting Paul if he proceeds to Jerusalem (Acts 21.10-11). The fact that both examples of Agabus' ministry involved speaking about suffering suggests a continuing and central part of the ministry of prophecy is that of bringing difficult messages to the church. It is even possible that Luke includes Agabus' messages within his account because they weren't ones that were popular within the church or even fully accepted at the time they were delivered.

The courage to bring such difficult messages to the church is still needed. This, of course, can be done by any of its members. But it is the clergy who particularly possess this responsibility as part of their commission to preach the word. Paul's instruction to Timothy shows that this commission involves being prepared "in season and out of season", presumably referring to being ready to proclaim this word whether the ground is receptive to it or not. It includes correction and rebuke, alongside encouragement and instruction. Crucially, it is also set in the context of many others saying 'what their itching ears want to hear' and the hardship that will always result from this calling (2 Timothy 4.1-5).

Just like the people of Israel and the early church, the Church of England needs prophets and preachers willing to speak out about the things that are wrong with its culture. However, this is no easy calling and honesty is needed about the courage that such a calling requires.

The Courage Needed to Recognise the Truth

This is the vital first step. But it is also extremely difficult for at least two reasons. The first, already mentioned, is how hard it is for people to critique the culture that they live within. The illustration commonly used for this, and one already quoted in this book, is that of a fish unaware that it is wet because living in water is all it has ever known.

New and younger clergy often feel that they are too junior or inexperienced to make judgements upon the culture of the church that they are entering. This is understandable. But older and longer-term clergy have got so used to that culture that many aspects of it have become completely normalised for them. Part of the problem is that the ritual, procedures and 'insider language' of the church frequently act as a cover for aspects of its culture that are extremely odd and questionable. Once someone has become assimilated into such a culture, it takes a great deal of insight, as well as courage, to recognise the things about it that are wrong.

Sometimes it is only reaction that awakens truth in this regard. Martin Luther is renowned for initiating the Reformation through his famous protest against indulgences from October 1517.[2] Indulgences represented God's forgiveness for sins and, in this case, were being sold on behalf of the church in nearby German territories. When Luther's Ninety-Five Theses against indulgences are examined, however, many are surprised at the limited extent of their critique. In many ways, Luther's protest was not even against the principle of indulgences, but simply against their abuse. Furthermore, acting as a theologian with a pastor's heart, Martin Luther appears to have been genuinely oblivious to the storm that his outspokenness would create. This was because Luther had no idea of the extent of the vested interest that his protest against indulgences was challenging; the financial deal made between Pope Leo X and Albrecht of Brandenburg over the indulgence being entirely secret. With years of dutiful obedience behind him, plus an introspective temperament, Luther was also largely unaware at this stage of the challenge that his action on indulgences was making to the entire penitential system of the Catholic Church.

What awoke Martin Luther to all of this, however, was the scale of the reaction that he then received. When Luther challenged the abuse of indulgences, he expected his arguments to be engaged with and, while the debate might be robust, for this to lead to practical change within the church. Luther was still, at this stage, confident that the church to which he belonged was invested in theological truth and open to being reformed by it. He fairly swiftly discovered that this was not the case at all. From his hearing before Cardinal Cajetan in 1518 to his disputation with John Eck in 1519 and finally his appearance before the Emperor Charles V at Worms in 1521, Luther instead experienced a consistent unwillingness to engage with his arguments and the demand that he simply accept the authority of the church and recant. It was the intransigence of his opponents, therefore, and their unwillingness to engage with his concerns, that led Martin Luther to the conclusion (unthinkable when he made his initial protest four years earlier) that the church to which he had taken two vows of obedience was institutionally corrupt, requiring wholesale exposure and reform.

At the risk of hubris, my claim is that the path towards the thinking contained in this book has been similar. When, as a relatively junior clergyman, I acted in response to the safeguarding issues surrounding the lay minister at my church, I had no idea that I was challenging an entire culture. I was simply doing what I considered to be right and, in my naivety, assumed that when the details of the case emerged, 'the church' would agree. The Church of England, in my fairly uncritical mind, was a sleepy but essentially good organisation which would eventually support what I had done and vindicate my actions. It was therefore as shattering for me, as it must have been for Luther, to discover the exact opposite. Through my poor experience in every subsequent safeguarding case and the consistent refusal of the church at every level to engage with my concerns, my eventual 'reformation discovery' was that the problem was far worse than I had imagined: that the Church of England's huge problems with safeguarding existed because its culture is utterly invested in untruth and injustice.

At the current time, presenting this assessment of the Church of England is generally limited to survivors of abuse within it. One of the most significant recent contributions to the safeguarding debate is the symposium *Letters to a Broken Church*, composed of thirty-three articles written by different authors, mostly survivors of abuse.[3] Just one of the many things that makes the volume so heartbreaking is the loss of faith that its writers display in the church's commitment to truth and justice. Its most chilling statement is that sent by Graham Sawyer to every member of the General Synod of the Church of England on the eve of their meeting in February 2018:

As one of the two people about whom Bishop Peter Ball pleaded guilty with respect to historic sexual offences I forgive Bishop Ball from my heart for what he did to me and wish him no ill will whatsoever. I also have absolutely no doubts about the personal integrity, competence and compassion of Bishop Peter Hancock as lead bishop for safeguarding.

That said, the enduringly cruel and sadistic treatment I have faced from the National Safeguarding Team in Church House and others in the Church of England hierarchy makes what Bishop Ball did to me pale into insignificance: this comes as a result, I believe, of a deep-rooted narcissism.

We cannot move forward as a church with respect to truth, reconciliation and peace until the National Safeguarding Team is abolished: it is, in short wicked in the way it treats survivors/victims of sexual abuse as I know only too well from my own experience.[4]

Such testimony is echoed by other survivors of abuse. Frequently remarkable in the forgiveness they are prepared to extend to their abuser, their greatest anger is often with the callous treatment that they have received from the church. This has led to the shattering realisation that, through their witness of its complete indifference to truth and justice, the Church of England cannot be seen as good. As another survivor of abuse at the hands of Peter Ball, Cliff James, put it:

If you look at ... (the church)... from the outside it is beautifully decorated and it has lovely stories, it promises so much – it promises everlasting life and redemption. But, if you strip away the veneer, it is a cold machine, its gun-metal coloured and, as with any corporation, its whole reason for being is to maintain itself, to reproduce itself from generation to generation. It is not about love or compassion or kindness or sympathy or any human quality like that...[5]

Such statements need to be recognised as deeply prophetic truth about the nature of the Church of England. They reflect Jesus' warning that those who claim to be his followers will be evaluated according to how they treat "the least of these brothers of mine" at their moment of greatest vulnerability (Matthew 25.31-46). When he spoke these words, Jesus was displaying his continuity with the Old Testament prophets, many of whom assessed the people of Israel with a similar criterion. Prophets such as Amos, Micah and Isaiah were outspoken in their declaration that Israel's worship and ritual was hateful to YHWH if it was accompanied by the neglect or ill treatment of those amongst her people who were vulnerable. The revelatory aspect of this process was crucial (Amos 3.7) with prophetic truth-telling forming an indispensable part of the coming of God's righteousness.

In terms of the Church of England, it represents a major scandal that the proclamation of prophetic truth about its treatment of the vulnerable is still left largely to the survivors of this abuse. The church needs fearless prophets to rise up who are prepared to speak on their behalf. But this can only begin through such potential prophets having the courage to recognise the truth about the church.

Such courage is also required in reference to the particular traditions within the Church of England. One of the most encouraging aspects of the aftermath of the revelations concerning Jonathan Fletcher at Emmanuel Wimbledon in 2019 was the response of the conservative evangelical leader, Vaughan Roberts. Roberts spoke of the need for his tradition to examine its culture and what needed to change within it.[6] For a conservative evangelical leader to acknowledge so publicly that their movement possessed a culture, rather than simply being built upon biblical truth, was striking. The pain involved in this process was clear and whatever its necessity at a moment of crisis for the tradition, it was a courageous and prophetic moment. It was also one not really paralleled within the Anglo-Catholic movement that has produced so much of the abuse within the Church of England. Further self-examination is needed by my own less conservative evangelical Anglicanism for the way in which the post-Keele ethos (mentioned in Chapter 1) has supported much of the institutionalism that has facilitated the cover-up of abuse within the church. The willingness to hear and engage with prophetic truth is needed in regard to all the traditions of the Church of England and the vulnerability this involves may even prove to be the key to developing greater understanding between them.

But another reason why courage is needed to recognise the truth about the church is because of the acknowledgement of personal frailty this can involve. Clergy, in particular, need immense courage to acknowledge the role that their weakness can play in creating environments where abuse is more likely to occur. Honesty about such personal frailty is needed to an even greater extent amongst the bishops of the Church of England. Just one aspect of this which will escape scrutiny otherwise is their frequent tendency to appoint timid, non-challenging personalities to safeguarding positions. For bishops to acknowledge such temptations and the role that their fears have in bringing about such decisions is difficult but a vital part of the courage that is required of them.

Biblical passages that repay study in this regard include Isaiah 6, where the prophet is commissioned to take God's word to his people. This process has to begin, however, with Isaiah's acknowledgement of the truth about the spiritual condition of both the people and himself. Once he has witnessed God's holiness, Isaiah can suddenly recognise the full sinfulness of both himself and the people that he lives among (Isaiah 6.5). The acknowledgement of this truth forms the vital prelude to both the forgiveness that Isaiah then receives and the prophetic commission that follows. Fear is present but it is fear of God. Such fear produces the courage with which Isaiah responds to the prophetic calling that God places on his life.

1 Corinthians 13 reminds us that even prophecy is only "in part" and will eventually pass away when our full experience of God takes place in the new creation. It is important for those with a 'prophetic ministry' to recognise that they are not given anything like the full picture of the truth but a partial one, however important. None of the prophets within the Bible, including Jesus, are given the full knowledge of everything, but instead an urgent message that God wanted to be delivered to the people of their day. 1 Corinthians 13, however, also uses the image of growing up and putting childish perspectives behind. This illustrates the growth in spiritual wisdom that Paul is advocating throughout the letter, and the need for its practical implementation within the life of the church, ahead of the new creation. The Church of England badly needs such greater maturity and this will begin when increasing numbers are prepared to take the painful path of acknowledging the truth about its strengths and weaknesses.

The Courage Needed to Speak and Act the Truth

Obviously it is not enough for those called to a prophetic ministry to recognise the truth about themselves and the culture that they live within.

They also need the courage to speak that truth and embody it. A crucial aspect of this is not being deflected from speaking out by the fear of the negative consequences that will follow.

A common attempt to deflect people from speaking about something wrong within the church is for them to be asked what they are hoping to achieve. Rather like Miriam to Amos in the dialogue that began this chapter, the truth about a given situation may well be agreed. But a greater significance is often given to *the reaction* that such truth-telling will provoke. This cautionary approach usually presents its perspective as judicious, wise and even moral. But the result of it is usually a strong case being made for not speaking the truth.

Sometimes this is right. When I was a teenager and said something mean about someone, my dad had a standard response. "Before you say anything," he would say, "ask yourself three questions: Is it true? Is it kind? Is it necessary?" In terms of personal relationships, this is good and important advice. It speaks powerfully to people so frustrated by something that they are tempted to say something cruel in response. In the proclamation of something seen to be true and necessary, kindness also has an important role. As an aspect of the fruit of the Spirit (Galatians 5.22), kindness will frequently stop gratuitously hurtful things being spoken or done. It needs to be borne in mind by those called to a prophetic ministry. But the danger comes when kindness (usually understood rather thinly as the desire not to upset anyone) is seen as possessing a power of veto over any statements of truth.

This occurs all too often in church life. Back in Chapter 3 we examined the prevailing influence of passive aggression within the culture of the Church of England. This included mention of the convention that someone should back off from speaking the truth at the first sign of discomfort in the person being addressed. This is particularly difficult when someone starts to cry or gets angry. Whether intended or not, this is often a very effective way of putting a stop to any further discussion. Especially in a mixed-gender setting, fear of being presented as a bully is often enough to make many men immediately back off. This is never beneficial for anyone, as its normal result is some sort of indirect or passive-aggressive response by these men to resolve the issue instead.

Such discomfort can just as easily be displayed when the critique is mounted towards a church, diocese or entire denomination. This is understandable when people are deeply invested in such a body, either because of what they have given to or received from it. More will be said shortly about the courage needed to see such criticism as a form of loyalty to the Body of Christ at such moments. Seeing truth as the friend, rather than the enemy, of any organisation that is good is another important ingredient of the courage needed at such points.

Another important part of prophecy is *symbolic action*. Rather than being limited to the oral proclamation of God's word, the prophets within the Bible frequently added powerful actions to the words that they spoke. It is when words and actions are combined that they frequently have the strongest impact. By the same token, however, this also provokes a much stronger reaction. If someone accompanies their words of protest in a church setting with some form of symbolic action, they are frequently accused of being immature or petulant. This can be the case. Just as often, however, it is because the symbolism has added massive potency to their protest causing major discomfort to those who resent the challenge being made. While people can switch off to words and pretend that they haven't heard them, this is much more difficult with symbolic action. Obviously, the use of such symbolism must be handled carefully and the need for it may be rare. But a prophetic ministry will be prepared to use such action and displaying truth often involves an even greater amount of courage than speaking it.

An example of this covered back in Chapter 6 was the response of a member of my church to the consistently poor behaviour of another of our members. Rather than just speaking words of rebuke, the decision of the former to withdraw from the 'home group' that they both belonged to, added powerful symbolism to these words. While any words spoken about the behaviour had been ignored, the tangible action of a friend leaving their 'home group' because of the continuing conduct made a significant impact. It also made some others uncomfortable because it challenged their desire to ignore the issue and the impact that it was having on the rest of the church. As mentioned, it also stood in stark contrast to the bishop's refusal to use either word or symbol in response to the destructive behaviour and its impact upon the church.

The Courage Needed to 'Go into Bat' for the Vulnerable

This is another important part of prophetic ministry. The prophets within the Old Testament consistently spoke up on behalf of those who were vulnerable and against those who were oppressing them. Mention was made earlier of the rise of the prophets coming alongside the ascendancy of Israel's monarchy. What they said and did was directly related to the oppression that came with the latter (see 1 Samuel 12). Again and again, we see the prophets speaking out against exploitation of the weak by the powerful and warning of the terrible judgement that would be incurred as a result of this.

Prophetic ministry within the local church will often involve speaking out in a similar manner on behalf of the vulnerable. Within many churches, power is held by a small group who expect most things to be done in accordance with their wishes. Clergy are expected to recognise this status and acknowledge these people's right to greater influence. Those who possess less power – most obviously children, newcomers and those more on the margins of the church and wider society – then pay the price for this. A major difficulty is that, because these groups are not used to having a voice, their expectations of change happening on their behalf are often very low. In a sorry cycle, this can lead to the perception that they are less committed to the church and therefore less deserving of influence within it.

A good deal of prophetic insight is needed to see through this sort of situation, and particularly the way in which the abuse of power undermines the entire calling of the church. Such insight will be able to discern the key moments when the church is under threat and the moments when a prophetic challenge needs to be made. Just one example of this at my church was when some of the members of our monthly lunch club, Grapevine, started to come to the service that preceded it, and sometimes to the evening service as well. Many attending these services were pleased at their presence and saw this as clear evidence that God was working through the project. Others were less happy, particularly when one of the members of Grapevine brought her dog. The dog, called Bailey, was quiet and well-behaved, but would also wander up and down the aisles during the service. The clear expectation of those who were unhappy with his presence, however, was that I would 'have a word' with the woman and make sure that Bailey no longer came.

What I realised, instead, was that a key moment for the church had arrived. The woman felt comfortable being with her dog and I realised that they very much came as a package. Demonstrating our care for the whole of God's creation, including all of his creatures, was another factor that I was keen to demonstrate. As a result of this, I made it clear that both of them were more than welcome to our services. I even had the opportunity to give this symbolic expression, with the dog receiving a blessing when he trotted up to the front during Holy Communion! When some members expressed anger at the 'disruption' to the service caused by the dog's presence, the most effective prophetic protest against this came from a woman in the church who was nearly ninety. In a way that displayed both kindness and challenge, she spoke out about the ridiculous nature of the attitudes being shown and the importance of what God was doing in bringing members of Grapevine to the church.

The prophetic aspect of this episode went on to bear considerable fruit. Seeing the woman and her dog at our Carols by Candlelight service, some of our less regular members expressed surprise that we welcomed dogs. Asking whether they could bring their dogs as well, they were delighted to be affirmed in this. As someone who had previously never viewed pets with any fondness, it made me reflect on the greater inclusion that becoming a dog-friendly church seemed to bring. I realised that, within New Malden, more and more people were getting dogs with very positive effects upon families as well as for those struggling with issues such as bereavement or mental health. The result of this was a pet service, widely publicised in the local area that brought numerous new people along to the church – alongside 38 dogs! The fascinating thing was the enormous amount of spiritual openness seen in 'outsiders' once the love they had for their pets was recognised and engaged with by the church. But all of this had its roots in the prophetic insight of the need to side with the vulnerable against those with greater power at a vital moment in the life of the church.

The need for courage in this regard is increased by the fact that little support is usually given to such an agenda. Regular churchgoers and bishops and archdeacons are generally far more concerned about offence being taken by powerful members of the church than the treatment of the vulnerable. When churchgoers say that a previous vicar was 'much loved', they often mean that he or she fulfilled the role of being 'chaplain to the club', rather than ministering to those on the margins. Complaints about clergy to their superiors overwhelmingly come from those who are established within churches rather than those more peripheral. The effect of this is that many clergy are frightened of doing anything to challenge the status quo within their churches. A great deal of courage, and probably a strong degree of self-sacrifice, is therefore needed if clergy are to fulfil the prophetic role of 'going into bat' for the vulnerable.

The Courage Needed to be Prepared to be Seen as Disloyal

It was Jesus, on his return to Nazareth, who commented that "no prophet is accepted in his hometown" (Luke 4.24). This phrase is often quoted but rarely analysed or its importance for churches duly unpacked. The reason why this is the case is because prophetic ministry is overwhelmingly concerned with bringing God's challenging word to the community from which the prophet comes.[7] While the prophets did pronounce God's judgement upon other nations, the primary focus of their critique was the people of Israel. Although there were plenty of false prophets prepared to underwrite Israel's condition (e.g. 1 Kings 22, Jeremiah 28), the authentic prophets were deeply courageous in their willingness to criticise their own nation and its culture. This is the reason why Jeremiah, and probably many other prophets, were seen as traitors. Most scholars agree that the overwhelming cause of Jesus' death was his symbolic act of judgement upon the Jerusalem Temple and the perceived disloyalty of this action. Stephen made it clear that the nation of Israel had constantly persecuted its prophets and was promptly killed himself (Acts 7). Genuine prophets will always be prepared to be seen as disloyal to their 'hometown' and persecuted as a result.

The tendency within many churches, and ironically many who pride themselves upon their 'challenging preaching', can be the precise opposite. Within such churches, challenging sermons can be delivered, but they are largely targeted at the world or church outside, and not at those people present. The challenging style can disguise the extent to which they are 'playing to the gallery', rather than being genuinely prophetic. In theory, the fact that Church of England clergy are paid centrally, rather than by their churches should help here. Within denominations where this is not the case, the financial impact of upsetting church members through prophetic preaching is often enough to deter many of its ministers from going anywhere near this. In reality, however, the pressure to concentrate on reassuring 'the faithful' rather than issuing any sort of genuine challenge is one that afflicts all churches. The danger with a great deal of preaching is that fairly immediate 'resonance' with the congregation is often taken as the greatest sign of its effectiveness. Genuine prophetic ministry, however, will have the courage to resist always aiming for such resonance, and will instead be prepared to receive the very opposite. Clergy also need to have the kind of courage that means they are willing to go through periods of being unpopular among their congregation because of the prophetic challenge that they are prepared to deliver.

Obviously balance is needed here. Endless challenges every week on numerous areas within church life will usually be inappropriate. It will also be ineffective and cause members to 'switch off' to the challenge being issued. The biblical prophets oscillated between issuing, on the one hand, deeply challenging messages to their hearers and, on the other, messages of comfort concerning God's future rescue and visions of this future. A great deal of preaching should be similarly comforting. Teaching sermons can also major on encouragement and practical suggestions for how to live the Christian life more fully. But if a preaching ministry is going to be authentic and biblical, it should at some points also include a prophetic challenge to the congregation even at the risk of the preacher's popularity.

An example in recent times is the willingness, in the wake of the murder of George Floyd and the 'Black Lives Matter' movement, to preach to congregations about their white privilege. There is also the damage that our Western lifestyles are doing to the environment and the role of our consumerism in creating and perpetuating global and national injustice. More local issues can include the need to be a properly welcoming church to outsiders, rather than an inward-looking club. Such preaching is rarely popular and usually creates a strong reaction. The hardest thing for clergy is when congregation members, upset by such challenge, find other ways of 'punishing' them for doing this. Where this looks like being the case, further honesty and courage is needed in calling this out, hopefully supported by other members of the church. It also needs to be made clear that, just as a true friend is prepared to be honest in speaking truth, prophetic challenge is an example of loyalty and commitment to a church, rather than the opposite.

The Courage Needed to Speak Truth to Power

As we have seen, courage is often needed to speak the truth, but never is this more so than when clergy have to summon the courage to speak truth to those in positions senior to them. Within the running of churches and dioceses, issues constantly arise and, as a result, there are plenty of concerns about particular situations and how they are being handled. The problem is not so much when clergy *initially* raise their concerns with bishops, archdeacons or other senior diocesan staff. An openness is normally present, as long as this is done in a polite and careful manner. The problem is how to respond when this communication meets with little or no response.

The difficulty here is that clergy who are most popular with bishops and archdeacons are those who make their job easier by not bringing up any difficult issues which need resolution. Or those who, having flagged up an issue only to receive an inadequate or non-response, are then prepared to drop the issue rather than persist in seeking an answer. During the twenty-two years that I have been ordained, I have lost count of the number of times that I have sent letters or emails to bishops or archdeacons that have received this treatment. Points and matters seen as important by me and/or my church have often been met with a deafening silence. At other times a 'holding email' or acknowledgement of receipt is received with a promise of a fuller response to come, which then doesn't materialise. This is normally because the issue is a difficult one and those receiving the communication hope that by ignoring it, the issue will disappear and will therefore be something that they can avoid dealing with.

The problem afflicting clergy is that, within the passive-aggressive culture of many dioceses, persistence at this point is seen as aggressive behaviour. Or – the ultimate crime within English middle-class society – being rude. One of the problems here is that the major characteristic of many bishops and archdeacons is that of being urbane and affable. They consciously see an important part of their role as travelling around churches being pleasant and, in the process, diffusing difficulties through their 'niceness'. This, of course, is quite difficult to find fault with. Until, however, it is recognised as a way of both avoiding difficult issues and, most significantly, making those who persist in raising them appear rude and unpleasant. This response extends to clergy who are open with others about the unsatisfactory way in which their concerns have been dealt with. The overwhelming pressure in such situations is to let matters drop and adopt a similar urbanity and 'niceness' to that being modelled.

Stepford Wives is a satirical thriller written in 1972 and made into film versions in 1975 and 2004. In its story, the once independent-minded wives of the town of Stepford are gradually reduced to fawning, docile and mindless accessories to their husbands. Within the different versions of the story, this change is achieved in different ways. But all of them involve replacement of those areas of the brain that enable independent thought, as the women increasingly become robots. Within the Church of England, a fairly low-grade equivalent of this can be seen. Bombarded by urbanity and 'niceness' and the rewards available to those who conform to this, many clergy lose any ability to express independent and critical thought about

8 / PROPHETS AND WHISTLEBLOWERS

their diocese. Perhaps the most common device used to remove the independent minds from clergy is that of making them into 'honorary canons' of the cathedral. This role is completely meaningless but very attractive to clergy who are insecure about their status and significance. In most cases, it represents a very public reward to clergy for upholding the status quo and not doing anything to make life more difficult for their superiors.

Within this context, it can take an extraordinary amount of courage and energy for clergy to persist in flagging up those issues which they consider to be important. It usually requires them to be completely indifferent to the negative impact that doing this will have upon their career, future moves and even their personal wellbeing. Sometimes this isn't possible or, especially when it impacts upon their health or that of their family, the right thing to do. However, the Church of England does need clergy who are prepared to show the necessary courage to speak truth in a prophetic way to those in power. This should always be done in a respectful manner and one that continues to acknowledge the authority of those to whom this truth is being spoken. Once again, the point should be made that a proper loyalty and respect for those in authority involves being honest about truth rather than suppressing this.

Once a certain amount of time has elapsed, such 'stands' are usually seen as extremely virtuous. All of the Christian traditions contain heroes and heroines who were prepared to speak what they considered to be truth to power, regardless of the consequences. Earlier in this chapter, mention was made of Martin Luther and the path he made towards recognising the truth about the state of the church in his day. Summoned before the Emperor Charles V at Worms in 1521, Luther knew any further refusal to recant would, in all likelihood, result in his death. "Here I stand" probably wasn't part of Luther's original speech. But the final part of the words that he is believed to have spoken are worth quoting: "…my conscience is captive to the word of God. I cannot and I will not recant anything for to go against conscience is neither right nor safe. God help me. Amen."

Within the church of today, a similar courage to that of Luther, and similar figures of other traditions, is badly needed. The church needs clergy who will have the courage to speak out about the abuses within it.

As mentioned, Luther's courage and insight into the problems with the church grew as he sought to speak out about those things that he knew to be wrong. The same is true today. This book has sought to show how the practical failures of the church in terms of its safeguarding are all linked to an underlying confusion and lack of confidence about Christian truth. More than ever, courageous Christian prophets are therefore needed to proclaim this truth and its application and take the consequences that come with this.

The Courage Needed to Risk Failure

This is important. For every Martin Luther (who, despite his expectations wasn't killed) and whose protest went on to meet with a fair measure of success, there are a greater number of Christian prophets who have met the fate of Jan Hus (1372-1415). Around a century before Luther, Hus made a very similar case for reform of the church. Despite receiving a promise of safe passage, Hus was tried by the Council of Constance in 1415 and burned at the stake as a heretic. The word 'martyr' was originally used of those prepared to witness to the truth of their Christian faith to the point of being killed for this by the pagan cultures in which they lived. Sadly though, many Christian martyrs like Hus have been created *by* the church as well.

In recent years a good deal of emphasis has been placed upon the importance of clergy wellbeing. Books such as *Driven Beyond the Will of God* are helpful for challenging Christian leaders about the unnecessary stress that they can place themselves under.[8] This emphasis can be overdone, however, with some clergy prioritising their 'protection' to such an extent that everything else about their ministry is built around their day off, holidays and emotional health. Within this context, the case for not speaking out about matters of truth can seem overwhelming, particularly if this will come at significant personal cost and is unlikely to meet with success. Many clergy within the Church of England appear to combine an individualistic piety with a low-grade cynicism which believes that little positive change is possible. It is this which enables them to believe they can maintain their personal integrity while keeping quiet about bad things in the wider church or outside world.

One of the indications of this is how Amos 5.13 is interpreted and then translated. In the passage containing this verse, Amos has been speaking out about the corruption and injustice prevalent in Israel, before declaring that in such evil times, the prudent or wise man keeps quiet. Given that throughout his prophecy, Amos is constantly doing the precise opposite, this seems a rather strange and contradictory thing to say. Particularly in the light of what follows as Amos' hearers/readers are exhorted to 'hate evil' and 'love good'. Despite this, most translations and commentaries continue to reflect the sense that Amos is advising a quietist response from his hearers. The Good News Bible is surely nearer to its intended sense when it gives the verse a tone of sarcastic scorn, saying: 'And so keeping quiet in such evil times is the clever thing to do!' According to this understanding, those seen as 'wise' in keeping silent about injustice, form part of the evil that Amos is exposing.

Mention was made earlier of how often those wanting to speak out are asked what they hope to achieve by doing this. The implicit logic here is that unless they can be fairly sure of bringing about the change that they desire, such an approach is futile and probably even morally wrong as well. Such thinking, however, ignores the wealth of biblical material exhorting the followers of Jesus to witness to the gospel regardless of the outcome. Jesus told his followers to place their priority on seeking the kingdom of God and his righteousness (Matthew 6.33). Central to the good news of Christianity is that because of the death and resurrection of Jesus Christ, the power of evil has been defeated, meaning that such seeking after God's righteousness is never in vain. This is why Paul ends his great chapter on the resurrection in 1 Corinthians 15 with the exhortation to: "Always give yourself fully to the work of the Lord, because you know that your labour in the Lord is not in vain" (1 Corinthians 15.58). This perspective, however, needs the eye of faith rather than being obvious. It includes speaking God's truth to those in power, even if the result of this is apparent failure. Just one example of this in the Bible is the fate of John the Baptist after he spoke out against the adultery of

Herod Antipas (Matthew 14.3-12; Mark 6.17-29). In human terms, this achieved little other than John's death and the cutting short of his ministry. Every Christian martyr has had to face precisely the same challenge, with all the courage and faith that this requires.

Such faith is based upon the vision that, because of the resurrection of Jesus Christ, everything built upon this foundation is building for something that will last forever. This is the message that Paul is presenting throughout 1 Corinthians. It is also contained within the last words that Stephen spoke, shortly before his fearless proclamation of the truth took him to his death. Stephen was able to see that what he had done had joined him to the ascended and vindicated Son of Man (Acts 7.56). Revelation and other parts of the New Testament present a very similar perspective. It is this theological basis that provides the vital foundation for Christians and particularly clergy, having the courage to speak truth to the church, even when the result of this is an apparent failure. Christians are never part of building the kingdom of God more than when they do the right thing regardless of the consequences.

THE RELATIONSHIP BETWEEN PROPHETIC VISION AND PERSONAL VANITY

Before we turn to the implications of this for safeguarding, this issue needs to be addressed. There will be some reading this chapter who find the whole talk of prophetic ministry insufferably arrogant and pretentious. It doesn't require the cynicism of a postmodern perspective on truth claims to be wary about those who claim to be able to see the truth more clearly than those around them. Surely this is just the sort of arrogant certainty that produces religious fundamentalism, with all of its terrible consequences for the world?

This is an important point which needs a response. The theme is explored in the film *Khartoum* produced in 1966.[9] The film focuses on the famous Christian soldier, General Charles Gordon, and his doomed attempt in 1885 to save the inhabitants of Khartoum from being massacred at the hands of the Islamic Mahdi. Despite its flaws, most notably its ridiculous portrayal of the British Prime Minister, W.E. Gladstone, as a faithless cynic, the film is a very interesting exploration of the thin line separating vision from vanity. Despite receiving explicit instructions from his political superiors that he was to leave Khartoum, Gordon believed that God was telling him to stay in the city knowing that this would force the British government to send an army to rescue its inhabitants. In the film, the ethics involved are discussed as well as the role of Gordon's personal vanity in this decision. Parallels with the convictions of the fundamentalist Mahdi are also made and indeed drawn by Gordon himself in the fictional scenes where the two figures meet and talk about the revelations that they have each received. But a crucial difference, pointed out by Gordon, is that his God has revealed to him what mercy is and that if, by his death, he could achieve the defeat of the evil represented by the Mahdi, his sacrifice would not have been in vain.

Two points can be made here. The first, already made in this chapter in the light of 1 Corinthians 13.9, is that any claim to possess a prophetic vision of truth will always be partial. This is shown by the very obvious flaws present within all prophetic Christian figures with General Gordon far from alone in this regard. Martin Luther, for instance, represented anything but the truth in the horrific response that he advocated against the German peasants in 1525 and the Jews in 1543. His namesake Martin Luther King was deeply prophetic in both his words and actions when it came to civil rights for blacks in 1960s America and anything but prophetic when it came to the adultery within his marriage. "We know in part and we prophesy in part" is important in approaching anything and anyone that appears to be prophetic. But the critical factor in distinguishing what is prophetic truth from what is not, is the extent to which it reflects the liberating self-giving love of God in Jesus Christ and the light that this brings into the darkness.

In recent times, it has been claimed that even the canonical prophets within the Bible should be approached in this manner, to distinguish what is truly prophetic within their writings from what is not. Gregory Boyd argues that acceptance of the death of Jesus Christ as the ultimate revelation of God requires such a critical response to truth claims made within the Old Testament.[10] Christians will disagree about this and many are worried about the implications of this hermeneutic for interpreting the Bible and understanding its authority. But in terms of evaluating and testing prophetic messages today, there should be little debate that the crucial factor in evaluating such messages is the extent to which they reflect the grace and truth represented in the ministry of Jesus Christ.

Prophetic Ministry and Safeguarding

The reason for the writing of this book is that the Church of England needs to receive an urgent message similar to that delivered by the prophets in the Bible. This prophetic message concerns the major and pervasive problems within its culture and the devastating impact that this is having upon every aspect of its ministry and mission but supremely, and most scandalously, upon its safeguarding. In many ways this book itself, with its many flaws and very partial vision, is seeking to be part of this prophetic message.

But change will only come if more prophets arise within the Church of England and are ready to show the different aspects of courage outlined in this chapter. Numerous prophets and prophetesses appear through the Old Testament, each with different insights and methods. Some make greater use of symbolism than others and some include greater visions of hope and restoration, alongside their messages of judgement. But what unites all of the prophets is their courage in proclaiming the insight that God has given them into the state of his people and the serious consequences of this. While it is difficult to establish quite as much clarity over the nature of prophecy in the New Testament church, it appears to have shared most of the same essential characteristics of being an urgent word from God that his people needed to heed. Prophets within the Church of England today will need the courage to recognise the truth, the courage needed to speak and act the truth, the courage to 'go into bat' for the vulnerable, the courage to be seen as disloyal, the courage to speak truth to power and the courage to be willing to fail. They will also need the courage that recognises that, whatever their flaws and personal failings and whatever the partial and incomplete nature of their vision, a genuine and urgent word from God has been given to them that they need to proclaim.

This is because the problems with safeguarding in the Church of England cannot and will not be solved without the truth about the wider problems within the church's culture being spoken and addressed. For those called to speak the truth to this culture, immense courage will be needed. It will involve losing favour with those in authority and all the advantages that come with this. It will include upsetting and disappointing those who love them and have their best interests at heart. It will involve them being presented as nasty, disloyal and arrogant. It will involve having their personal weaknesses and failings exploited and used as the reason for discounting the message they are seeking to speak. The writer has experienced all of these things in speaking out about the weaknesses of safeguarding in the Church of England and the underlying problems within its culture that have caused this. It is a somewhat lonely but very necessary calling. It is also one that God will be making right now to many of those who are reading this book.

CHAPTER 9

Tough on Safeguarding, Tough on the Causes of Safeguarding

*A Vision for Restoring Truth to the
Centre of the Church's Culture*

This book has sought to argue that, given the prevailing culture within the Church of England and the normative status of its attitudes and practices, it should be no surprise that it is so immensely poor at safeguarding. It has also made the case that the problems that the Church of England has had with safeguarding simply represent the most serious outcome of its dysfunctional and problematic culture. While this culture may help to sustain the church as an institution, it is deeply detrimental to the church's provision of effective ministry and mission, and catastrophic in its effect on its safeguarding.

However, it is this very truth which, paradoxically, holds out hope for the Church of England and its renewal. Over the past two decades in particular, there has been an increasing recognition that much of the Church of England is moribund. Falling attendances and ageing congregations are symptomatic of a church that, in overall terms, is largely incapable of speaking and acting with any credibility and relevance to the surrounding culture. There are significant exceptions to this with some wonderfully dynamic examples of the church in action occurring within the Church of England. However, hardly any of its hierarchy and leadership reflects or represents the healthy life that has produced this. The situation has been masked in recent times by having an Archbishop of Canterbury in Justin Welby who, whatever his failings on safeguarding, was able to speak with a public credibility that eluded most of his episcopal colleagues. Dominant within the House of Bishops and particularly the 'Civil Service' of the Church of England, at national and diocesan levels, however, lies the deeply unhealthy culture examined in this book.

The Church of England is uncomfortably aware of its decline. Past reports such as *Breaking New Ground* in 1994 and *Mission Shaped Church* in 2004 have sought to signal the need for radical change. Fresh Expressions of Church and their practical incarnation in movements such as Messy Church have been enthusiastically endorsed and championed as part of the necessary way forward.[1] The research of church growth analysts such as Bob Jackson has played an important role in flagging up what needs to change if the decline in the church is to be reversed.[2] Very little of this, however, appears to have impacted upon the *culture* of the Church of England. Most churches that experience growth and have a dynamic and imaginative approach to ministry and mission would say, if they were honest, that these things are occurring *despite* the structures and culture of their diocese and the overall Church of England, rather than because of them. This is why many of their leaders are uncomfortable for their churches to be used as part of the PR for their diocese and wider church. These leaders are resistant to the good practice and healthy culture within their churches being used to sustain the image of a wider church that represents neither of these things. The situation, in overall terms, is a church that knows that it has to change but is terrified at the implications of the challenge this represents to the culture of complacent incompetence that runs throughout the Church of England.

Safeguarding, however, while representing the most serious aspect of this dysfunctional culture, also presents the greatest chance of it being changed. This is because of the current non-negotiability of the seriousness of safeguarding. Since the revelations emerged about Jimmy Savile and the resulting work of Operation Yewtree, a consensus has rapidly established in Britain that all institutions, however venerated, must be held more accountable with their entire credibility resting upon their handling of safeguarding. This has only grown as other scandals, such as those involving the Post Office and the NHS, have emerged.

A paler and more nervous version of this was developing within the Church of England before the publication of the Makin review. For the most part, its efforts with regard to safeguarding up to now have been invested in establishing more secure processes and procedures. Every diocese now has to have safeguarding officers and policies in place. As indicated at the beginning of this book, these measures are both good and positive. They are also, however, largely taken up with ensuring that a proper *response* is made to the emergence of safeguarding issues rather than having much of a *preventative* nature. The current effort of the Church of England in regard to preventative safeguarding is through the requirement for those in key positions of authority and involved in work with children and vulnerable people to undergo DBS (Disclosure and Barring Service) checks. The speed with which such checks are now processed is a major step forward.

However, the entire point of this book is to make clear that such policies and procedures, while important, are relatively minor in their significance for genuine safeguarding. Reflecting the case set out in Chapter 5, their major significance probably lies in the greater safety that they bring to the institution of the church, rather than those to whom it actually ministers. What is needed for a genuine advance in safeguarding to take place, is a cultural overhaul of much of the Church of England.

The title of this chapter is a fairly obvious play on the slogan that the Labour party used as it sought to make itself electable again in the first half of the 1990s. Tony Blair, then Shadow Home Secretary, used the slogan 'tough on crime, tough on the causes of crime' to indicate his party's fresh commitment to being tough on law and order alongside its traditional commitment to addressing the injustice that it saw as creating many of these problems in the first place. The aim of this chapter is not to denigrate safeguarding policies and procedures, but rather to argue that these are, at best, largely responsive rather than proactive and preventative, and that they need to be set within a broader context where the Church of England is equally serious about being tough on the causes of safeguarding offences. It is this attempt to change the culture of the Church of England – and only this – that will produce a church that can move beyond its current delusions of adequacy when it comes to safeguarding.

9 / TOUGH ON SAFEGUARDING, TOUGH ON THE CAUSES OF SAFEGUARDING

Most of these words were drafted before the seismic events in the Church of England that occurred in November 2024. Before these events, it was common to hear people saying that the culture of the Church of England around safeguarding needed to change. When I heard this, I was always ambivalent, since it could be taken to mean that safeguarding in the Church of England could be responded to separately from addressing the rest of its culture. In the light of the Makin review and the resignation of Justin Welby, far more commentators have spoken about the culture of the Church of England, in overall terms, needing to change. Whether this belief, and crucially what it means, is genuinely shared and understood by those invested in the institution, only time will tell. But there is no doubt that the context has now been provided for widespread cultural change within the Church of England to be firmly on the agenda.

The exciting implication of the central thesis of this book is that, if this is done, then plenty more than the reform of safeguarding will come with it. Safeguarding abuses and scandals are definitely the most egregious result of the dysfunctional culture within the Church of England. But they are by no means the only ones. Again and again, the result of this culture is an undermining of the effectiveness of the ministry and mission for which the church exists. If the wider cultural factors within the church impacting upon its safeguarding are addressed, the result will be gain in every direction.

A point is needed here about cultural change within institutions. While it is usually painful, slow and difficult, institutions *can* change their cultures. The fact that this is often only as a result of these institutions having to endure crises or major scandals does not alter the fact that this change can and does occur. As a result of the scrutiny of the wilful and corrupt incompetence with which they handled the murder of black teenager Stephen Lawrence in 1993, the Metropolitan Police Force has very definitely undergone a major cultural shift. While the speed and the extent of this change may be debatable, it is nonetheless a reality, with elements of the struggle against this representing part of the evidence for its existence. I was a schoolteacher for seven years back at the school where I had once been a pupil, providing a great deal of insight into the stark difference between these periods of 1980-87 and 1993-2000, specifically with regard to the greater culture of accountability and professionalism within the teaching profession. While some teachers may resent these developments and hark back to a 'golden age of teaching', there is little real desire to turn the clock back on these cultural changes, particularly in relation to inclusion. Within all sorts of institutions, the necessity for cultural change is being engaged with and in many cases, albeit fitfully and incompletely, such change is occurring.

Within the Church of England, the lack of accountability (similar to that felt by many institutions) is often bolstered by something of a 'superiority complex', particularly amongst the conservative evangelical and Anglo-Catholic traditions. A further point, already indicated in this book, is how many clergy seem attracted to ministry within the Church of England precisely so that they can escape the scrutiny or accountability present within their previous occupations. All of this makes the process of changing the culture within the Church of England and its traditions more difficult. But it is not impossible, particularly following the events of November 2024. What follows, therefore, are practical suggestions, based upon the contents of the previous chapters of this book, about those changes needed to bring about the necessary overall change within the culture of the Church of England.

Grace and Truth

At the root of all of these suggestions is the development of a much greater culture of honesty, and one that possesses a far greater confidence about the goodness and power of truth, in particular. It is in John 1.14 that Jesus Christ is described as being "full of grace and truth" and a few verses later in 1.17 that "grace and truth came through Jesus Christ". A contrast is made with the earlier revelation that God provided in the law given through Moses. Rather than claiming that grace and truth were completely absent from the law of Moses, John is declaring their revelation within the Old Testament law to have been partial, and that both grace and truth were revealed to their fullest extent in Jesus Christ.

Over the last thirty years churches across Britain have experienced a powerful rediscovery of the concept of grace. When I was a child and then

9 / TOUGH ON SAFEGUARDING, TOUGH ON THE CAUSES OF SAFEGUARDING

a teenager growing up within evangelical subculture, grace was spoken about a great deal. In virtually every instance, however, grace was used exclusively to refer to the act of God in sending his Son, Jesus Christ to die so that those who repented might be forgiven of our sins and accepted into his family. This is a wonderful truth and remains the non-negotiable basis for everything else that can be said about grace. In the last three decades, however, and running alongside their recognition of the decline of Christendom, many churches have started to recognise the vital role that this grace has in the ongoing ministry and mission of the church. Grace has indeed come through Jesus Christ and supremely through his death. But the message of this grace now needs proclaiming, not only in words, but in the deeds and actions of the church. Through the ministry of the Holy Spirit, this holistic proclamation of God's grace by his people is just as much an act of God as the earthly ministry of Jesus Christ.

Within evangelical culture, the book that made a particular impact in this regard was *What's so Amazing about Grace* in 1999 by the American writer Philip Yancey.[3] To many Christians, including the author, Yancey's book came at just the right time to clarify the vital role that churches had in embodying God's grace. It was an interesting experience to reread Yancey's book twenty years on and be surprised by how unradical it felt. The reason for this, however, was entirely contextual and because of what has happened in the intervening years. For me and many other evangelical Christians in Britain, the priority of the church displaying God's grace in every aspect of its ministry and mission had become utterly central.

The biblical basis for this lay in greater attention being given to the nature of Jesus' earthly ministry within the gospels. Stories such as Jesus meeting with Matthew/Levi (Matthew 9; Mark 2; Luke 5), Zacchaeus (Luke 19) and the Samaritan woman at the well (John 4) were read with fresh eyes which recognised the amazing power of God's grace to transform the lives of those whom Jesus encountered. Christians started to suggest that, rather than being known as 'the story of the prodigal son' or 'the lost son', Jesus' most famous parable in Luke 15 should perhaps be known as 'the story of the forgiving father', in order to draw out more explicitly what is being proclaimed in the story about God's grace. Running alongside this exegesis were attempts to embody this grace more energetically and fully, particularly within the church's mission. All of these developments are wonderful.

A similar revolution is now needed within the Church of England in regard to truth. Without this, the rediscovery of grace and the desire to see its expression within the church's ministry and mission swiftly reveals its darker side, leading to many of the problems that this book has highlighted. Understood separately from truth, 'grace' all too easily justifies the apparently kind but ultimately lazy and uncourageous pragmatism that makes passive aggression the model for approaching every problem within the church. Dietrich Bonhoeffer saw, perhaps more clearly than anyone else, that any attempt to understand or practice grace without a corresponding emphasis upon truth simply produces a false understanding of grace – what Bonhoeffer referred to as 'cheap grace'.[4] Without truth, grace loses its power to bring God's powerful, redeeming love because it distorts and disguises the reality that needs to receive that love.

The Contemporary Crisis in Regard to Truth

Before anything further can be said about the church and truth, the problems with truth in wider society need comment. Here we have to mention the cultural force known as postmodernism. The roots of postmodernism lie in its rejection of the modernist philosophy that preceded it. The claim of modernism was that the scientific advances of the eighteenth and nineteenth centuries were now leading the way to the truth that really mattered. Central to its philosophy was the idea that the Western countries were in the vanguard of this exciting project and the rest of the world simply needed to follow.

Postmodernism represents the collapse of confidence in this philosophy. A key role in its development was played by the horrors of the twentieth century as the utopia or ideal world promised by the modernist project failed to materialise. People also started to recognise how many of the truth claims of modernism had been used to gain power. In response, certain forms of postmodernism claimed that all 'metanarratives' –

9 / TOUGH ON SAFEGUARDING, TOUGH ON THE CAUSES OF SAFEGUARDING

i.e. the big stories of the world that attempted to explain its truths – were self-serving narratives that were being told as part of an attempt to gain power over others.

Much of the culture in which today's Western Church exists is located somewhere between postmodernism and an awareness of its inadequacies. A widespread cynicism about universal truth has established a deep suspicion around the motives of politicians, religious leaders and institutions seeking any sort of globalising influence. At a popular level, many appear happy to believe that the best answer is for every individual to believe and follow 'what is true for them'.

In parallel with this, however, and holding back the triumph of postmodernism is the realisation that a completely subjective or relativist approach to truth will not do. Courts in the United Kingdom, for instance, still require their witnesses to tell "the truth, the whole truth and nothing but the truth", and few would want this changed. People still believe it is reasonable to expect their politicians and other public officials to 'tell the truth' and that distortions or corruptions of 'the truth' – i.e. lies – do exist and need to be called out as such, even or perhaps especially when they bear the label 'spin'.

Furthermore, there is an increasing awareness of how easily those in power can themselves use the weapons of postmodernism to dismiss attempts to hold them to account. Perhaps the most obvious example of this in recent times is Donald Trump's response to any criticism of his presidency as 'fake news' and his denial of the legitimacy of the election in November 2020 that saw him replaced by Joe Biden. Western society, despite the advance of postmodernism, knows that such a thing as truth exists and is important. But it remains deeply confused about truth and therefore completely unsure about how to go in search of it.

THE CURRENT CRISIS OF THE CHURCH IN REGARD TO TRUTH

Unfortunately, Western Christianity has not been immune to the impact of either modernism or postmodernism. Part of the agenda of modernism was to establish categories whereby claims about spiritual truth could be kept separate from those established by science and reason. 'Religion' was therefore largely retired from public life and repackaged as a private source of hope and comfort. Most evident in the eighteenth-century constitutions of republican France and America, this secular/spiritual divide was less overt in this country with the retention of the established status of the Church of England and its continuing role in public life.

Despite this, the effect of this ideological separation was still felt across the different traditions of the Church of England. While the 'broad church' movement (the precursor to today's liberal tradition) bought into the modernist agenda by giving increasing priority to 'reason' over 'revelation', the evangelical and Anglo-Catholic traditions were also shaped by it through largely accepting the category of private faith into which 'religion' had been relocated. There were notable exceptions to this, such as Wilberforce's evangelical campaign against the slave trade. But in both evangelicalism and Anglo-Catholicism, the truth revealed through Jesus Christ became increasingly restricted to an 'otherworldly' salvation that brought a personal relationship/communion with God in the present followed by a place in heaven after one's death.

It is these developments that explain the crisis with regard to truth within all of these traditions of the Church of England in the wake of the rise of postmodernism. The collapse of modernism has brought with it the almost complete demise of the liberal tradition that had bought so strongly into the truths revealed by reason. Meanwhile, stuck within the categories they accepted from modernism, evangelicalism and Anglo-Catholicism are also in crisis. Part of this is because both have struggled to defend their truth claims in the face of the postmodern critique that their doctrines represent the attempt to gain power over people's lives. The safeguarding scandals that have afflicted the church have obviously played a crucial role in providing damning evidence for this charge.

But at a deeper level, all traditions within the Church of England have struggled to meet the desire for holistic truth that much of the current culture (somewhat inconsistently) also demands. Suddenly people everywhere are becoming more than open to encountering spiritual truth that

9 / TOUGH ON SAFEGUARDING, TOUGH ON THE CAUSES OF SAFEGUARDING

will speak into the whole of their life experience in a manner that is deeper than modernism allowed. But, having trimmed their sails to a modernist wind and retreated into the sphere of private spirituality, both Anglo-Catholicism and evangelicalism (including its charismatic elements) possess little confidence in speaking such holistic truth. Jesus said, "If you hold to my teaching, you are really my disciples. You will know the truth, and the truth will set you free" (John 8.31). But rather than having a scope that can speak with confidence into every aspect of the human experience in this world, the truth of which Jesus spoke has been restricted to the rituals of Anglo-Catholicism and the largely escapist understanding of salvation represented by evangelicalism.

This provides the link to the central thesis of this book. At the root of all of the current problems of the Church of England and the deeply dysfunctional behaviour within it is a fundamental lack of confidence about truth. Having accepted for so long the separation of theological truth from most of life and its issues, the various traditions within the Church of England have retreated into increasingly odd and fearful subcultures that appear to possess no confidence at all about the power and clarity that Christian theology can and should bring to the practicalities of everyday life and its problems. It is this that has resulted in the pragmatism and culture of passive aggression with which the Church of England tends to approach every problem that it faces and its utter fear of honesty and transparency. At the heart of this is quite simply a lack of faith in Jesus Christ as the truth that can set us free.

Jesus and Truth

The answer, therefore, to all of the problems recounted in this book is quite simply a rediscovery of the truth brought by Jesus Christ and its transforming power. At the centre of this will be the rediscovery of the new creation theology within the New Testament that was the biggest casualty of the restrictions that Western Christianity accepted from modernism.

It is within John's Gospel that the clearest connection is drawn between this theology of new creation and the theme of truth.[5] The world into which Jesus came, according to John, was a world of darkness. Central to this darkness is people's refusal to acknowledge their enslavement to the evil that has corrupted the world (John 8.33-34). Its people are unable to see the light/truth and therefore the source of life (1.5). This is the basis for the, at first sight, strange connection that Jesus makes between the devil as "the father of lies" and being "a murderer from the beginning" (8.44). This connection is the message of evil that seeks to deny the source of eternal life and, as a result, brings death into God's good creation.

What Jesus brings into the world, by contrast, is the life-giving truth of new creation – what God is doing to heal and restore creation from the evil that has infected it. Jesus, because he comes from the Father in heaven, is the one who brings the words of eternal life into the world as the fulfilment of God's purpose. A central feature of John's Gospel is the dialogues that Jesus has with successive characters within it. Within each of these episodes we see Jesus confronting these people with the untruth contained in their present existence and the challenge to accept the truth of the eternal life that he holds out to them. The climax of the dialogues in John's Gospel is the one that Jesus has with Pilate as the representative of the ultimate kingdom of the world (18.28-19.16). When Jesus says that he comes to reveal the truth, Pilate cynically asks his famous question: "What is truth?" This, however, is immediately followed by its full revelation in Jesus' death on the cross. It is this supreme embodiment of the truth of divine love that then brings the start of God's new creation through Jesus' resurrection from death.

This, incidentally, forms the answer to postmodernism's valid concern about truth and the manner in which the kingdoms of the world have often used claims about it as a means of oppression. Within John's Gospel, Jesus makes the strongest and most exclusive claims about truth that it is possible to make (e.g. 14.6). But the supreme form of this truth being the sacrificial death of Jesus and the resulting self-giving love of his followers shows that this claim to truth is the very opposite of an oppressive power play.

The really significant part of this for our purposes is what Jesus says in John's Gospel about 'the Spirit of truth' and his role in leading the followers of Jesus 'into all truth'. Part of this will happen through the Holy Spirit

9 / TOUGH ON SAFEGUARDING, TOUGH ON THE CAUSES OF SAFEGUARDING

leading the disciples to love one another, thereby revealing themselves to the world as Jesus' followers (14.15-17). But another important feature of the Spirit's work is to:

... convict the world of guilt in regard to sin and righteousness and judgement: in regard to sin because men do not believe in me; in regard to righteousness because I am going to the Father, where you can see me no longer and in regard to judgement, because the prince of this world now stands condemned. (16.8-11)

Within this dense statement, Jesus is speaking of how the Holy Spirit will testify to the truth that he has brought into the world. The Spirit will show how the world is in the wrong in three ways. It is in the wrong because it has missed the mark of 'life in all its fullness' through its failure to recognise Jesus. It is in the wrong about justice because the one whom it crucified has been vindicated by the Father. And it is wrong about judgement because God is putting the world right in a manner that overturns all of the things to which it has ceded sovereignty.

All of this means that truth-telling is a vital part of the calling of the Spirit-filled followers of Jesus Christ. The grace and truth that came into the world in Jesus Christ is further displayed through the love and the truthfulness lived and spoken out by his followers. Paul says something similar when he urges Christians to speak the truth in love (Ephesians 4.15). He also speaks of "setting forth the truth plainly" without secrecy, deception or distortion (2 Corinthians 4.2). This is the basis of the prophetic calling of the church as, through its actions and words, the followers of Jesus speak truth about God and the world using the paradigm of creation, judgement and new creation. Christians are called to speak truthfully of the goodness of the world that God made but also, equally truthfully, of the ways in which the world has become corrupted and lost its way. But this will always be followed by equally truthful words and actions that point to God's new creation and the supreme truth of how God's love in Jesus Christ disarms and defeats the power of evil.

This involves followers of Jesus having the courage to confront the surrounding world with the faith that the Spirit will provide the words of truth that need to be spoken at that moment (Matthew 10.19-20; Mark

13.11; Luke 12.12; Ephesians 6.19). An important aspect of this is that those through whom the Spirit of truth speaks will encounter a similar hostility from the world to that received by Jesus (John 15.26-27). All of this has important implications for the church which, long before its accommodation to modernism, was tempted to downplay its calling to speak truth to power. What the world needs now – particularly in the West with its mixture of confusion and continuing deep desire for truth – is churches having the courage to speak and live out the truth of God as creator, judge and the bringer of new creation.

But this calling to truth telling – and again especially relevant to our context – is given so that the church will speak the truth to itself as well. The epistles in the New Testament exist because the apostles were called to speak God's truth to the church through precisely the same paradigm of creation, judgement and new creation. Paul makes it clear that this calling to speak the truth and to call one another to account is extended to every member of the church, declaring: 'Let the word of Christ dwell in you richly as you teach and admonish one another in all wisdom…' (Colossians 3.16).

Like every part of the work of the Holy Spirit, the calling of the church to 'speak the truth in love' is eschatological in its nature – i.e. it is given to bring part of God's future into the present. The Bible is clear that one day the nature of everything in this world will be fully exposed – that God's judgement will be an encounter with truth. This particularly extends to the work of the church which will be brought fully into the light in a manner that will "test the quality of each person's work" and reveal whether it has been built with "gold, silver" and "costly stones" or "wood, hay and straw" (1 Corinthians 3.11-15). Prophecy, as already mentioned several times in this book, will always be partial in its vision and part of how for now "we see but a poor reflection, as in a mirror". Like other aspects of the Spirit's ministry, the calling to such courageous truth telling will no longer be needed once we see "face to face", "know fully" and are 'fully known' (1 Corinthians 13.12). But it nonetheless has a vital present role in speaking the truth that reveals God's judgement as well as his redemption and restoration through the coming of his new creation.

The Challenge of Encounter with Divine Truthfulness

One of those who saw this with particular clarity was C.S. Lewis.[6] Within the Narnia stories, for instance, the interactions that its characters have with Aslan bear a strong resemblance to the encounters of Jesus with individuals in John's Gospel as they are summoned to an uncomfortable engagement with truth. With Edmund but also Peter in *The Lion, the Witch and the Wardrobe*, Eustace and Lucy in *The Voyage of the Dawn Treader*, Aravis in *The Horse and His Boy*, Digory in *The Magician's Nephew* and Puzzle in *The Last Battle*, Aslan leads all of these characters to an honest engagement with what they have done and its consequences. Aslan represents the presence of complete truthfulness as his silent gaze, in response to attempts at evasion or excuses for wrong conduct, eventually leads to these actions being confessed, resulting in forgiveness and restoration. Rowan Williams comments that Lewis wants to lead his readers to prosaic honesty through developing the habit of undeceiving ourselves. He further comments that "most often this is allowing ourselves to see what we already know, at a level we try to ignore."[7]

But the stories also make clear how painful and difficult this process is, with some remaining imprisoned within their self-deceit. Examples of this include Uncle Andrew in *The Magician's Nephew* and the dwarfs in *The Last Battle*. Fear and the desire for self-protection at all costs leads these characters to remain trapped within a wilful denial of reality. They lose the ability to hear Aslan's voice or acknowledge the reality of the new world that they have experienced or that stands before them.

Relationship with the divine truthfulness represented by Aslan/Jesus Christ is therefore presented as the path to the new creation. What determines whether people can follow this path is whether they are seeking the truth and can therefore bear the fear and pain of Aslan's silent gaze through which everything is unmasked. This priority is seen in Aslan's acceptance of the Calormen soldier called Emeth (the Hebrew word for 'truth') who thought he had served the false god Tash but, through his quest for truth, had really served Aslan. The journey towards the new world is thus presented as the tough and demanding process of allowing Aslan to strip away the untruthful versions of reality that serve to enslave, so that the truth of the new world can then be accepted and experienced in an ever-deepening story 'which goes on forever: in which every chapter is better than the one before.' [8]

The challenge currently facing the Church of England is that of embarking upon a similarly painful and challenging engagement with divine truthfulness. There needs to be a willingness to allow the Jesus Christ whom we claim to follow to strip away the deeply untruthful narratives which the Church of England has adopted in its fear and its desire for self-preservation and survival at all costs. Like the characters in the Narnia stories, this will involve an honest engagement with the church's actions and non-actions and the deeply damaging consequences of this. The most demanding part of this process is overcoming the fear of the 'death to self', or in this case the 'death to the institution', that this involves. For it will, undoubtedly, involve the death of much of what many presently hold dear within the Church of England.

However, time and again in the Narnia stories, and other works of Lewis such as *The Screwtape Letters*, we see death presented as not the worst thing that can happen. This is because the key factor leading to God's eternal life and the reality of his new creation is the willingness to put our fears and quest for survival aside, through allowing Jesus Christ/the Holy Spirit to 'lead us into all truth'. Everything that is real and solid in our present experience – supremely the ultimate truth represented in self-giving love – will form part of this future with everything that is false, untrue or only ever intended to be temporary, falling away (1 Corinthians 3.10-15, 13.1-13). Belief in the reality of the resurrection of Jesus Christ and the new creation is therefore meant to banish the fears that have imprisoned the church for too long within a false and damaging perception of reality and guide the whole of our agenda (1 Corinthians 15). The great prize that should encourage the church to persist in this 'encounter with divine truthfulness' is the greater experience of the joy and richness of God's new creation that the willingness to go on this journey with Jesus Christ always then brings.[9]

9 / TOUGH ON SAFEGUARDING, TOUGH ON THE CAUSES OF SAFEGUARDING

What follows, therefore, are practical suggestions about how truth can and must be taken more seriously within the Church of England if we are going to change the culture that has had such disastrous consequences. It will be apparent in every area that being prepared to recognise truth is a vital first stage, followed by the second of allowing truth claims to be both spoken and discussed. It is only when these occur that the third vital stage of implementing change in the light of this truth can happen. In line with the earlier sections of this book, the issue will be looked at in its broadest application before reference is then made back to safeguarding and how such cultural changes will result in the response to this then becoming radically different.[10]

BUILDING A CULTURE OF TRUTHFULNESS WITHIN LOCAL CHURCHES

We begin here partly because the author is a vicar and doesn't want to be seen as laying all the blame on bishops and diocesan structures! But it is also because local churches provide most people with their experience of the Church of England and represent an area where a greater embracing of (and confidence in) truth is needed. If this change can occur, it will not only revitalise the ministry and mission of these churches but have a dramatic impact upon the effectiveness of their safeguarding.

TRUTH ABOUT RELEVANCE

This is perhaps the most important place to start. One of the hardest questions for clergy and congregations within the Church of England to ask, let alone seek the truth about, is their relevance to the surrounding population. The church is meant to be the body of Christ continuing his work on earth, with a particular calling to be his ambassadors to the surrounding world (2 Corinthians 5.20). There are many wonderful examples of this happening, with just one of the best recent developments being the growth of winter night shelters for people who are homeless. These are held overwhelmingly in churches. The most heroic examples of such ministry are often in relatively small churches with an astonishing degree of faith and fortitude being displayed. Plenty of other examples of similarly faithful and inspiring ministry by local churches could be cited, with one of the most notable examples of this in recent times being Messy Church. Many older Christians show astonishing degrees of commitment to schemes such as 'Open the Book' assemblies in local schools or active love and care for others through clubs for people at their churches. All of this is rightly praised and valued. But it also faces the danger of being used to suggest that this sort of dynamic relevance in local churches is common.

Honesty requires mention of the other side of the picture and the numerous Church of England churches where any relevance to their local community is either negligible or non-existent. The characteristics are all too common: an ageing and dwindling congregation within an increasingly unsuitable and unsustainable building with insecure clergy uncomfortably aware that even the faithful attend the church more through habit or for reasons other than being nourished there by the exciting, dynamic and utterly relevant reality of God. This is not to say that those attending do not find a certain reassuring peace by coming to their church. However even this is often because of its detachment from a changing world rather than because it represents any sort of helpful engagement with it.

None of this is meant to be harsh, judgemental or negative. It is simply an appeal for greater honesty about this question and truthfulness in response to it. In fact, clergy simply allowing the question to be asked and then discussed is usually a crucial moment for churches. This can and does lead to a greater clarity about how the gifts that God has always given to its members can have their proper impact upon the locality. Allowing the question of relevance to be raised and discussed will also bring immense blessings to the existing members because the ministry of the church will then have to make some sort of attempt to respond to their needs. For churches unused to such honesty being expressed, this will represent a seismic shift in culture but a vital one for all of the reasons outlined in this book.

9 / TOUGH ON SAFEGUARDING, TOUGH ON THE CAUSES OF SAFEGUARDING

Truth about Power

Once unleashed, such honesty needs to move into other even more uncomfortable areas of church life. One of the most vital questions for churches to ask (with vital implications for safeguarding) concerns those who hold the greatest and the least power within them. This is found by asking who those people are whose opinions carry most weight in the church and need to be 'onside' if any change is able to happen within it? The swiftest path to the answer here is often found by asking who are the people most feared within the church – by the congregation and by the vicar? A vital corollary to this question is identifying which people connected with the church have the least amount of power? What are the signs of this?

A really brave church will then proceed to ask even deeper questions about how power is commonly exercised within the church. This might be found by asking how power is used by those who hold most of this? What effect does this have upon the church's mission and ministry? Perhaps the most vital question of all to ask is what reactions and behaviours do we see within the church when the status quo and existing balance of power within it is threatened?

Any discussion about power within the church will include searching questions about the use of the church's resources and for whose benefit most of these resources are usually being deployed. Priority in terms of the use of church buildings, for instance, is often based upon purely historical factors and fear of challenging those who currently possess power in the church, rather than any honest evaluation of how these buildings are best used to serve the ministry and mission of the church. Another area where questions should be asked in church life is in terms of its use of financial resources. Many Church of England churches spend more of their budget each year on flowers than on any provision for children and young people. If this is the case, asking honest questions about what this fact reveals is a vital stage in the process of addressing the imbalance of power that it represents.

Once questions about power are pressed within churches they should eventually become theological or more specifically ecclesiological in their focus. Infant baptism is practised throughout the Church of England but with hardly any reflection about what this should then mean in terms of the status and power of those baptised. As I have argued elsewhere, for infant baptism to be practised with proper integrity, churches must accord all those who are baptised the status of full members of that church.[11] The fact that baptised children are often treated instead as, at best, 'members of the church in waiting' is telling when it comes to asking why they are so frequently and disproportionately the victims of safeguarding abuses. Churches need to think through the practical implications of Paul's statement about baptism and its significance in Galatians 3.27-28 and what needs to change about the power structures within their community in the light of this.

Truth about Behaviour

This is closely connected with questions about power. In Chapter 6 we saw that, within many churches, completely different standards can often exist in terms of the behaviour expected of different people within the church. This perspective is often so entrenched that it is barely recognised. Children and those more marginal to church life can be held to quite rigorous standards of behaviour. Meanwhile established, longer-term and 'respectable' members of the church, particularly when any threat occurs to their power, frequently get away with behaviour that should be seen as outrageous.

Truthfulness about such behaviour in churches should not exclude compassion. In fact, compassion requires truth in order for the behaviour to be understood and properly responded to. One of the greatest contributors to men behaving badly in church life, for instance, is their feelings of loneliness or disempowerment in the wider world. Those who have been made redundant or have seen their hopes disappointed in other ways can sometimes, largely unconsciously, see their church as the place that can compensate for this with consequent expectations about the power they seek to wield. Poor behaviour by women in churches can be similarly complex in its causation.

Able women, in particular, who may in the past have been frustrated by their lack of access to power and influence in church life, may seek power in inappropriate ways. This is the reason why traditional areas of female influence within churches such as the running of the church kitchen, the organisation of 'the flower rota' and even children's ministry can become areas of such tyranny and unreasonable behaviour. They also become largely unaccountable with nervous, male clergy, in particular, seeing and sometimes even stating that it is more than their life is worth to try and resolve this!

A recurring theme of this book has been the way in which a great deal of the habitual practice within the Church of England appears to work as a means of maintaining the institution but is disastrous for its ministry and mission and catastrophic for its safeguarding. Allowing questions to be asked in church life about power and behaviour will definitely bring short-term instability into local churches. If such questions have never been asked, this instability will extend for a longer period, and often this will be presented as then placing any actual or potential ministry and mission of the church in jeopardy. The reality is the precise opposite. Such questions are indispensable for churches if they are to avoid being clubs or cliques and become genuine communities of relevant ministry and mission, with care and safeguarding for the most vulnerable at their centre.

The gains here will be in every direction. Poorly behaved adults, just as much as children, are being neglected when their behaviour is ignored rather than responded to appropriately. Developing a greater culture of honesty within churches about poor behaviour and its impact is the indispensable first step towards those who display this receiving the support and help that they need. Plenty of resources are now emerging to help with this, including the books by Peter Scazzero.[12] Many of those who most need such help will, of course, be most closed off to acknowledging this. But this is where establishing a culture of honesty is so important with clergy and other leaders of churches needing to work hard to change the culture, usually through displaying a greater emotional honesty and openness themselves. Pastoral care of those displaying poor behaviour is obviously of crucial importance within any Christian community. But this begins with honesty about the impact of such behaviour both upon others within that community and also the detrimental impact upon its calling to wider ministry and mission.

Truth about Competence

This is another related area where honesty in churches is urgently needed. The culture of evasion discussed in Chapter 3 means that within many churches no one is prepared to confront issues of basic competence. The writer of the comedy *Only Fools and Horses*, John Sullivan, also wrote a 'spin-off' called *The Green Green Grass*.[13] Part of the humour of the programme was derived from a situation where the key employees on the farm were all so settled there that no expectation existed whatsoever that they would actually do the work indicated by their job titles. As is often the case in comedy, the dysfunctional scenario was of course exaggerated. But it bore a disturbing similarity to some churches, with vergers/caretakers, administrators, youth workers and children's workers often performing at an extremely poor level and without anyone holding them to account for this. The cause of this is once again the fear about dealing with anything difficult. This factor is made worse in churches by the way that responding to such problems is regularly spiritualised away. Challenging problems of, for instance, poor performance is presented as somehow 'unchristian'.[14]

Honesty and truthfulness in this matter are essential for all concerned. This includes fairness to those whose performance needs to be challenged because a common scenario is one where endless toleration of a church employee suddenly gives way to their dismissal. Building a culture of proper assertiveness in this regard starts with establishing really clear job descriptions and structures of accountability and review. This then needs to be followed by these structures being properly 'owned' by those with responsibility for their maintenance. Perhaps most crucially of all, the whole of the church – or at least its clergy, churchwardens and PCC – needs to take responsibility for actively supporting rather than undermining this culture of clarity and accountability. While creating initial 'waves', all of this will head off many problems and potential problems at source and result in a far more secure, healthy and productive working situation than that present in many churches. More broadly, it will also contribute to the general atmosphere of honesty and openness that is so crucial for churches to possess if they are ever going to be communities that practise proper safe-

9 / TOUGH ON SAFEGUARDING, TOUGH ON THE CAUSES OF SAFEGUARDING

guarding. One of the factors commonly preventing this is incompetence on the part of the vicar, whose inability to supervise others often relates to their own insecurity, isolation and lack of accountability and supervision. This will be further addressed in the sections below on the selection and training of clergy and the changes required of bishops and dioceses.

Before we turn from this area, an issue common to a number of evangelical churches needs to be addressed. This is the lack of honesty that can exist in terms of the missionaries that such churches may support and what is being achieved through their work. This is a sensitive subject with the potential to cause hurt and offence. Clearly there is some exceptional missionary work supported by such churches. It is also true that some mission takes place in such demanding circumstances that the outcome of such work should be measured with a care that avoids worldly perspectives and values. What is being challenged here, however, are situations where missionaries are so revered by their supporting churches that a completely uncritical attitude is taken towards their work. One of the tell-tale signs of this is when most of the information and prayer requests concern the missionary and their family rather than their actual mission, and where questions pressed about the latter meet with an evasive or annoyed response. Honesty is also needed about the extent to which such uncritical support and sometimes fervour for supporting overseas missionaries, might be understood as a distraction exercise by those least committed to the church becoming more missional in its locality. As said, this is a very sensitive area. But it is mentioned here because the author has seen too many examples in churches of a lack of candour about missionary work making a very significant contribution to a lack of truthfulness and honesty in the church overall.

The problem is that establishing a culture of truthfulness about competence and also relevance is impossible if it doesn't come from the top down. With many parish clergy and bishops deeply insecure about their personal status in regard to these issues, it is not surprising that they wish to avoid any searching questions. This is where questions of selection, training and supervision become vital and will be addressed later in this chapter.

Truth about Claim and Practice

Mention was made earlier in this book of the 'urban myths' that can spring up within churches. The point was made that, whilst appearing harmless, such stories can play a very significant role in establishing a culture of untruthfulness. The way of telling whether such stories need to be challenged is when a clear 'lesson', explicit or implicit, is attached to the story and if there is a person or grouping whose position or power is obviously benefitting because of the story continuing to be told. One of the strategies that can be helpfully used to combat this is when churches actually talk about their history with members being actively encouraged to give their views on it. The results of this are many, including a helpful diversity of perspectives, the prevention of one telling of its history becoming 'canonical' and the establishment of a greater spirit of truthfulness and honesty.

Closely related to this is allowing theological and ethical truth to be explored with much greater honesty in church life. Once again the author is speaking largely from an evangelical perspective in commenting on the lack of truthfulness that can be present within churches in this regard. Often there will be an official position taken on a certain issue which, in practice, is far from possessing consensus amongst congregation members. This has all sorts of applications but the one most relevant here is the major inconsistency between the official line of many evangelical churches on sexual ethics and the true opinion and practice of their members: particularly in terms of cohabitation and the appropriateness of sexual relationships outside of marriage. The debates over gay emancipation and more recently transgender issues have obscured a more basic shift that has taken place over the last generation. This is that many Christians, including many evangelicals, simply do not believe that the promotion of anything other than more or less full sexual freedom amongst young people, is realistic or perhaps even natural. Where this shows itself more than anywhere else is the 'blind eye' that Christian parents show to their children's conduct in this regard and the consequent loss of confidence about Christian truth more widely that this causes to these parents and their children.

9 / TOUGH ON SAFEGUARDING, TOUGH ON THE CAUSES OF SAFEGUARDING

The point here is not to bemoan this change in sexual ethics. Discussion of the rights and/or wrongs of this belongs elsewhere. The point here is the impact upon these churches of such a significant difference between what is officially believed and what is actually believed and practised and the culture of dishonesty and untruthfulness fostered by this. As with most dishonest cultures, the level of collusion occurring at this point is very deep with a vested interest on all sides in uncomfortable facts not being stated and/or truthfulness allowed to emerge. This is particularly damaging in evangelical churches, because of the very strong emphasis simultaneously being made about the importance of biblical truth.

The inconsistency here can be one of the major reasons why some young people who have grown up within such cultures reject the Christian faith of their parents with such vehemence. Others, sometimes within the same family, adopt a completely uncritical approach to such a faith, which perpetuates the avoidance of any difficult questions. Both results are tragic and avoidable. Particularly within cultures that claim to be evangelical, searching questions must be allowed, the existence (which does not necessarily mean the rightness) of divergence in the congregation acknowledged and confidence expressed about a collective desire to seek God's truth and what, if anything, needs to change in the light of this.

Truth about Fear

Many clergy and church members reading this will already be becoming fearful at the prospect of seeking truth about such matters. Some will be terrified at the prospect and will find all kinds of reasons for avoiding this challenge. But one of the very best questions that a church leader can ask is what makes them most nervous and why? In virtually every case, it is the prospect of having to deal with difficult issues with all the fallout that will then come their way. This explains why most clergy are committed to not allowing the most basic questions about church life to be asked. The one time that clergy have to do this is at the Annual Parochial Church Meeting, or APCM, which Church of England churches are required by law to hold each year. The agitation that many vicars feel about this meeting, and especially the opportunity that it provides for any and every question to be asked about church life, demonstrates the scale of the problem here. This of course has implications for the support of clergy and other church leaders, which will be addressed within what follows.

But this is where there is no substitute for clergy and other church leaders recognising that one of the most common injunctions in the Bible is about showing courage and resisting fear. This involves demonstrating in practical ways that we really do believe Jesus' words, that we hold to his teachings as the meaning of our discipleship, and that when we know and acknowledge the truth, *the truth will set us free* (John 8.31-32). Rather than restricting Jesus' reference here to the means of us gaining a purely personal and escapist salvation, we need to understand this truth as pointing to the fullest understanding of salvation: what makes God's new creation possible – including further liberation from all the effects of fear, sin and falsehood that damage and destroy life in the here and now. Once again it is important to stress that, on this side of the new creation being realised, such truth will not be fully revealed – that for now, to quote once again 1 Corinthians 13.12, "We see but a poor reflection, as in a mirror". But within this, Christians (and particularly clergy) need to be demonstrating that there is nothing to fear from seeking the truth because this truth is central to who Jesus Christ is, and the salvation, in all its many and wonderful forms, that is received through him.

How Safeguarding Changes when a Culture of Truth is Established in the Local Church

The last few sections have looked at establishing a culture of greater truthfulness within the local church on a fairly broad canvas. This is because, in line with the thesis of this book, no amount of good safeguarding procedures and practices will change anything while they remain embedded in a culture that is so geared towards creating and perpetuating the very problems these procedures and practices are claiming to address. If a general fear about upsetting the status quo exists within the church, and asking searching questions about church life is feared and avoided, this will inevitably shape the whole approach that the church takes to safeguarding. However, by the same token, the establishment of a greater culture of truthfulness and honesty will transform the state of safeguarding within the Church of England.

Much of this will be at the level of preventative safeguarding. This is most obviously true in terms of behaviour, since a culture that acts in response to unacceptable behaviour will send out all the right messages to potential abusers about it not being a soft touch. But at a deeper, crucial level, safeguarding will improve because congregations are no longer being trained by the culture to ignore or suppress their instincts when they see things that seem wrong. A culture of collective responsibility will have been established instead, with congregation members actively encouraged to ask searching questions about everything within church life and with clergy expressing how important it is for the church to be questioned and kept accountable. This will require a major shift within the mindset of clergy. It will have implications for selection, training and supervision, as we shall see.

The development of such a renewed culture will also shape the church's selection of safeguarding officers. As well as clergy and PCCs being required to acknowledge their safeguarding responsibilities, congregations within the Church of England are now required to have a Parish Safeguarding Officer, with good practice further stipulating that they should also have a deputy. In most churches, this position is given to whoever is most keen to possess the role. This is problematic because, within the culture as it currently exists, people are often motivated by a fear of truth and a strong desire to contain it and protect the status quo. The fact that this agenda is unstated and largely subconscious makes it particularly difficult to prevent. But there can also be deeper problems with those seeking the role of Parish Safeguarding Officer actively wanting the sort of illegitimate power within church life, referred to earlier. It was after unfortunate experiences of people in this role that one of my churchwardens said that, as with those wanting to be rugby referees, anyone seeking the post of Parish Safeguarding Officer should be automatically barred from it! What we eventually discovered was that those best suited to the role of Parish Safeguarding Officer were people with other key responsibilities in church life. This meant that they were not defined by the role and were less likely to draw status and inappropriate power from it. Just as crucial were the criteria of candidates being invested in solving rather than avoiding problems within church life, and being committed to its wider ministry and mission.

Building a Culture of Truthfulness within Clergy Recruitment, Selection and Training

While local churches retain cultures independent of their leadership, the changes necessary within these cultures will rarely occur without a key role being played by the clergy. For this to happen, a completely new breed of clergy needs to emerge, developed by a system far more committed to encouraging courage and truthfulness.

Reforming Clergy Recruitment and Selection

This needs to become much more rigorous. One of the strengths of clergy selection at present is the emphasis rightly placed upon identifying those with unprocessed 'baggage', because of the pastoral damage to others that can result from this. What needs just as much attention is evidence that potential clergy will seek to confront problems and difficulties rather than avoid dealing with them. Obviously the manner in which such problems and difficulties are confronted is crucial, with the wrong sort of approach carrying the potential to make matters worse. Arguably, however, ensuring that clergy will take the right approach to resolving problems and difficulties should come within the orbit of clergy training – both within their college/course training and then within their curacy. Once the principle of confronting rather than evading problems and difficulties is accepted, effective training of the clergy will be about the best way to do this. Over the 6-7 years set aside for their training, this should not be difficult. What is difficult, perhaps impossible, is to create that basic desire to confront rather than evade problems. This is why it is so crucial that it becomes an element within the criteria for clergy selection.

The test for this would look for evidence of capability. Candidates for ordination should be expected to speak about a problem or difficulty, particularly within a work context, and how they approached it. They should be expected to be able to talk about the fears that dealing with such problems provoked, and how they dealt with these fears. Vitally, they should be asked about the role that their Christian faith played in their thinking and approach, and the various tensions within them that this may have created. Rather than looking for a perfect response to these situations, selectors should be looking for evidence of lessons learned from past experiences and, in particular, a current emotional readiness on the part of the candidate to confront problems rather than hide from them. When it comes to assessing candidates' aptitude for confronting issues in the future, tests should be constructed that reveal their actual or potential weaknesses. This can and should include those prone to being too 'gung-ho', as well as those whose danger lies in the opposite direction. If candidates proceed to training for ordination, these assessments can then be shared with them, so that their response and an expectation of progress form an important part of their preparation for future ministry.

Reforming Clergy Training

A major problem here is the serious level of dysfunctionality present within institutions responsible for training clergy. As mentioned earlier, this is demonstrated by the fairly regular scandals that afflict theological colleges within the Church of England, often accompanied by shady pay-offs and NDAs. It is common to hear such colleges and courses spoken of as places committed to the spiritual formation of ordinands, as well as their training for ministry. This makes it particularly important that these institutions are communities where the truth is honestly stated about problems and difficulties and the approach being taken to deal with them. Rather like the Church of England overall, the factor usually preventing such honesty in theological colleges and courses is fear about the reputation of the institution and the potential damage to its ministry. In the long term, openness will actually bring the precise opposite, with confidence in the institution's integrity and an appropriate sympathy for its problems built up by such honesty. Crucially, ordinands will also see an honest engagement with problems and difficulties as the courageous but right approach to take.

Another important issue here is the staff within such institutions. Reference was made in Chapter 3 to the 'Captain Darling' characters prevalent within diocesan structures: people who have little or no parish experience and who are invested in keeping their distance from such posts. Sadly, such attitudes are found in even greater numbers within the theological and ministerial educational institutions that train ordinands. There is a great deal of investment, largely subconscious, in the system that has facilitated their retreat from 'front-line service'. One of the problems here is the growth in an expectation that ministerial tutors should possess PhDs rather than ministerial experience, leading to a significant gulf between those who 'do ministry' and those who train them for this task. A shift is needed here, with more clergy within theological education being people who have spent significant time within parish ministry and who are committed to returning to it, or perhaps doing both at the same time. While many colleges and courses do presently have a 'tutor in ministry' who might tick these boxes, the ethos that makes such positions necessary should change; all tutors should be 'tutors in ministry'. During their two or three years of training, ordinands need to be taught and helped in their spiritual formation by a good number of tutors who have a track record of confronting difficulties and problems within parish ministry and who can therefore speak honestly of their successes and failures in this regard. The presence of those invested in avoiding such settings should be the exception rather than the norm.

This is particularly important, because much of the focus of such ministerial training should be upon the difference made by biblical theology to the very practical task of leading a church and especially confronting its problems and difficulties. During their training, ordinands need to be prepared, not just for the problems that will confront them in parish life but the overwhelming pressure they will face to avoid dealing with these problems. The proper integration of theology with ministerial practice is crucial here. Honesty about the frequent personal cost to clergy of 'doing the right thing' can then be combined with a theological emphasis on 'death to self' followed by 'resurrection life' that encourages future clergy to experience and nurture the courage they will need. This training should be integrated into the assessment of ordinands that took place during their selection process, so that they are encouraged to think about their natural tendencies when it comes to handling difficulties or conflict, and the temptations they will most often need to resist. No type of training is foolproof, but such an approach will add much greater honesty, realism and theological wisdom to the present emphasis on safeguarding processes and procedures. Nothing can guarantee that clergy will make the right choices when confronted with safeguarding situations and issues. But the aim should nonetheless be to produce clergy who are able to recognise the right and wrong choices in front of them in such situations, rather than being able to plead ignorance about this.

Reforming Curacies

All of this then needs to be reinforced during the four-year curacy that follows. The curacy should be one of the greatest strengths within the Church of England, with a wise and experienced training incumbent taking the curate through the situations that arise in parish life and being committed to a process where both learn and progress together. As already mentioned, many curacies represent the opposite of this, partly as a result of the motives that lead dioceses to allocate curates. Curates are meant to be allocated to parishes on the basis of the availability of accommodation, the training potential of the parish and, most importantly, the training ability of the incumbent. In reality, they are used as a reward for clergy prepared to take on roles that prop up the diocese as an institution – such as area deans and others. Little evaluation takes place of even the most disastrous curacies, enabling the suitability of training incumbents to go largely unquestioned.

All of this needs to be swept aside. We need training incumbents who see it as their aim to grow curates who will be, among other things, confident about dealing decisively and clearly with problems and difficulties rather than evading them. Lessons should be learned from other areas of life, such as the army and business, about how such skills and confidence are to be encouraged. Crucially, and to head off the lazy accusation that the development of such skills belongs to a 'secular management mindset', a good amount of theological work should be done to demonstrate the firmly biblical basis of such an approach. As part of their Initial Ministerial Education, curates should be expected to log the problems and difficulties that occur within their parish, how these issues are dealt with and their evaluation of these responses. Part of their IME should be a focus on the theological principles involved, and where they should find the support needed to help them to be courageous rather than cowardly in their future ministry.

Some of those reading this will see such proposals as hopelessly idealistic. They certainly are aiming high, but it is only through being clear about the ideal that we will come close to making the progress desperately needed. The aim should be to produce clergy for our parishes that seek to be appropriately courageous and proactive in the face of problems, rather than evading them through 'the Pac-Man approach to leadership' described in Chapter 3. The benefits of such a cultural change will surely be immense in all areas of the church's ministry and mission.

How Safeguarding Will Change Once Clergy Selection and Training is Reformed

The differences that will occur as a result of such changes should not be exaggerated. Once they are in their parishes and immersed in practice rather than theory, clergy will continue to face the temptation to avoid dealing with anything that will make their lives more difficult. The temptation will also continue to spiritualise away uncomfortable issues and to suggest that doing nothing is a credible and even godly action. But, particularly when it comes to safeguarding issues, the crucial change will be the much greater extent to which the internal voice or conscience of these clergy will tell them that such avoidance is cowardly, dangerous and wrong. Concrete examples discussed during their training will come to mind and, especially in emotional terms, make 'doing nothing' in the face of actual or potential safeguarding situations less easy. These clergy must, of course, be encouraged by their bishops, archdeacons and diocesan safeguarding officers when they show such courage rather than being rebuked or punished for being proactive, and this is where change to the culture of dioceses is desperately needed.

Building a Culture of Greater Truthfulness Within Dioceses

This is perhaps the biggest challenge. The general public is largely unaware that the Church of England is an essentially diocesan rather than a national organisation. This means that, in many ways, its dioceses are left to 'do their own thing'. This makes reform considerably more difficult. When, for instance, it was proposed a number of years ago that annual reviews should be mandatory for Church of England clergy, this was only accepted through the concession that each diocese should be allowed to construct its own review system. This 'solution' enabled some dioceses to 'tick the box' of clergy accountability while avoiding much of its reality. The culture of different dioceses within the Church of England can be very varied, with some of these cultures more problematic than others. None of them, however, are without very significant institutional problems which need to be reformed.

Dismantling Cultures of Patronage

This needs to be at the heart of any change. At present patronage is the major way bishops and others within diocesan structures exercise power. This is partly disguised by official use of the term being reserved for those (sometimes including the bishop) who hold the right to nominate potential clergy to parishes. A more significant patronage within the Church of England is the unofficial system of 'rewards' that bishops can bestow upon 'their' clergy. Mention has already been made of the way that the placement of curates (in direct contradiction of the official criteria for their allocation) is often done as a reward to those prepared to take on duties within the diocese, and the detrimental effect of this. Another reward involves appointing clergy as honorary canons of the cathedral. For insecure clergy, such status carries immense personal esteem and can serve as an effective screen for their ineffectiveness. Like the honours system used by politicians, the existence of such 'gongs', whatever their official justification, is both corrupt and corrupting, chiefly through their usefulness for both rewarding and encouraging conformity. If honorary canons can be found in the Church of England who have been willing to 'rock the boat' within their diocese and continue doing so after their appointment, they are a rare species indeed. As with so many of the factors examined in this book, such patronage is helpful for maintaining the Church of England as an institution, but at the heavy price of damaging its effectiveness and ultimately its safeguarding.

Part of the evidence for how deeply such patronage is embedded within the culture of Church of England dioceses is the upset expressed at any curtailment of this. Dioceses are under increasing pressure to have greater perspicuity over appointments to senior positions. This most obviously includes the proper advertisement of these posts. Such change is, at present, patchy and inconsistent. Much of it appears to be done to hold at bay any wholesale change. Listen carefully and it's not unusual to hear clergy in a diocese bemoaning the departure of 'the good old days' when a bishop would 'tap you on the shoulder' and suggest you come over for a coffee and 'a chat about your future'. What is being bemoaned here is the erosion of the comfortable 'club mentality' that ensured 'jobs for the boys'. The advent of women clergy might have been expected to improve this situation. However, with the continuation of the culture of male patronage, the vulnerability of women clergy within this culture has, if anything, made it worse.

Another example of this is the financial grants that dioceses can make to clergy. It may seem churlish to critique a system where clergy are given extra money to spend on, for instance, summer holidays. It is overly cynical to suggest that this is administered by bishops and their teams with any corrupt intent. In the majority of cases, perhaps all, it is sent with genuine concern for the welfare of its recipients and the hope that it will be part of renewing them. However, the effect of such a system, whether consciously intended or not, is to create a certain measure of debt owed by these recipients towards their bishops. This makes challenge more difficult. It is not uncommon to hear bishops being praised for having a personal manner that is 'disarming', with the assumption that such disarming is always positive. However, if the effect is that those with legitimate concerns and grievances feel less able to express them, it is very problematic.

The answer is, quite simply, to dismantle such patronage. All appointments within dioceses should be advertised and become completely transparent in their process. Grants to clergy should not be at the discretion of bishops and their teams, but should operate completely independently, with input from officers allowed in a manner conducive to complete scrutiny. The post of honorary canon has no legitimate justification and should be abolished. The path towards this will begin with clergy having the courage not only to refuse such 'gongs', but to be open and public about the reason for their decision. Once again, truthfulness about the nature and role of such 'honours' is the key thing here. When it comes to reforming curacies, such truthfulness is equally essential. Dioceses should be completely open about the basis on which incumbents and parishes have been selected to have curates, so that this reasoning can be fully examined and scrutinised. If the allocation of a curate can in any way appear to be a form of 'payback' to someone prepared to take on a job in the diocese, it should be made quite clear why this is not the case.

As ever, good theological work is the path to making and sustaining such change and showing its rightness. Biblical scholars are starting to recognise how much of the New Testament is very deliberately written to display the difference between the kingdom of God and the kingdoms of the world, specifically that of Rome. The Roman Empire rested from top to bottom on a system of patronage with interlocking patrons and clients at every level. Jesus was very clear that within the kingdom of God, power and authority is exercised in a manner totally different from this (e.g. Mark 10.35-45; Luke 22.24-30). Much of St Paul's letter to the Philippians is based upon a very similar contrast between what is involved in acknowledging that Jesus, rather than Caesar, is Lord of the world. Greater theological work needs to be done on scrutinising diocesan structures which are officially based upon the servant model of the kingdom of God while, in reality, they are far more based on the 'patrons and clients' model of Rome, with all the corruption and oppression that resulted from this.

Dismantling Diocesan Subcultures

Part of what will follow the dismantling of patronage within dioceses will be the lessening of the power of people who, in addition to those in senior positions, have sought to benefit from this culture. Within every diocese, as examined in Chapter 4, there are numerous 'Captain Darlings' – those with little aspiration to proceed to high office themselves, but who readily benefit from the culture of patronage by securing a 'cushy number'. Examples exist among clergy who, beyond their curacy, stay entirely within such diocesan roles – proceeding, for example, from being bishop's chaplain to a role like canon chancellor, to archdeacon, and then to bishop, without any experience of incumbency at all, and even when their suitability for each of these roles is widely questioned. This can also occur at a parish level, usually among clergy aspiring to such positions. Often doing remarkably little in their parishes, such clergy are able to gain prestigious titles and roles such as 'bishop's adviser on self-supporting ministry' or a place on the diocesan trustees. The effect of this is to solidify an unhealthy investment within dioceses as job and status-creating institutions, increasing both their dysfunctionality and their lack of scrutiny.

All of this should and must be swept away. The best way of working towards this outcome is doing away with continuous career tracks for non-parish 'staff officer' clergy. The most obvious of these would be the convention of clergy being required to return to a parish post after completing a diocesan one, with any exceptions to this having to be openly explained and justified. The issues here, as mentioned in Chapter 7, are complicated by the fact that diocesan posts are seen as 'safe spaces' for gay clergy. This issue will be addressed in the section below on changes needed

9 / TOUGH ON SAFEGUARDING, TOUGH ON THE CAUSES OF SAFEGUARDING

within the wider Church of England. Progress will also be made if there is greater truthfulness about the negative impact upon those clergy who spend much of their time occupying posts within the diocese. The results are, virtually always, low self-esteem and poor mental health brought about by the nagging awareness that they are feeding off the church, rather than contributing meaningfully to its ministry and mission. In the famous final episode of *Blackadder Goes Forth*, Captain Darling is finally sent to the front line. Part of the considerable pathos involved is the measure of redemption that Darling is receiving in resuming proper service, even when it involves his almost certain death.

Another aspect of this reform should be the abolition, or at least reform, of deanery synods. The point was made back in Chapter 4 that the bizarre nature of deanery synods means that membership of them is often only attractive to those anxious for status, to fill an otherwise empty evening, or as an easy way of getting onto a PCC. Frequently it is all three, resulting in such members remaining on PCCs for many years and, through their status in the diocesan structure, heavily invested in the status quo. If the continued existence of deanery synods is seen as necessary, a very significant change in reducing their problematic impact upon churches would be the removal of their members' automatic right to a seat on the PCC of their church. The frankness of the comments here may seem hurtful to those who have served on such synods for years. This is another example, however, of where 'niceness' and 'urbanity' should not be allowed to trump the basic truthfulness needed by dioceses and churches if they are to achieve any level of effectiveness in their ministry and mission.

Dismantling Cultures of Wilful Incompetence, Manipulation and Passive Aggression

As mentioned back in Chapters 3 and 4, the management of clergy within dioceses is frequently maintained by such means. The commonest form for this is the use of meetings where agendas are kept deliberately unclear to those intended to be 'managed' by this method. This approach is so entrenched within dioceses that bishops, archdeacons and other officers using such means are hardly aware that they are doing it. Even when the problematic nature of this approach and its consequences for eroding trust and effectiveness are pointed out, this is usually met with a mystified response that suggests no alternative exists. Much the same goes for poor communication, where clergy are deliberately kept in the dark and then suddenly confronted by a *fait accompli*. Another frequent tactic is that of 'divide and rule', whereby bishops and archdeacons refuse to manage situations of conflict between or within parishes. Disastrous in its undermining of effective mission and ministry, this is all-too-common as a means of preserving the church as an institution and maintaining its status quo.

We will move to the crucial issue of the selection of people suitable to be bishops in a moment. But a crucial part of the induction of both bishops and archdeacons should be a programme that points them to the temptation that will exist to use such tactics, and both the wrongness and danger involved in doing this. For existing bishops and archdeacons, repentance for the past use of such approaches should take place and a very clear and official renunciation made of such tactics. This should include the establishment of clear protocols about the proper conduct of meetings, with clear agendas sent out in good time and agreed notes being taken to ensure the accountability of those involved. Such protocols should also cover communication and the approaches that will be taken to resolve conflict. [15]

Should such change take place – and it will require an enormous shift in the culture of most dioceses in the Church of England to bring this about – the results of this will surely be immense. With a clear commitment to openness, bishops and archdeacons will start finding the respect that they crave from their clergy, but which so often seems to elude them. Much of the frustration, cynicism and eventual depression that afflicts many clergy will be cut off at source, even if this change in culture will be as much of an adaptation for them as their leaders. More crucially, much of the dysfunctionality impeding ministry and mission before it even starts, will be prevented. Most important of all, dioceses and their churches will start moving closer to being safe havens for those who are vulnerable, rather than those who would exploit and abuse them.

9 / Tough on Safeguarding, Tough on the Causes of Safeguarding

The Establishment of Proper Structures for Lay Accountability and Discipline

In Chapter 6 we saw how the Church of England has no effective structure of discipline for its lay members.[16] Liberals may most obviously applaud this aspect of the Church of England, but members across all of its traditions take advantage of it. Few would argue that this should change – until they open their eyes to the catastrophic impact that a message about lack of discipline and accountability among its members has for safeguarding.

Change will occur through having a proper and appropriate mechanism for the discipline of lay members of the church that is equivalent to the Clergy Discipline Measure. This could start by a simple code of behaviour which dioceses establish for their lay members, and to which churches and their members are invited to commit themselves. This could be expressed very positively, speaking in terms of standards of politeness, courtesy and kindness which few people could question in their appropriateness. The crucial addition to this would be an agreement to accept the discipline of the church in maintaining these standards, and the role of the diocese within this discipline.

Operating such a process could be completely in line with the principles spoken of by Jesus in Matthew 18.15-20. Within this passage we see a careful but clear movement from informal discussion about poor behaviour to the matters becoming formalised. Such a process would combine, at every stage, a desire to avoid escalation with the willingness to escalate matters if the problem remains unresolved. The final step would be the church being prepared to place that person, in sacramental terms, outside of its community. The point about excommunication made in Chapter 6 bears repeating. Despite its historical associations, such action is not about casting an offender 'into outer darkness'. It is instead a member's removal, hopefully temporarily, from full membership of the church community until they repent of their destructive behaviour and its impact upon that community. Needless to say, such a step should never be taken without absolute fairness, rigorous process and widespread consensus over the unacceptability of the continuing behaviour.

Once in place and properly established, the final form of such a process would rarely need to be used. In most cases, its earlier stages would be enough to make unacceptable behaviour able to be seen as such and, as a result, be discontinued. Crucially it would introduce, after a long absence, proper accountability for the behaviour of adult members of churches that causes so much disruption and dysfunctionality within them.

The writer can hear the screams of protest going up as some read these words. Even to mention the word 'discipline' in the context of church, let alone 'excommunication' can be made to appear utterly backward and barbaric. The only alternative, however, is the present 'free for all' in terms of adult behaviour in churches, with the message it gives out about churches being a completely soft touch. For such a process of lay discipline to work, it would require bravery on the part of all concerned, with complete 'buy-in' to the principle of responding to misbehaviour rather than ignoring it. This would require an enormous movement in the mindset of bishops and archdeacons. From doing their best to avoid dealing with problems, they would need to shift to recognising that they are in post precisely to deal with such matters. If this happens, the respect of clergy for their leaders, and their confidence in them, will grow enormously. Most crucially, it will establish a general atmosphere where church leaders know that ignoring difficult issues is always wrong and that to do 'the brave thing' in any situation (when accompanied by appropriate care and process) is virtually always to do 'the right thing' as well.

How Safeguarding Will Change When the Cultures of Dioceses are Reformed

If changes such as those set out above occur within the culture of dioceses, their combined implications for safeguarding will be immense. This is because all of these changes represent a decisive movement from the ethos of protecting an institution and affording illegitimate forms of 'protection' and 'safety' for those who cling to it most strongly. It is this that leads to the insecurity and fear that drives the pragmatism, secrecy, manipulation and passive aggression that so often mark the practice of the dioceses

9 / TOUGH ON SAFEGUARDING, TOUGH ON THE CAUSES OF SAFEGUARDING

within the Church of England and then has such a devastating impact upon their safeguarding.

With the sorts of changes outlined in this chapter, all of this will be replaced as dioceses become committed to bringing the light of God's grace and truth to bear upon every situation they encounter. Much of the impact of this upon safeguarding will be at a preventative level, as an atmosphere of openness, honesty and confidence about truth and its transforming power replaces the previous one of secrecy, duplicity and fear. Create a culture that has confidence about truth, and several things will then happen which all have important implications for safeguarding. Searching questions will be asked without fear of recrimination about any part of the status quo of the diocese that feels wrong. Diocesan positions will move from being hiding places for those fearful of truth to being places to which people gravitate if they wish to contribute to giving grace and truth its fullest expression within the diocese. Rather than being tolerated and even rewarded, poor behaviour at whatever level will be swiftly and decisively called to account in a way that demonstrates very clearly that churches are no longer soft touches for people who would bring harm to others.

Crucially, a different type of safeguarding officer will be appointed. Rather than anxious introverts with the unofficial brief to defuse as many difficult situations as possible, dioceses will start appointing safeguarding officers of a quite different calibre. A crucial characteristic of these officers will be a greater confidence about the power of truth and the determination to uncover it and expose everything to the light, however uncomfortable this may be. The present ethos of only acting in relation to safeguarding issues when it is unavoidable, and the institution of the church is under threat, will give way to the energetic desire to follow up on everything that smells bad and looks or feel suspicious in any way. The immediate fear of some is that anything like this will lead to a 'gung-ho' culture where false allegations can thrive and innocent people are victimised. A culture built upon asking searching questions and bringing everything into the light should actually produce the very opposite, because any allegations will have to be based upon clear evidence that is thoroughly and openly scrutinised. Once again it will be built upon total confidence that Jesus was right when he said "the truth will set you free".[17]

The horror with which some will respond to such suggestions shows how much dioceses within the Church of England have become places of secrecy and hiding – often telling themselves, with considerable irony, that this results in them being 'safe places'. Such cultures represent anything but genuine safety for those who are most vulnerable. It is a false form of safety even for those people that they are trying to protect. This is where we will inevitably need to return to the issues of sex explored in Chapter 7, and to the changes needed to the culture of the Church of England in overall terms if these factors are to be addressed.

Building a Culture of Truthfulness Within the Church of England as a Whole

While the Church of England is essentially diocesan in terms of its nature, a crucial role in changing its culture still exists at a national level. Crucial decisions need to be taken by the General Synod of the Church of England and its House of Bishops if the critical changes are to take place.

Honesty About the Impact of an Ethos of Survival-Based Pragmatism

Back in Chapter 3 the ethos of pragmatism at the heart of the Church of England was examined. Some of the reasons for the development of this ethos from the Elizabethan Settlement onwards were also suggested, although this by no means received comprehensive treatment. Many do regard this ethos as 'the genius of Anglicanism'. Given the extraordinary breadth within the Church of England, this characteristic has undoubtedly aided its survival. However, as repeated throughout this book, it is this very pragmatism and the survival-driven agenda behind it that has been disastrous for much of the ministry and mission of the Church of England and catastrophic for its safeguarding.

An urgent task of the Church of England is to re-examine, with complete honesty and openness, the negative impact of this ethos. Plenty of time and energy has been invested in recent times in the development of safeguarding procedures and processes which dioceses and churches now have to adopt. But given that 'culture eats strategy for breakfast', none of this will amount to anything without truthful scrutiny of the impact upon safeguarding (and probably numerous other areas of incompetence) played by the ethos of survival-driven pragmatism.

There have been efforts to name this problem in seeking to bring truth to bear upon other areas. In 2003 Tom Wright published *For All the Saints*, a short book in which he challenged the confusion reflected in the Church of England's liturgy with regard to those who had died. In one particular section, repeated on the book's back cover, he wrote: "We have been drifting into a muddle and a mess, putting together bits and pieces of traditions, ideas and practices in the hope that they will make sense. They don't. *There may be times when a typical Anglican fudge is a pleasant, chewy sort of thing, but this isn't one of them. It's time to think and speak clearly and decisively.*" (italics added) [18]

The final sentence here applies, with bells on, to safeguarding. Just as widespread repentance is now taking place about the impact of the British Empire upon those affected by slavery, so a similar repentance is needed for the devastation brought about by the survival-based pragmatism of the Church of England. Long before his resignation, Justin Welby regularly expressed shame about the Church of England with regard to the findings of the various reports into its safeguarding. The continuation of such rhetoric without any genuine change eventually compounded the pain and frustration of those involved. The repentance by the church that is now needed goes well beyond shame and regret. It requires a complete U-turn based upon the renunciation of an entire way of thinking and the adoption of a completely fresh one.

Fortunately, this does not involve singling out one particular tradition. Repentance is needed across the entire Church of England. This is because virtually all parts of the Church of England have colluded with this ethos through receiving its 'benefits'. This may seem a strange claim, given that conservative evangelicals have railed for decades against the Church of England and its liberalism. But while this has happened, many clergy and churches within this tradition have also exploited to the full the easy-going, survival-based ethos that has generally decided to 'let sleeping dogs lie' and allowed many conservative evangelical churches to (more or less) make their own rules. A direct line can be drawn between this and the safeguarding scandals that have afflicted this tradition. My own less conservative evangelical tradition is no less guilty of protesting against the woolliness of the Church of England, while exploiting the lack of accountability resulting from this. For those in the know, *Common Worship* can be painful reading for those aware of the moral compromises that accompanied the liturgical ones being inscribed within it. Within each tradition of the Church of England, work needs to be done on recognising the specific ways in which they have each benefitted from a pragmatic, survival-based ethos, and genuine repentance then expressed over the contribution that this has made to the church's disastrous safeguarding.

The most obvious sign of the repentance from survival-based pragmatism within the Church of England will be the appearance of a new type of bishop. At present, the system for selecting bishops is undoubtedly a thorough, careful and prayerful one. But the result of this process is one single characteristic overwhelmingly found in the bishops of the Church of England – disarming niceness. If anything, this has increased since the advent of women bishops, with most of them (understandably in the light of the opposition to their introduction) committed to being conciliatory rather than confrontational.[19]

The problem is that thoughtful confrontation is precisely what is needed when it comes to the cultural changes so badly needed within the Church of England. A completely different type of bishop is therefore needed if the church is to make the major cultural change that is now required, an issue which will be returned to as this book reaches its close.

Resolution of the Church's Wilful Inconsistency in Regard to Sexuality

Before this we need to turn once again to the single most controversial issue within the Church of England. And, if the argument of Chapter 7 is accepted, the cause of a great deal of disastrous handling of safeguarding by the Church of England. To recap and summarise, the Church of England has a policy in relation to homosexuality that is wilfully and irresponsibly ambiguous. In official terms, actively gay relationships are not consistent with the Church of England's position that sex belongs exclusively within the marriage of a man and a woman. In practice, such relationships, not least within the clergy of the Church of England, are actively endorsed and encouraged.

The argument of Chapter 7 is that this situation has had a disastrous effect on safeguarding. In specific terms, it means that any expressions of sexuality that exist outside of the Church of England's official position are completely unaccountable. In broader terms, it contributes to a general complacency about untruthfulness in regard to sex and relationships. The point, to reemphasise, is not that people who are gay are more likely to commit abuse. The evidence from outside of the church shows that this is patently not the case. The point is that the Church of England's wilfully dishonest policy in regard to sexuality directly contributes to the culture that has fostered abuse of all kinds and particularly the same-sex abuse (more specifically male-to-male abuse) disproportionately found within it.[20]

There are three basic options here. *The first option is to bring the practice into line with the official position.* This would involve the clear message that sexual relationships outside of heterosexual marriage are not permitted for clergy within the Church of England. While the law would make it difficult to remove someone from a post for this reason, it could be used to prevent clergy selection and appointments. If enforced, and even if it was impossible to remove clergy from their posts, this resolution would almost certainly lead to the resignation of a number of bishops (some of whom are in such relationships). While strong support for this would be found within the most conservative evangelical sections of the church, it would gain nothing beyond a tiny minority of support in overall terms. Within the majority of evangelical churches, let alone those of other traditions, the prevailing view is now that gay/homosexual relationships should be given complete equality with straight/heterosexual ones. For all sorts of reasons, the adoption of such a decision would effectively end what is left of the Church of England.

The second option is to bring the official position in line with current practice. This appears to be the option overwhelmingly favoured by the general public within the country, and the majority of churchgoers. This would involve the Church of England accepting and endorsing gay marriage. Some would present this as automatically solving the problem of unaccountability within the church's non-heterosexual clergy.

Matters, however, are considerably more complex. Gay relationships within the church have been unaccountable for so long that the sudden introduction of such accountability would appear completely intrusive. Partly because any questions about sexual conduct will seem inappropriate to those not used to this. But it is also because the official acceptance of gay relationships within the clergy will inevitably involve their greater regulation. Clergy in a gay sexual relationship, like their heterosexual counterparts, would in short be expected to get married. Whilst some would regard this as the 'holy grail' of gay emancipation, it is actually far from clear whether this would be welcomed by all, after years of gay clergy being left to their own devices. It would, in other words, be a massive and very challenging change for almost every section of the church to get used to, not least those clergy who are gay. This is the reason why, largely on the quiet and with considerable levels of dishonesty, the third option is probably still the most favoured one by those who currently lead the Church of England.

The third option is that the situation stays more or less as it is. In spite of the impression given by the most vocal advocates of gay emancipation within the church, there is a very heavy investment across the church in maintaining the existing approach to sexuality. However it was presented, the measure on same-sex blessings that General Synod passed in 2023 was, in reality, not so much about working towards the resolution of this complex issue as preserving the status quo in regard to it. This is why the bishops (in overall terms) were the only ones happy with it. Deeply uncomfortable about dealing with anything that would make their job more difficult, the measure satisfied their desire to 'kick the can down the road'. Shockingly, even if the catastrophic implications of the current handling of sexuality within the church for safeguarding are recognised, this is probably still not enough to disturb the complacency of its leaders.

9 / TOUGH ON SAFEGUARDING, TOUGH ON THE CAUSES OF SAFEGUARDING

It is easy to be judgemental about this approach. But in many ways, it is simply an extension of the mentality of the majority of middle-class Christians within the Western world, unwilling to open our eyes to the consequences for others of our comfortable lifestyle choices.

However, Option 3 is an intolerable one and must be recognised as such. Even without its consequences for safeguarding, it makes a complete mockery of the Christian claim to believe in truth. The crucial factor here, however, is its devastating effect – how the lack of sexual accountability for clergy within the Church of England has led to so many being abused on its watch. This simply has to change.

The only answer, therefore, is the proper implementation of Option 2. What is being proposed is obviously a huge change to the church's traditional understanding of marriage. For many, it will be shocking that this is being proposed by someone who considers himself to be an evangelical Christian committed to the authority of Scripture. Throughout most of my life, I have understood the only form of marriage sanctioned by God to be that between a man and a woman, with this partnership fundamental to human beings representing the image of God. I have now changed in this regard and fully support gay marriage. The process by which I have reached this conclusion, however, is significant.

It started with my recognition that nothing short of this will create a safe church. While still non-affirming of same-sex marriage, it became clear to me that addressing both the evil of abuse within the church and the church's inadequate response to this had to be the greatest priority. Once clear on this, I realised that endorsing same-sex marriage represented the only way of introducing proper accountability for the sexual behaviour of the church's clergy and addressing the devastating consequences of the long-term neglect of this. The motivation here was the thoroughly biblical one of placing the greatest priority upon the safety of those vulnerable people who must be the church's greatest concern (Matthew 25.31-46). For around a year, which included writing the bulk of this book, I took the view that my conservative position on the nature of marriage had to be subordinated to the church fulfilling its calling to protect people rather than wilfully sanction their harm.

Further change in my thinking, however, then followed. Realising that the position that I was advocating lacked intellectual coherence was a major factor. Another was the impact of a course on St Paul that I led at my church over eighteen months in 2022-24, which included a particular focus upon the cultural context of his writings. I had also been increasingly realising the destructive impact on gay Christians to be told that their every impulse for sexual intimacy is sinful – even when it is within a committed, faithful relationship. Seeing the earnest desire of these same people to follow Jesus and reflect his love for the church through the covenant bond of marriage made me realise the need to re-examine the biblical material on same-sex relationships.

All of this formed the background against which I read *God and the Gay Christian: The Biblical Case in Support of Same-Sex Relationships* by Matthew Vines. In this book Vines examines the biblical texts about same-sex relationships with meticulous care. He acknowledges that all of its references to same-sex sexual behaviour are negative. His key point, however, is that read with proper attention to the cultural context in which these texts were written, as well as to their language and literary context, such conduct is being rejected because it represents uncontrolled sexual excess and/or oppression. Vines also makes compelling points about the voluntary nature of celibacy within the Bible (see particularly Matthew 19.10-12; 1 Corinthians 7.9; 1 Timothy 4.1-5). He combines all this with showing how, given the sexual nature of human beings and the need within the vast majority for this to find expression, its repression within people incapable of being attracted to the opposite sex has had devastating consequences.

Vines, understandably, concentrates on the effect of this upon those who are gay, including heart-breaking stories of the loss of faith, depression, and suicide. Reading his book in the light of the safeguarding scandals of the Church of England makes it impossible to ignore the equally terrible devastation that the situation has brought upon many others as well. I remain convinced that the Bible presents marriage between a man and a woman as normative, archetypal, and unique in key aspects of its fruitfulness. Alongside this, however, I now believe that the supposed biblical case for the rejection of faithful and committed same-sex relationships is far weaker than the claims made about this. It is on this basis, and still led by my prior reflections on safeguarding, that I now see the church's endorsement of same-sex marriage as not only permissible but essential to creating a safe church.

As I have said, I am aware that many, including close friends and relatives, will be horrified at my change. This is not primarily a book about homosexuality. It is probably still right to share my view, however, that those who remain non-affirming of faithful and committed gay relationships need to, at the very least, admit the theological steps that are required to arrive at this position from the biblical texts that they have appealed to. Such an admission among those who remain conservative on same-sex relationships will bring a dramatic change of tone to the overall debate and hopefully encourage a similar change of tone within those committed to a revisionist agenda.

But my major appeal to those who remain non-affirming of same-sex relationships remains related to safeguarding. The likelihood that some of those reading this book will only be interested in my change in regard to homosexuality, points once again to the appalling complacency within much of the church about safeguarding. Back in Chapter 7, the illustration was used of the church's divisions in regard to sexuality resembling the stand-off between Russia and Austria-Hungary before the First World War. As decaying superpowers aware that their best days were behind them, these empires largely accepted the unsatisfactory status quo that existed in regard to their influence in the Balkans, reserving their energy for resisting any major 'slippage' in favour of their rivals. The point was made that, just as these insecure empires were indifferent to the fate of the Slav peoples caught in the middle of this power struggle, so the opposing sides on the sexuality debate within the Church of England appear indifferent to the safeguarding implications for people's lives of the church's current chaotic and unprincipled status quo in regard to sexuality.

Conservatives, in particular, need to be honest about how they have often been happier with the continuation of the status quo on sexuality than they would care to admit, with their greatest anxiety reserved for any change to the official position of the church rather than what actually happens in practice. The impact caused by the current status quo appears not to concern them and when I have talked to conservatives about the safeguarding implications of this situation, they have shown little interest. This may be because it is something that hasn't occurred to them before. But it is now time to engage with this reality and the utterly biblical principle of our care for the vulnerable being the most authentic guide to our faithfulness to Jesus Christ (Matthew 25.31-46). If conservatives see the endorsement of gay marriage by the church as a 'necessary evil' to prevent the much greater evil of abuse within that same church, then so be it.

If the outcome being proposed here does prevail, it is of the greatest importance that 'Anglican fudge' is no part of this, because if we end up with a mixture between Option 2 and Option 3, the result will be disastrous on every level. The introduction of same-sex blessings in February 2023 was misguided because it was a step in this direction. This is where the new breed of bishop talked about in the previous section is an indispensable part of managing such a seismic change. Speaking frankly, the current cohort of bishops is so invested in pragmatism and duplicity that, in most cases, they are simply incapable of exercising the leadership and courage that this major change to the status quo will require. With the best will in the world, most of them have simply not got it in them.

The Purge of Leaders Needed to Bring About Genuine Cultural Change

This is where the most dramatic change proposed in this chapter has its place. For many it will seem appalling in its extremity and ludicrous as a suggestion. But having thought about it as much as the proposal in the previous section and informed by virtually all of my experience since ordination, I sincerely believe that it represents the best and possibly only way of bringing the change needed to the culture of the Church of England. It can be illustrated by the key turning point of the English Civil War. This was in 1644-5 when, following years of military disasters largely caused by incompetent leadership, the Parliamentarian side decided that only a deeply radical solution would result in victory over the Royalists. This was

9 / TOUGH ON SAFEGUARDING, TOUGH ON THE CAUSES OF SAFEGUARDING

the famous 'Self-Denying Ordinance' passed by Parliament in April 1645, which required all MPs to relinquish their military commands. Given his military brilliance, an exception was made for Oliver Cromwell. The effect upon the culture was immediate with the New Model Army's dramatically different approach swiftly leading to victory.[21]

Given its catastrophic failure in regard to safeguarding and the role of its culture in facilitating this, all of the Church of England's current bishops should be reviewed as to their suitability to stay in office. A report in *The Church Times* in 2020 revealing that some thirty bishops and cathedral deans were being investigated for the mishandling of safeguarding issues, shows that this is far from an overreaction.[22] Such a clear-out of leaders is always one of the vital first steps in changing a culture. Some exceptions could and perhaps should be made for those bishops with obvious Cromwell-like brilliance who already stand distinct from the current ethos. But these exceptions will be few.

When I first drafted these words, long before November 2024, they looked ridiculously radical and impossibly idealistic. I kept returning to them, thinking that this book would lack credibility, unless they were deleted. Each time I was convinced of the need to retain them, chiefly through the necessity of such resignations if the practical changes contained in this chapter are to have any chance of occurring. I was further aware that the likelihood of such prophetic calls being ignored or ridiculed should not prevent them being made. The last thing I expected to occur before the publication of this book was the resignation of the Archbishop of Canterbury over a safeguarding matter and the widespread calls for other bishops to go as well. Such calls, for all those found to have suppressed safeguarding matters, are entirely correct. The resignation of Justin Welby will have a negative effect upon safeguarding if, by taking this action, he has 'taken one for the team'. A wider clear-out of the Church of England's senior leaders is desperately needed.[23]

It is an immensely radical solution, but desperate times call for desperate measures. To borrow the language coined during the Coronavirus crisis of 2020-21, a cultural 'circuit-breaker' is needed for the Church of England since, at present, most new bishops inevitably adopt the ethos

229

of the group that they are joining. The humility and courage required by the present bishops to resign their office would make an enormous impact upon the general public and demonstrate the church's repentance more clearly than any other action. These resignations should include, at the very least, all of those bishops found guilty of dealing inadequately with safeguarding issues. Another perhaps more vital step, would then be to deal with the numerous 'Sir Humphrey Appleby' figures present within the 'civil service' of the Church of England who essentially act as trustees of its culture.[24] It is important to note that some of those with the greatest knowledge of recent safeguarding scandals view the little-known, but highly influential, figures working at Lambeth Palace as the biggest problem in this regard.[25]

The extremity of these proposals should, at the very least, make those in power within the Church of England recognise that nothing other than the most wholesale change is needed for the church to regain its credibility. The incompetence that dare not speak its name must be banished for ever as the Church of England, in deep repentance, becomes committed instead to believing and acting on the basis of the liberating and transforming power of the truth revealed in Jesus Christ.

Select Bibliography

O'Grady, Ron, *The Hidden Shame of the Church: Sexual Abuse of Children and the Church* (WCC Publications, 2001).

Sue Atkinson, *Breaking the Chains of Abuse: A Practical Guide* (Lion Books, 2006).

Sue Atkinson, *Struggling to Forgive: Moving on From Trauma* (Monarch Books, 2014).

Fife, Janet and Gilo, *Letters to a Broken Church* (Ekklesia Publishing, 2019).

Rosie Harper and Alan Wilson, *To Heal and Not to Hurt: A Fresh Approach to Safeguarding in Church* (Darton, Longman and Todd, 2019).

Lisa Oakley and Justin Humphries, *Escaping the Maze of Spiritual Abuse. Creating Healthy Christian Cultures* (SPCK, 2019).

Rob Merchant, *Broken by Fear, Anchored in Hope: Faithfulness in an Age of Anxiety* (SPCK, 2020).

Fiona Gardiner, *Sex, Power, Control: Responding to Abuse in the Institutional Church* (Lutterworth Press, 2021).

Andrew Graystone, *Bleeding for Jesus: John Smyth and the Cult of Iwerne Camps* (Darton, Longman and Todd, 2021).

Julie MacFarlane, *Going Public: A Survivor's Journey from Grief to Action* (Between the Lines, 2021).

Marcus Honeysett, *Powerful Leaders: When Church Leadership Goes Wrong and How to Prevent It* (IVP, 2022).

Notes

PREFACE

1 'Published and be damned' is a phrase first attributed to the Duke of Wellington in 1824 when he was threatened with blackmail by his former mistress Harriette Wilson.
2 Keith Makin, *Independent Learning Lessons Review: John Smyth QC* (Church of England, November 2024).

CHAPTER 1

1 *Exposed: The Church's Darkest Secret* was originally broadcast on BBC2 in two episodes on 13th and 14th January 2020. It is now available on YouTube. See: https://www.youtube.com/watch?v=bNep7fCaj2g and https://www.youtube.com/watch?v=adoDCbr5_SA
2 *An Abuse of Faith: The Independent Peter Ball Review*, June 2017, was conducted by Dame Moira Gibb DBE and can be found at https://www.churchofengland.org/sites/default/files/2017-11/report-of-the-peter-ball-review-210617.pdf
3 *Exposed: The Church's Darkest Secret*, Episode 1.
4 *Ibid*
5 *Ibid*, Episode 2.
6 For more on Fulcrum, see: https://www.fulcrum-anglican.org.uk/
7 Interview on ITN News, 9th November 2012, https://www.itv.com/news/update/2012-11-09/rev-stephen-kuhrt-welby-will-be-credible-leader/
8 I was appointed Priest-in-Charge (Vicar Designate) in July 2007 because of the common practice of 'suspension of the benefice' while a new vicarage was being built. The construction of the vicarage encountered many delays but on its completion in September 2016, I was duly licensed and instituted as Vicar of New Malden and Coombe.
9 An earlier draft of this book reflected my view that it was unnecessary to refer to the person's name. Legal advice, however, confirmed the possibility of this leading to misidentification, hence the change.
10 Online articles related to my suspension and the issues surrounding it include two by my brother Jon Kuhrt on his blog *Grace and Truth: Faith, Transformation and Social Justice*. These were 'Whistleblow and the Sheep-guarders: a parable', https://gracetruth.

blog/2021/06/25/whistleblow-and-the-sheep-guarders-a-parable/ and 'A Tale of Two Vicars: One exploiting the status quo, the other challenging it'. See: https://gracetruth.blog/2021/10/06/a-tale-of-two-vicars-one-exploiting-the-status-quo-the-other-challenging-it/

11   'Betrayal of Trust: Lay preacher who fondled teenager is spared jail', by Alita Howe, *Kingston Guardian*, 23rd October 2008.

12   Those I shared the paper with included Andrew Graystone, an advocate for survivors of abuse within the Church of England and author of *Bleeding for Jesus* (Darton, Longman & Todd, 2021), a book about the mishandling of the abuse of John Smyth; Lee Furney, a key witness in the allegations about Jonathan Fletcher; and Janet Fife, co-editor of *Letters to a Broken Church* (Ekklesia Publishing, 2019), a collection of essays about safeguarding failures in the Church of England.

13   Statement by the Christ Church members of the PCC of New Malden and Coombe, June 2021. See: https://ccnm.org/files/pdf/PCC%20Statement%2024%20June%202021.pdf. This was reported in the *Church Times*, 31st July 2021, in an article by Madeleine Davies entitled 'PCC accuses Southwark diocese of "weaponising" safeguarding against its vicar'. See: https://www.churchtimes.co.uk/articles/2021/30-july/news/uk/pcc-accuses-southwark-diocese-of-weaponising-safeguarding-against-vicar

14   'The Power of the Internet to bring change in the Safeguarding World', by Stephen Parsons, on his blog *Surviving Church*: https://survivingchurch.org/2021/08/16/the-power-of-the-internet-to-bring-change-to-the-safeguarding-world/

15   While it is disappointing that my paper on safeguarding has never been engaged with, these supervision meetings with the Southwark DSA, Pamela Chisholm, have otherwise been excellent. This is chiefly because Pamela welcomes rather than closes down questions and discussion about safeguarding and is clearly committed to bringing about the necessary cultural change. My experience of the Deputy DSA, Rebecca O'Neill has also been excellent for similar reasons.

16   See *Letters to a Broken Church*, edited by Janet Fife and Gilo (Ekklesia Publishing, 2019).

17   'Gaslighting' is the subjective experience in which an individual's perception of reality is repeatedly undermined or questioned by another person through their constant repetition of an unsubstantiated narrative. Derived from the 1944 film *Gaslight*, this term appears to have entered colloquial English usage as recently as the mid-2010s.

18   My interview on GB News about my treatment by Southwark Diocese can be found on https://www.youtube.com/watch?v=rEz4R7WtG6o

19   See: https://gracetruth.blog/2024/11/10/why-justin-welby-must-resign-by-stephen-kuhrt/ This article then led to a number of TV interviews with Sky News https://www.youtube.com/watch?v=XM_Gjkqq5CA, GB News https://www.youtube.com/watch?v=KomCRIJcFyk and Channel 5 News https://www.youtube.com/watch?v=IiQ4xNuip8s

20   George Carey was Archbishop of Canterbury from 1991-2002.

21 Debates exist over whether Peter Drucker originated or popularised this phrase.
22 See Stephen Kuhrt, *Church Growth through the Full Welcome of Children: The Sssh Free Church* (Grove Books, 2009); *Tom Wright for Everyone: Putting the Theology of N.T. Wright into Practice in the Local Church* (SPCK, 2011); *Using Film with Older People* (Grove Books, 2012); *I Heard It Through the Grapevine: Developing a Social Mission Project within the Local Church* (Grove Books, 2014); 'Messy Church and the Challenge of Making Disciples' in Ian Paul (ed.) *Being Messy, Being Church: Exploring the Directions of Travel for Today's Church* (Bible Reading Fellowship, 2017); and, with Gordon Kuhrt, *Believing in Baptism: Understanding and Living God's Covenant Sign* (Bloomsbury, 2020). An exception to the positive nature of these writings was an article that I wrote called 'How to encourage bullying in the Church of England' published on Ian Paul's blog *Psephizo*, in October 2022 https://www.psephizo.com/psephizo/how-to-encourage-bullying-in-the-church/

CHAPTER 2

1 'It takes a village to raise a child' is commonly believed to be a conflation of several expressions, all of which originated in Africa
2 See Rosie Harper and Alan Wilson, *To Heal and Not to Hurt: A Fresh Approach to Safeguarding in the Church* (Darton, Longman & Todd, 2019).
3 The Lucy Faithfull Foundation is the only UK-wide charity dedicated solely to dealing with child abuse, including responding to abusers. See: https://www.lucyfaithfull.org.uk/
4 *Exposed: The Church's Darkest Secret*, Episode 2 and *An Abuse of Faith: The Independent Peter Ball Review*.
5 An independent lessons-learned review concerning Jonathan Fletcher and Emmanuel Wimbledon was published on 23rd March 2021. See: https://walkingwith.s3-eu-west-1.amazonaws.com/Final+Report+of+ECW+Review_March+2021.pdf
6 'Concerns about Canon Mike Pilavachi were voiced in 2004', *Church Times*, 8th June 2023. See: https://www.churchtimes.co.uk/articles/2023/9-june/news/uk/concerns-about-canon-mike-pilavachi-were-voiced-in-2004
7 A national expert on safeguarding, commenting in an address to ordinands at Wycliffe Hall, Oxford, 2001
8 'Poor bloody infantry' appears to have been coined during the First World War (1914-18), with the initials PBI used by an anonymous contributor to a magazine published by British soldiers called *The Wipers Times*.
9 Dietrich Bonhoeffer, *The Cost of Discipleship* (SCM Press, new edition, 2019)
10 *Ibid.*
11 N. T. Wright, *Evil and the Justice of God* (SPCK, 2006), pp. 1-20.
12 Martin Luther's understanding of *simul iustus et peccator* is expressed in greatest clarity in his *Lectures on Galatians* (1535), *Luther's Works*, Vol. 26, pp. 232-236.

NOTES

CHAPTER 3

1. Dave Walker's books include: *The Dave Walker Guide to the Church* (Canterbury Press 2006); *My Pew: Things I have seen from it* (Canterbury Press 2008); *The Exciting World of Churchgoing* (Canterbury Press 2010); *Heroes of the Coffee Rota* (Canterbury Press 2015); and *How to Avoid the Peace: Tips for Advanced Churchgoing* (Canterbury Press 2017); *Revenge of the Flower Arrangers* (Canterbury Press 2019).
2. Books about proper procedures and process at PCCs include Gordon Kuhrt, *A Handbook for Council and Committee Members: A Practical Guide to their Work* (Mowbrays, 1985) and John Pitchford, *An ABC for the PCC: A Handbook for Church Council Members* (Continuum, 2019).
3. Stephen Neill, *Anglicanism* (Pelican/Penguin, 1958), pp 395-398.
4. *Ibid*, p 397-8
5. See Tracy Borman, *Elizabeth's Women* (Vintage, 2010).
6. See Dairmaid MacCulloch, *Thomas Cranmer* (Yale University Press, 2016).
7. See David Gilmour, *The British in India: A Social History of the Raj* (Penguin, 2019) and Jon Wilson, *India Conquered: Britain's Raj and the Chaos of Empire* (Public Affairs, 2016).
8. Mike Marqusee, *Anyone But England: An Outsider Looks at English Cricket* (Aurum Press, 2005).
9. This illustration is not intended to disparage children with English as their second language, but purely to convey the problems of communication between those for whom language and culture are so different.
10. 'Women "to change C of E forever"' by Trevor Timpson, BBC website, 7th March 2009. http://news.bbc.co.uk/1/hi/uk/7916214.stm
11. In early 2021 there were 24 women bishops in the Church of England, with twelve of them married to a clergyman also ordained within it.
12. The term 'girls' is used here simply because it is the counterpart of 'boys'. 'Women' is, of course, the proper term that should be used.
13. The best recent account of the D'Oliveira affair is found in Peter Oborne, *Basil D'Oliveira: Cricket and Conspiracy: The Untold Story* (Time Warner, 2004), with pp 191-3 particularly insightful on the personality of Colin Cowdrey. Interestingly, Oborne is married to a vicar in the Church of England.
14. David Hopps, *A Century of Great Cricket Quotes* (Robson Books Ltd, 2000), p 201.
15. https://www.espncricinfo.com/england/content/player/13340.html

CHAPTER 4

1. More polite alternatives to the term 'cock-up' were considered but its ubiquitous use for something inadvertently done badly/disastrously and its frequent juxtaposition against 'conspiracy' gave it a centrality to the main claim of this chapter.

2   Derek Nimmo starred as the Rev. Mervyn Noote in *All Gas and Gaiters* from 1966-71, Brother Dominic in *Oh Brother* from 1968-70 and Dean Selwyn Makepeace in *Hells Bells* in 1986. Frank Williams played the Rev. Timothy Farthing in *Dad's Army* from 1968-77 and Gerald Sim 'The Rector' in *To the Manor Born* from 1979-81.

3   Rowan Atkinson's roles as a clergyman include several sketches in *Not the Nine O'Clock News* from 1979-82, Father Gerald in *Four Weddings and a Funeral* in 1994 and the Rev. Walter Goodfellow in *Keeping Mum* in 2005.

4   Various Church of England clergy appeared in *Only Fools and Horses* between 1981 and 2003: John Pennington played the vicar in *Christmas Trees* (1982) and who buries 'Grandad' in *Strained Relations* (1985), Rex Robinson the vicar in *Video Nasty* (1986), Angus MacKay the vicar in *The Frog's Legacy* (1987), and Treva Etienne the vicar who christens Damien in *Miami Twice* (1991). The Roman Catholic Father O'Keith was played by P.G. Stephens in *The Miracle of Peckham* (1986).

5   Dawn French starred as the Rev. Geraldine Granger in *The Vicar of Dibley* between 1994 and 2007, with some further short episodes, such as those shown during the Covid pandemic at Christmas 2020.

6   Tom Hollander starred as the Rev. Adam Smallbone in *Rev* between 2010 and 2014.

7   This phrase originates from George Whyte-Melville's 1858 novel *The Interpreters: A Tale of the War* about the author's experiences during the Crimean War.

8   *Yes Minister* and *Yes Prime Minister* ran from 1980-88. Hugh Grant's performance as diffident English 'chaps' include *Four Weddings and a Funeral* (1994), *Nine Months* (1995), *Mickey Blue Eyes* (1999), *Notting Hill* (1999) and *Music and Lyrics* (2007).

9   https://www.itv.com/news/update/2012-11-09/rev-stephen-kuhrt-welby-will-be-credible-leader/ and 'Archbishop's honesty and courage are truly remarkable' by Stephen Kuhrt, *The Sun*, 10th April 2016. The latter article included the following comments: "Whilst previous archbishops have sometimes struggled with their public profile, Welby has managed to convey the image of an ordinary human being, endeavouring to bring his Christian faith to bear upon the public and personal issues with which he has to deal… Rather than seeking to hide or sensationalise the story, the archbishop has used it as an opportunity to speak simply and clearly about the circumstances and express his solidarity with those whose lives have been affected by similar issues… He has also been clear that at the heart of his response is his firm belief in a God of love who enters into the mess and complexities of life in Jesus Christ to bring healing and hope. In a world full of pain and suffering, we can all be grateful for an archbishop able to embody this identification and show that the Church exists, not for those with perfect lives, but for everyone."

10 See particularly Stephen Kuhrt, *Church Growth through the Full Welcome of Children: The Sssh Free Church* and *I heard it through the Grapevine: Developing a Social Mission Project within the Local Church*

11 Bob Jackson, *Hope for the Church: Contemporary Strategies for Growth* (Church House Publishing, 2002) and *The Road to Growth: Towards a Thriving Church* (Church House Publishing, 2008).
12 Bob Jackson, *Hope for the Church: Contemporary Strategies for Growth,* p. 177.
13 Jon Kuhrt 'The Seven Deadly Sins of Managing People Badly' https://gracetruth.blog/2022/03/17/the-7-deadly-sins-of-managing-people-badly-2/
14 Colin Buchanan, *Anglo-Catholic Worship: An Evangelical Appreciation after 150 years* (Grove Books, 1983) p. 6, note 2.
15 See Jon Kuhrt, 'Women Bishops? I think the jury is still out on male bishops…' *Grace and Truth: Faith, Transformation and Social Justice* https://gracetruth.blog/2013/11/22/women-bishops-i-think-the-jury-is-still-out-on-male-bishops/
16 Captain Darling in *Blackadder Goes Forth,* from 1989, was played by Tim McInnerny.
17 A 'pyrrhic victory' is one that comes at such a cost that this outweighs any gains that might have been achieved. The expression refers to Pyrrhus, king of Epirus, who lost enormous numbers of his troops defeating the Romans in 279 BC.
18 *Exposed: The Church's Darkest Secret*, Episode 2.
19 *Ibid*.
20 This episode from *Yes Minister* was entitled 'The Compassionate Society', from 1981.
21 *The Office* starring Ricky Gervais as David Brent first appeared on the BBC from 2001-3.
22 Thirty-one *Carry On Films* were produced between 1958 and 1978 with another in 1992.

CHAPTER 5

1 *A Safe Church: Safeguarding Policy of Southwark Diocese.*
2 *Exposed: The Church's Darkest Secret* and *An Abuse of Faith: The Independent Peter Ball Review.*
3 See 'British Post Office Scandal' on Wikipedia: https://en.wikipedia.org/wiki/British_Post_Office_scandal
4 See my article 'Why Stephen Cottrell should resign as Archbishop of York', written after the revelations of his mishandling of the David Tudor case: https://safeguardingtheinstitution.com/2025/01/23/why-stephen-cottrell-should-resign-as-archbishop-of-york/
5 Proprietary Chapels originally belonged to private individuals but with the intention of being open to the public for worship. Able to have a Church of England clergyman licensed to them, they are somewhat anomalous, existing outside the parish system and, in the case of Emmanuel, Wimbledon, largely outside the financial structures of their diocese.
6 For some of the background to 'Nobody's Friends' see https://en.wikipedia.org/wiki/Nobody%27s_Friends

SAFEGUARDING THE INSTITUTION

7   The Greek word *koinonia*, central to early Christianity, and particularly significant within Paul's letter to the Philippians, needs several English words to catch the fullness of its meaning. It is therefore variously translated as 'partnership', 'fellowship' and 'community'.
8   See particularly N.T. Wright, *What St Paul Really Said* (Lion, 2003); *The Meaning of Jesus: Two Visions* (SPCK, 1999); *The Resurrection of the Son of God* (SPCK, 2003); *Paul: Fresh Perspectives* (SPCK, 2005) and *Paul and the Faithfulness of God* (SPCK, 2013).
9   Tom Holland, *Dominion: The Making of the Western Mind* (Abacus, 2020).
10 See N.T. Wright, *Luke for Everyone* (SPCK, 2001), pp. 20-24
11 See N.T. Wright, *What St Paul Really Said* (Lion, 2003), p. 57; *Paul: Fresh Perspectives* (SPCK, 2005), pp. 71-9 and *New Tasks for Renewed Church* (Hodder, 1992), p. 80.
12 *Ordinal* of the Church of England.
13 Rosie Harper and Alan Wilson, *To Heal and Not to Hurt* (Darton, Longman & Todd, 2019).
14 William Hazlitt, quoted in C.L.R. James, *Beyond a Boundary* (Yellow Jersey, 2005), p. 217.
15 See Desmond Tutu, *No Reconciliation without Forgiveness: A Personal Overview of South Africa's Truth and Reconciliation Commission* (Rider, 2000).
16 Jon Kuhrt and Chris Ward, *Grace and Truth with Homeless People* (Grove Books, 2013).
17 Stephen Kuhrt, *Church Growth through the Full Welcome of Children* (Grove Books, 2009).
18 This expression typically sums up the willingness to include unpleasant or unattractive aspects in a public presentation. Its origin is often attributed to Oliver Cromwell, Lord Protector of the Commonwealth of England, Scotland and Ireland in the 1650s, when speaking to the artist Sir Peter Lely about his desires for the latter's portrait of him.
19 See Chapter 1 note 21.
20 *Liar Liar,* starring Jim Carrey, appeared in 1997.
21 C.S. Lewis, *The Lion, the Witch and the Wardrobe* (Harper Collins, 1950), p. 89.

CHAPTER 6

1   See George Lings (ed), *Messy Church: Exploring the Significance of Messy Church for the Wider Church* (BRF, 2013); Lucy Moore and Jane Leadbetter, *Messy Church: Fresh Ideas for Building a Christ Centred Community* (Barnabas, 2006); Ian Paul (ed.), *Being Messy, Being Church: Exploring the Direction of Travel for Today's Church* (BRF, 2017).
2   Stephen Kuhrt, *Church Growth through the Full Welcome of Children: The Sssh Free Church* (Grove, 2009) and, with Gordon Kuhrt, Believing in *Baptism: Understanding and Living God's Covenant Sign* (Bloomsbury, 2020), particularly Chapters 9,11,14.
3   *The Parenting Children Course: For Those Parenting 0 to 10 year olds, Guest Manual* by Nicky and Sila Lee (Alpha International, 2011), Cpt 3, 'Setting Boundaries', pp 35-

46. See also their *The Parenting Teenagers Course: For Those Parenting 11 to 18 year olds, Guest Manual*, Cpt 3, 'Setting Boundaries', pp 31-43 (Alpha International, 2011).

4 Early in 2024, the establishment of procedures to respond to lay misbehaviour within churches was discussed at General Synod, with further progress on this expected to follow.

5 'Home groups' exist in many churches, where around eight to ten church members meet together to study the Bible, pray and support one another.

6 See Stephen Kuhrt, *I Heard It Through the Grapevine: Developing a Social Mission Project within the Local Church* (Grove, 2014).

7 The part of the Archdeacon Robert in *Rev* was played by Simon McBurney. He also played the choirmaster Cecil in four episodes of *The Vicar of Dibley*.

8 *Exposed: The Church's Darkest Secret*, Episode 1 and *An Abuse of Faith: The Independent Peter Ball Review*.

9 Ibid

CHAPTER 7

1 'Concubinage' is a term once commonly used to refer to a relationship possessing many of the characteristics of a marriage but lacking the latter's official status.

2 "The love that dare not speak its name" is a phrase from the last line of the poem *Two Loves* by Lord Alfred Douglas, written in September 1892 and published in the Oxford magazine *The Chameleon* in December 1894. It was mentioned at the trial of Oscar Wilde for gross indecency in 1895 and is usually interpreted as a euphemism for homosexuality, although Wilde denied that this was the case.

3 Jeffrey John, *Permanent, Faithful, Stable: Christian Same-Sex Partnerships* (Darton, Longman & Todd, 1993).

4 One of the earliest examples of this in print was Michael Vasey, *Strangers and Friends: A New Exploration of Homosexuality and the Bible* (Hodder and Stoughton, 1995). A recent evangelical network established in August 2023 to express support for same-sex relationships is Inclusive Evangelicals https://www.inclusiveevangelicals.com/

5 See Vaughan Roberts, *Battles Christians Face* (Authentic Media, 2013), Chapter 7 and Sam Allberry, *Is God Anti-Gay?: Why Does God Care Who I Sleep With?* (The Good Book Company, 2020).

6 Church of England House of Bishops Pastoral Statement on Civil Partnerships, 2004.

7 In Acts 15, the Council of Jerusalem agreed not to impose obedience to the Law of Moses, particularly circumcision, upon Gentile converts. For the sake of church unity, however, it also told Gentile Christians to observe certain elements of that law to acknowledge the legacy they had received from Judaism.

8 The different understanding of the measure on same-sex blessings by those in different positions within the church appears to be indicated by the voting patterns within the

General Synod in February 2023. While the measure received overwhelming support in the House of Bishops (36 for, 4 against, 2 abstentions), matters were very different within the House of Clergy (111 for, 85 against, 3 abstentions) and House of Laity (103 for, 92 against, 5 abstentions).

9 Matthew Vines, *God and the Gay Christian: The Biblical Case in Support of Same-Sex Relationships* (Convergent Books, 2014), Chapters 4-7.
10 The concept of 'approach-avoidance conflict' as a cause of stress was first introduced by Kurt Lewin, one of the founders of modern psychology in *A Dynamic Theory of Personality* (McGraw-Hill, 1935).
11 Stephen Neill, *Anglicanism* (Pelican/Penguin, 1958), p. 398.
12 This phrase is attributed to Harry Day, a First World War fighter ace in the Royal Flying Corps
13 Bishop Alan Wilson, while still in post as Bishop of Buckingham and approaching retirement, died suddenly as this book was being written in February 2024.
14 The case against an essential equivalence between the issues is set out in R.T. France, *A Slippery Slope: The Ordination of Women and Homosexual Practice – a Case Study in Biblical Interpretation* (Grove Books, 2000).
15 See Andrew Graystone, *Bleeding for Jesus: John Smyth and the Cult of Iwerne Camps* (Darton, Longman & Todd, 2021).
16 *Exposed: The Church's Darkest Secret*, Episode 1.

CHAPTER 8

1 John Goldingay, *God's Prophet, God's Servant: A Study in Jeremiah and Isaiah 40-55* (Clement Publishing, 2002).
2 An accessible account of the career and significance of Martin Luther can be found in Graham Tomlin, *Luther and his World* (Lion, 2012).
3 Janet Fife and Gilo (ed) *Letters to a Broken Church* (Ekklesia Publishing, 2019).
4 Graham Sawyer, 'Enduring Cruelty' in *Letters to a Broken Church*, p. 143.
5 *The Church's Darkest Secret*, part 2
6 'Fixing our eyes on Jesus' (Hebrews 12:2), a talk by Vaughan Roberts on 25 June 2019 at Emmanuel Church, Wimbledon. https://walkingwith.uk/Fixing_our_eyes_on_Jesus.pdf
7 Amos, admittedly, travelled north from Tekoa, in the kingdom of Judah, to prophesy to the northern kingdom of Israel. But his proclamation of God's judgement was still to the covenant people to whom he belonged and also included an oracle just about Judah (2.4-5).
8 Pamela Evans, *Driven Beyond the Will of God: Discovering the Rhythms of Grace* (BRF, 1999).
9 *Khartoum* was a British film produced in 1966, written by Robert Ardrey and directed

by Basil Dearden. It starred Charlton Heston as General Gordon and Laurence Olivier as the Mahdi.
10 Gregory Boyd, *The Crucifixion of the Warrior God* (two volumes, Fortress Press, 2017) and also *Cross Vision: How the Crucifixion of Jesus makes sense of Old Testament Violence* (Fortress Press, 2017).

CHAPTER 9

1. See Graham Cray, *Mission-Shaped Church: Church Planting and Fresh Expressions of Church in a Changing Context* (Church House Publishing, 2009); *Ancient Faith, Future Mission: Fresh Expressions of Church and the Kingdom of God* (Canterbury Press, 2010); David Goodhew, Andrew Roberts, Michael Volland, *Fresh! An Introduction to Fresh Expressions of Church and Pioneer Ministry* (SCM, 2012); Graham Cray, Ian Mobsby, Aaron Kennedy, David McCarthy, *Seeing Afresh: Learning from Fresh Expressions of Church* (St Andrew's Press, 2019) but also Matt Stone, *Fresh Expressions of Church: Fishing Nets or Safety Nets* (Grove Books, 2010) and Andrew Davison and Alison Milbank, *For the Parish: A Critique of Fresh Expressions* (SCM, 2010).
2. Bob Jackson, *Hope for the Church* (Church House Publishing, 2002) and *The Road to Growth* (Church House Publishing, 2005).
3. Philip Yancey, *What's so Amazing about Grace* (Zondervan, 2002).
4. Dietrich Bonhoeffer, *The Cost of Discipleship* (SCM, 2015).
5. This section is indebted to Tom Wright's *Creation, Power and Truth: The Gospel in a World of Cultural Confusion* (SPCK, 2013), Chapter 3 and *Broken Signposts: How Christianity makes sense of the World* (SPCK, 2020), Chapter 6.
6. See Rowan Williams, *The Lion's World: A Journey into the heart of Narnia* (SPCK, 2012).
7. *Ibid.*, p. 77.
8. C.S. Lewis, *The Last Battle* (Harper Collins, 1956), p. 224.
9. The irony of this section being so dependent upon the analysis of the Narnia stories by Rowan Williams, who was Archbishop of Canterbury between 2003 and 2012, needs to be acknowledged here.
10. For another interesting engagement with the vital nature of truthfulness for proper human living, see Jordan Peterson, *Twelve Rules for Life: An Antidote to Chaos* (Penguin, 2019) and its Rule 8: 'Tell the truth – or at least, don't lie'.
11. Stephen Kuhrt, *Church Growth through the Full Welcome of Children: The Sssh Free Church* (Grove, 2009) and, with Gordon Kuhrt, *Believing in Baptism: Understanding and Living God's Covenant Sign* (Bloomsbury, 2020).
12. Peter Scazzero, *Emotionally Healthy Spirituality: It's Impossible to Be Spiritually Mature, While Remaining Emotionally Immature* (Zondervan, 2017); *Emotionally Healthy Church: A Strategy for Discipleship that Actually Changes Lives* (Zondervan, 2010); *The Emotionally Healthy Leader: How Transforming Your Inner Life Will Deeply Transform*

Your Church, Team, and the World (Zondervan, 2015); *Emotionally Healthy Discipleship: Moving from Shallow Christianity to Deep Transformation* (Zondervan, 2021)

13 *The Green Green Grass*, ran for 32 episodes between 2005 and 2009.
14 See Jon Kuhrt, 'The seven deadly sins of managing people badly', *Grace and Truth: Faith, Transformation and Social Justice*. https://gracetruth.blog/ethics/the-seven-deadly-sins-of-managing-people-badly/
15 The primary reason that I wrote the article 'How to encourage bullying in the Church of England' in the form of a C.S. Lewis 'Screwtape Letter', was to encourage new bishops and archdeacons, in particular, to renounce the common tactics often used by their peers to manage clergy. This article can be found at https://safeguardingtheinstitution.com/2025/01/25/how-to-encourage-bullying-in-the-church/
16 The General Synod began to discuss this matter in 2023, particularly in response to the bullying of clergy by lay members of churches. What will result from this is currently uncertain.
17 The reported change that will come during 2025, with Diocesan Safeguarding Advisers (DSAs) becoming Diocesan Safeguarding Officers (DSOs), will be crucial. This is because they will be able to instruct bishops on safeguarding matters, rather than merely advise them.
18 N.T. Wright, *For All the Saints: Remembering the Christian Departed* (SPCK, 2003).
19 There are, of course, exceptions; and one of these was the courageous call of the Bishop of Newcastle, Dr Helen-Ann Hartley, for Justin Welby's resignation in November 2024. So was Hartley's publication of the letter from the archbishops putting pressure on her to reinstate the 'Permission to Officiate' of the former Archbishop of York, John Sentamu, following his refusal to accept findings about his previous mishandling of safeguarding.
20 This is a point very specific to the Church of England and its culture. As noted in Chapter 7, within the non-Episcopal Protestant churches in North America, for example, the overwhelming amount of sexual abuse by church leaders appears to be committed by men against women.
21 For the significance of the 'Self-Denying Ordinance' of 1645, see Christopher Hill, *God's Englishman: Oliver Cromwell and the English Revolution* (Penguin, 1990), pp. 63, 74-5, 137, 205-6.
22 *The Church Times*, 7th August 2020. The report quoted a Church House spokesman who said: "We have approximately 30 national cases, with the majority being where senior clergy or church officers have not reported allegations of abuse to the relevant safeguarding adviser, the local authority or the police or made other inappropriate decisions." It added that there were 104 active bishops and 42 deans in the Church of England, although some of those being investigated were retired.
23 This point about Justin Welby's departure aiming to 'take one for the team' and stop the necessity of further resignations is made in the article that I wrote calling for the

resignation of Stephen Cottrell as Archbishop of York. This followed the revelations about Cottrell's mishandling of the case of David Tudor, when he was Bishop of Chelmsford and can be found at https://safeguardingtheinstitution.com/2025/01/23/why-stephen-cottrell-should-resign-as-archbishop-of-york/

24 Sir Humphrey Appleby was the fictional Permanent Secretary for the Department of Administrative Affairs, and then Cabinet Secretary, in the political TV comedies *Yes Minister* and *Yes Prime Minister,* where much of the humour was drawn from his generally successful attempts to thwart any potential changes to the status quo upholding his social privilege.

25 "She knows where the bodies are buried … probably because she has buried most of them!" was a quote that I heard from one well-informed supporter of survivors with regard to a senior figure at Lambeth Palace.

Index

absolution 152
accountability xiii-xv, 3, 70, 75-6, 125, 128-30, 133, 142, 146-9, 151-4, 181, 184, 199-201, 205, 211, 216-18, 222-5
agendas 16, 19, 26, 32, 47-50, 81-4, 90, 94, 99, 109, 118, 134, 141, 169, 187-8, 194, 205, 215-16, 220, 227
aggression 38-40, 117 *see also* passive aggression
allegations 2, 9, 26, 28, 83-5, 87-8, 95, 127, 219, 233, 242
Amos 15-7, 162, 165, 175, 240
Anglicanism 4, 53, 55-6, 65, 67-8, 74, 90, 113, 123, 141, 148, 163, 220-1, 228, 232, 235, 240
Anglican Communion xiv, 33, 141
Anglo-Catholicism 11, 27, 31, 53-4, 136, 138, 141, 148-9, 152-3, 163, 184, 188-9, 237
Annual Parochial Church Meeting (APCM) 203
annual reviews 80, 125, 211
area deans 9, 72, 79, 90, 209
archdeacons 4-5, 11, 45-48, 52, 59-60, 68, 74-5, 77, 80-1, 90, 100, 108, 121, 125, 129, 169, 171-2, 211, 214-16, 218, 239, 242

arrogance 130, 132-3, 143, 149, 151-3, 176, 179
assertiveness 38-41, 43, 46, 57, 60, 76, 200
Aslan 11, 193-4
Atkinson, Rowan 65, 236
Austria-Hungary 150, 227

Bailey (dog) 168
Ball, Bishop Peter 1-3, 5, 11-12, 26-29, 32, 34-5, 45, 83-4, 87-8, 131-2, 151-2, 161-2, 232, 234, 237, 239
baptism 66, 115, 197-8, 234, 238, 241
BBC 1, 17, 26, 84, 89, 232, 235, 237
behaviour in churches xiv, 9-10, 23, 25, 27, 30, 34, 42-4, 48-9, 57, 59, 65, 69, 77, 110, Cpt 6, 143, 166-7, 172, 189, 197-9, 205, 217-19, 225-6, 239
bishops x, 1-3, 5, 7-13, 45-8, 52, 54, 56-61, 67-8, 74, 77-84, 86-90, 95, 99-101, 108, 121-3, 131, 135, 138-40, 142-6, 153, 161-4, 166, 169, 171-2, 180-1, 195, 201, 211-16, 218, 220-1, 223-4, 228-30, 233, 235-7, 239-43
'Black Lives Matter' 58, 171
Blackadder Goes Forth (TV sitcom) 78-9, 215, 237
Bonhoeffer, Dietrich 33, 186, 234, 241

boundaries 22-25, 76, 118, 127, 238-9
Boyd, Gregory 177, 241
British Empire 57, 95-6, 221, 235
Buchanan, Bishop Colin 74, 237
bullying 129, 165, 234, 242

cant 61, 100-1
Carey, George (former Archbishop of Canterbury) 1, 3, 12, 32, 34, 45, 88, 233
Carry On films 85-6, 237
celebrity 19, 27-8, 88
celibacy 134-6, 138, 143, 226
Charles, Prince/King 3, 88, 131
Changing Attitude 144
Charge of the Light Brigade 66
charismatic leadership 88, 98
charismatic traditions 11, 28, 35, 76, 138, 189
'cheap grace' 33-6, 186
children 18, 21-4, 37, 60, 69-70, 73, 77-8, 96, 103, 106-8, 112-116, 118, 126, 128, 130, 136, 164, 167, 182, 184, 197-200, 202, 234-6, 238, 241
choirs 113, 154, 239
Christ Church, New Malden xi, 8, 10, 19, 23-4, 40-2, 49-50, 69, 104-8, 126-8, 233
Christendom 69, 185
Christie, Agatha 14
church discipline 8, 33-4, 81, 99, 115, 121-4, 128-9, 217-18
church planting 48, 71, 241
church services 19, 21, 24, 36, 41, 53-4, 58-9, 63, 67, 73, 76, 95, 102, 106-7, 112-13, 117-18, 123-4, 143, 167-9
Church Times, The 229, 233, 234, 242
Churches Together 73

churchwardens 8-10, 58, 78, 98, 116-17, 119, 122, 128, 200, 205
civil partnerships 139, 239
Clergy Discipline Measure (CDM) 8, 121, 217
Clifford, Max 151
'cock-up' 63-4, 66, 68, 81-2, 84, 235
colonialism 57-8
competence 45, 56, 59, 67, 75-6, 79-80, 85, 162, 200-1
complacency 3, 181, 223-4, 227
concubinage 135, 239
confession 36, 152
conflict 10, 39, 41, 43-4, 46, 64, 72, 74, 82, 98, 119-21, 125, 142, 149, 209, 216, 240
congregations 8, 19-20, 22-4, 37, 41, 43, 51, 69, 74, 76, 78, 107, 116, 119, 121, 138-9, 141, 145, 170-1, 180, 195-7, 202-3, 205
conservative evangelicalism 11-12, 20, 27, 29, 31, 37, 59, 69, 136, 138, 144, 149-50, 152, 163, 184, 221-3
conspiracy 63-4, 153, 235
corruption 34, 89, 175, 187, 214
courage ix, xiii-xv, 9, 46, 83, 91, 102-3, 116, 124, 137, 153, 155-60, 163-7, 169-71, 173-5, 178-9, 186, 191-2, 194, 204, 206, 208-11, 213, 228, 230, 236, 242
Cotton, Roy 11, 26, 132
Cottrell, Stephen (Archbishop of York) 90, 237, 242-3
cover-ups 2, 12, 96-100, 106, 163
Covid-19 pandemic 8, 236
Coward, Colin 144
Cowdrey, Colin 62
Cranmer, Thomas 56, 135, 235
cricket 23, 58, 61-2, 100, 235

curates and curacies 5, 32, 41, 50, 58, 76, 78-81, 106, 118, 209-11, 213
Curry, Bishop Michael 67

Darling, Captain (*Blackadder Goes Forth*) 78-9, 208, 214-15, 237
deanery synods 72-3, 77, 90, 215
deceit 43, 89, 110, 193
decline of the church 74, 181, 185
Dexter, Ted 62
dioceses 60, 72, 74, 79, 171-2, 201, 209, 211-21
diocesan safeguarding advisers/officers 8, 13, 60, 91-2, 182, 211, 219, 242
diocesan structures 77, 195, 208, 211
discipleship 28-30, 204, 234, 241-2
discipline 8, 33-4, 81, 99, 115, 121-4, 128-9, 217-18
Disclosure and Barring Service (DBS) 18, 182
dishonesty 2, 30, 45, 48, 58-9, 62, 67, 71, 78, 94, 101, 130, Cpt 7, 203, 223
disloyalty 95, 169-71, 178-9
'divide and rule' 120, 216
D'Oliveira, Basil 61-2, 235
Drucker, Peter 13, 234
duplicity 2, 53, 62, 82, 110, 144, 219, 228
dysfunctionality 39-44, 46, 50, 52, 55, 71, 77, 81, 120, 180-1, 183, 189, 200, 207, 214, 216, 218

Elizabethan Settlement 55-6, 220, 235
Emmanuel Church, Wimbledon 26, 90, 149, 163, 234, 237, 240
English Civil War 228
Engel, Matthew 62
entitlement 3, 133

evangelicalism 4-5, 11, 41, 53-4, 69, 74-5, 113, 119, 136, 138, 141, 148-9, 152-3, 185, 188-9, 201-3, 223, 225, 237, 239 *see also* conservative evangelicalism
evil 3, 16, 35-7, 57-8, 89, 93, 103, 130, 156-7, 175, 177, 190-1, 225, 228, 234
excommunication 122-4, 217-18
Exposed: The Church's Darkest Secret, The (BBC documentary) 1, 12, 26, 232, 234, 237, 239-40

false prophets 158, 169
families 21, 69, 106, 168
fear 3, 9, 18, 20-21, 28, 41, 43, 48, 53, 71, Cpt 5, 142, 147, 151-3, 155, 157, 163-5, 176, 189, 193-4, 197, 200, 203-5, 207, 218-19, 231
fiefdoms 70-2, 75
Fife, Janet 231, 233, 240
First World War 79, 150, 227, 234, 240
Fletcher, Jonathan 11, 26-9, 90, 132, 136, 149, 163, 233-4
Floyd, George 58, 171
forgiveness 33, 103, 110, 152, 160, 162, 164, 193, 238
Forward in Faith 148
Fresh Expressions of Church 98-9, 181, 238, 241
Fulcrum 4, 60, 232
funerals 102-103
Furney, Lee xi, 233

GAFCON 141
'gaslighting' 10, 23
Gatting, Mike 62
General Synod of the Church of England 60, 139-41, 161, 220, 224, 239-40, 242

Gibb, Dame Moira 1
Gordon, General Charles 176-7, 240-1
Grant, Hugh 66, 236
grace 23-4, 33-6, 51, 103, 110, 124, 127, 131, 178, 184-6, 191, 219, 232-3, 237-8, 240-2
grants 212-13
Grapevine (lunch club) 126-7, 167-8, 234, 236, 239
Graystone, Andrew 231, 233, 240
Green Green Grass, The (TV sitcom) 200, 242
grooming 16, 18-26, 41, 130
guilt 24-5, 45, 120, 152, 161, 191, 222, 230

Hancock, Bishop Peter 162
harassment xiii-xv, 10, 33
Harris, Rolf 133, 151
Harry, Prince 67
heterosexuality 135, 146, 223-4
home groups 70, 239
homosexuality Cpt 7, 222-8, 239
honesty ix, xv, 14-15, 45, 48-9, 52, 62, 107, 119, 127, Cpt 7, 155, 159, 163, 171, 173, 181, 184, 189, 193-4, 196-7, 199-202, 205, 207-9, 219-21, 227, 236
honorary canons 173, 212-13
Holland, Tom 93, 238
Holy Communion 21, 122-3, 168
Holy Spirit 76, 92, 158, 185, 190-2, 194
House of Bishops 139, 181, 220, 239-40
Hughes, Bryn 5, 19-20, 28, 34, 41, 105-7, 161
Huntley, Ian 35
Hus, Jan 174

incompetence Cpt 4, 153, 181, 183, 201, 215-16, 221, 230
Inclusive Church 137, 148-9
Inclusive Evangelicals 239
Indian Civil Service (ICS) 57
induction of bishops and archdeacons 216
inertia 3, 82
inconsistency 24, 67, Cpt 6, 143-4, 153, 188, 202-3, 212, 222
initial ministerial education (IME) 210
injustice xiii, xiv, 37, 110, 131, 156, 161, 171, 175, 182
insecurity 14, 30, 52, 86, 88, 108, 145, 149-50, 173, 196, 201, 212, 218, 227
integrity xiii, 34, 51-2, 74, 97, 107, 115, 137, 151, 162, 175, 198, 207-8
Isaiah 158, 162, 164, 240
Israel 156-9, 162, 167, 169-70, 175, 240
Iwerne camps 12, 136, 231, 240

Jackson, Bob 71, 74, 181, 237, 241
James, Cliff 84, 162
Jeremiah 158, 169, 240
John, Jeffrey 138, 239

Keeler, Christine 132
Keswick Convention 27
Khartoum (film) 176-7
King, Bishop Edward 78
King, Martin Luther 177
Kuhrt, Jon xii, 76, 103, 232, 237-8, 242

Lambeth Palace 3, 83, 90, 230, 243
Lang, Cosmo Gordon (former Archbishop of Canterbury) 78, 135
Lawrence, Stephen 183
Lee, Nicky and Sila 115, 238-9
Lewes 1-2

Lewis, C.S. 76, 110-11, 193-4, 238, 241-2
Liar Liar (film) 110, 238
liberalism 74, 138, 147-8, 188
loyalty 50, 166, 170-1, 173
Lucy Faithfull Foundation 24, 234
Luther, Martin 36, 135, 160-1, 173-4, 177, 234, 240
lying 13, 43, 110, 120-1

Makin Review x, 12-13, 182-3, 232
manipulation 18, 25-6, 43, 45-9, 59, 76, 215-6, 218
martyrs 174, 176
Markle, Meghan 67
meetings 9-11, 22-3, 47, 59, 63, 81, 99, 108, 203
mental health 24, 52, 71, 103, 168, 215
Messy Church 114, 181, 196, 234, 238
middle-class society 126-7, 172, 225
missionaries 201
Mr Bates versus the Post Office (TV drama) 89
modernism 186-9, 192

Narnia, The Chronicles of 111, 193-4, 241
National Evangelical Anglican Congresses 4, 74
National Health Service (NHS) 17, 89, 181
National Safeguarding Team and Panel of C of E 7, 84, 192
Neill, Bishop Stephen 53-4, 142-3, 235, 240
new creation 34-5, 164, 189-94, 204
New Wine 27, 78
newspapers 16, 35-6, 68, 236
Nimmo, Derek 64, 236
Nixon, Richard 97

Nobody's Friends (dining club) 90
non-disclosure agreements (NDAs) 97, 207
North American Church 146, 242

Office, The (TV sitcom) 85, 237
Only Fools and Horses (TV sitcom) 65, 200, 236
Open the Book 196
Operation Yewtree 105, 151, 181
ordinands 29-30, 33, 57, 97, 138, 146-7, 207-9, 234
OutRage (protest group) 144

Pac-Man (video game) 44, 210
paedophile offences 21, 25-6, 34, 36, 41
parents and parenting 21, 68, 107, 112-115, 202-3, 238-9
parish safeguarding officers 23, 205-6
parish share 74-5, 90
Parochial Church Councils (PCCs) 8, 10-11, 24, 41, 49-50, 63-4, 73, 98, 127-8, 200, 205, 215, 233, 235
passive aggression 10, Cpt 3, 86, 102, 165, 186, 189, 215-16, 218
Past Cases Review (PCR 2) 6-7
pastoral care xv, 45, 91, 102-3, 118, 146-7, 199, 206
patronage 58, 80, 93, 211-14
Paul, St 29, 39, 50-51, 55, 93-4, 136, 158-9, 164, 175-6, 191-2, 198, 213, 226, 238
Pilavachi, Mike 11, 28, 234
Pontius Pilate 96, 190
poor behaviour *see* behaviour
police xv, 1, 3, 12, 21-3, 32, 41, 88, 151, 183, 242
politeness 10, 13, 59, 171, 217, 235
postmodernism 176, 186-8, 190

Post Office scandal 89, 181, 237
power xv, 3, 20, 27, 29, 37, 39, 51, 65-6, 68-72, 75, 78, 83, 85-9, 94-6, 98, 101-4, 106, 108, 110, 118, 122, 126, 129, 132-3, 137, 150, 158, 165-7, 169, 171-5, 178, 184-92, 197-9, 202, 205-6, 211, 213-14, 219, 227, 230-1, 233
pragmatism 48, 56-7, 60-1, 105, 143, 222
Prayer Book controversy of 1927-28 53-4, 143
preventative safeguarding 18, 31, 182, 205, 219
Pritchard, Colin 11, 26, 132
Profumo, John 132
prophets 14, Cpt 8, 191, 229, 240
public schools 57-9, 62, 136

reconciliation 47, 103, 123, 162, 238
'relative expendability' 31-3, 42, 79, 94, 130
relevance of the church 3, 34, 65-7, 72, 77-9, 104, 180, 195-6, 201
repression 149, 226
Rev (sitcom) 65-6, 129, 148, 236, 239
Rideout, George 11, 132
righteousness 96, 156, 163, 175, 191
Roberts, Vaughan 138, 163, 239, 240
Roman Catholic Church 17, 65, 107, 134, 160, 236
Roman Empire 93-6, 213
Royal Family 17, 67
rudeness 57, 59, 81, 110, 117, 172
Russia 150, 227

sacraments 122-3, 217
same-sex marriage 139-41, 225, 227-8
Savile, Jimmy 17, 19, 26, 88-9, 105, 132-3, 181

Sawyer, Graham 161-2
scandals ix, 2, 6, 11-13, 53, 96, 101, 130, 132, 146, 154, 181, 183, 188, 207, 222, 226, 230
Scazzero, Peter 199, 241-2
schools 2, 22-3, 31, 57, 59-60, 62, 115, 136, 183, 196
selection of clergy 146-7, 201, 205-7, 210-11, 223
self-deprecation 66
sex and sexuality Cpt 7, 222-8, 239
Shipman, Harold 35
sin and sinfulness 36-7, 59, 64, 158, 191, 204
single-sex subcultures 30-1, 149
Smyth, John x, 11-13, 28-9, 35, 132, 149-50, 231-3, 240
Soul Survivor 11, 27, 28
Spring Harvest 27
Stepford Wives (book, films) 172
Stockwood, Bishop Mervyn 144
Stott, John 4, 136
Suez Crisis 66, 85, 132
The Sun (newspaper) 68
Sunday schools 112-13
suicide 102-3, 226
Sullivan, John 65, 200
supervision 8, 80, 201, 205, 233
survivors of abuse xiii, 9, 17, 21, 32, 82-4, 91-2, 109, 161-3, 233, 243
suspension of Stephen Kuhrt xi, 8-9, 47, 232-3
symbolism 122, 124, 135, 166-8, 170, 178

television 11, 64-66, 68, 85, 89, 232, 236, 243
theological colleges xiv, 29-30, 33-4, 56-7, 97, 207-9

Thompson, Robert 35
Titus Trust 150
Todd, Neil x, 1, 3, 131
training of clergy 32-3, 50, 76, 79-80, 108, 201, 205-11
transparency xiii, xv, 49-50, 99-100, 105, 108, 144, 189, 213
Tudor, David 90, 132, 237, 243
Trump, Donald 187
trust 7, 18, 52, 95, 97, 99, 108, 216, 233
Truth and Reconciliation Process 103, 238

unaccountability 3, 70, 125, 129, 149, 199, 223-4
urban myths 104, 202
urbanity 59, 81, 101, 172, 215

vanity 132, 176-8
Venables, John 35
Vennells, Paula 89
veneration of leaders 3, 26-8
Vicar of Dibley, The (TV sitcom) 65-6, 148, 236, 239
vicars xi, xiii, 4-5, 8-11, 26, 32, 40-1, 43-5, 49-50, 52, 63-7, 71-2, 75-6, 79-80, 98-100, 104, 106-8, 116, 125, 127, 129, 148, 152, 169, 195, 197, 201, 203, 232-3, 235-6, 239
victims of abuse *see* survivors of abuse
vindication 85, 91, 105, 109-10
Vines, Matthew 226, 240

vulnerability xv, 16, 43, 65, 83, 93-4, 110-11, 162-3, 167-9, 178, 182, 199, 216, 220, 225, 228

Walker, Dave 44, 71, 235
Walsh, Bishop Jeremy 2-3
Watergate scandal 97
weaponising of safeguarding 8-10, 233
weddings 66-7, 236
Welby, Justin (former Archbishop of Canterbury) x, 5, 12-13, 68, 78, 89, 180, 183, 221, 229, 232-3, 236, 242
wellbeing xiv, 34, 46, 74, 80, 89, 93, 97, 128, 137, 173-4
West, Fred and Rosemary 35
whistleblowers 155, 158, Cpt 8, 232-3
Wilberforce, William 188
wilful incompetence *see* incompetence
Williams, Rowan (former Archbishop of Canterbury) 193, 241
Wilson, Bishop Alan 144-5, 234, 238, 240
wisdom xiv, 29, 33, 40, 51, 99-100, 151, 164, 192, 209
women bishops 60-1, 222, 235, 237
women's ordination 135, 149
worship 27, 63, 69, 98, 113-14, 120, 156, 162, 237
Wright, Tom 35, 221, 234, 238, 241-2

Yancey Philip 185
Yes Minister/Yes Prime Minister (TV sitcoms) 44, 66, 84, 236-7, 243
youth ministers 154, 200
youth work 20, 31, 70, 112-14

www.ingramcontent.com/pod-product-compliance
Lightning Source LLC
Chambersburg PA
CBHW061936220426
43662CB00012B/1928